The Draft

and

Its Enemies

The Draft
and
Its Enemies

A DOCUMENTARY
HISTORY

edited by
John O'Sullivan
and
Alan M. Meckler

University of Illinois Press
URBANA CHICAGO LONDON

Library of Congress Cataloging in Publication Data

O'Sullivan, John, 1939–   comp.
  The draft and its enemies.

  Includes bibliographical references.
  1. Military service, Compulsory—United States—
History—Sources. I. Meckler, Alan M., 1945–
joint comp. II. Title.
UB343.O85   355.2′236   74–10979
ISBN 0–252–00395–0

To R.D.B.
ne plus ultra
and
to James P. Shenton
for believing

Contents

☆

1861–1900:
The Beginning of
Federal Conscription

1900–1940:
Conscription
Comes of Age

1940–1965:
Conscription in War
and Cold War

1965–the Present:
The Draft: Institution
in Crisis

Foreword

To EXAMINE and analyze the enemies of the draft on this continent since colonial times is a massive undertaking, which Messrs. O'Sullivan and Meckler have admirably accomplished. Their approach is objective in the sense that they do not presume to pass judgment —implicit or explicit—on the worth or value of military conscription in our society by either their choice of materials or their comments. Throughout the book they present a summary of each era of our nation's history, a summary of issues surrounding military manpower procurement, and documentation from each period in question to illustrate the different positions of the men of the times relative to the draft.

While there was conscription in many of the colonies before and after independence, there was no federally centralized draft until the War between the States, the South being the first to institute it. After the conclusion of the war until World War I our country was without conscription. Again, the draft lasted only for the duration of the conflict and over significant public protest. With the inception of conscription during the First World War, the public outcry did not turn to violence to the extent it had one-half century earlier when hundreds of men died in draft riots.

In 1940 we experienced our third national military draft. Through World War II it was in full operation until it was allowed to lapse for almost two years. It was again revived in 1948 with the press of the cold war and the fear that we could not meet our military manpower requirements through voluntary enlistments. Since then until June 30, 1973, we had, for the first time in our history, conscription without a declaration of war.

Messrs. O'Sullivan and Meckler do an excellent job in giving fabric and substance to the history of conscription by thoroughly documenting the varied opinions of each era relative to the draft and describing the environment in which the issue was debated. Seen from this perspective, it is incumbent upon us now to evaluate military conscription in light of the termination of the President's induction authority on July 1, 1973. While the authority to induct is no longer in effect, the draft mechanism, the Selective Service System, remains intact.

In any book with the title *The Draft and Its Enemies*, as Messrs. Meckler and O'Sullivan would agree, I would be listed as an enemy. I am one who views the draft as inherently inequitable, inefficient, and unjust—a form of involuntary servitude striking at the very heart of the principles which have made this country strong, vital, and creative. Consequently, any comments that I might make with respect to the draft must be taken with this in mind.

As the authors have described in great detail, the draft has a fascinating history in our society, but, for the time being at least, it is no longer an institution claiming authority over the lives of our young men. Yet the debate over the draft will continue, not only because of the switch to an all-volunteer military in July, 1973, but also because of the continued existence of the Selective Service System and the persistent efforts of many in private and public life to repeal the funds supporting the system. The issues surrounding abolition of the draft mechanism vary somewhat from those involving the induction authority. The latter debate focused on foreign policy, accession rates, racial justice, budgetary outlays, economic priorities, congressional versus executive prerogatives, constitutionality, and individual and governmental morality. The former focuses on governmental efficiency, bureaucratic self-perpetuation, military contingencies in the atomic age, constitutional issues between the congressional and executive branches of our government, and the central question of governmental authority over the individual.

In keeping with the authors' approach in the body of their book, I would like to briefly describe both sides of the present debate. As I mentioned above, the issue currently revolves around the institution of the Selective Service System: Should it be continued? Proponents of its continuation argue the need for $55 million in fiscal year 1974 to fulfill its functions. What are those functions? First, argue proponents, the Selective Service System is needed in case of war or national emergency. Therefore, continued registration of 100,000 men annually is required. Second, if we are unable to meet our manpower requirements for the armed forces under a totally voluntary enlistment program, we need to have a standby draft ready to be activated. Third, there are a few-score men to be monitored who have conscientious objector status and are performing their alternative service.

Opponents of continuing the Selective Service System, including myself, argue that in case of war or national emergency the National Guard and the Reserves are our second line of defense behind the active-duty forces. It takes at least four months to train an inductee anyway, so the draft could not be, nor has it ever been, used as an immediate backup for our active-duty forces in times of danger. Furthermore, we argue, to register 100,000 men each year is pointless because of the small number of men relative to potential future needs, should the draft be reinstated, and the rapidly changing status of men in that age group. If we were to need a draft, opponents assert, one could be established quickly enough to meet our contingencies just as it was prior to World Wars I and II. To spend $55 million to employ approximately 4,500 men and women to monitor men fulfilling alternative service is inefficient. Another agency or department, such as the Department of Health, Education, and Welfare or the Department of Labor, could take over that job and thereby eliminate another needless expenditure—a prime example of a bureaucracy trying to perpetuate itself after its original purpose for existence has vanished.

Finally, some opponents argue, there should be an amendment to the Constitution requiring voter approval before military conscription is initiated again unless there is a war or national emergency, in which case only congressional approval would be required. This amendment is necessary because of the singular nature of conscription: it, more than any other institution in our society except our justice system, can take away the rights, and indirectly the life, of individual citizens of our country. The concept underlying this proposal is that if a foreign policy of a government cannot induce its citizens to support its military through voluntary enlistments, that policy should not be followed. In wartime a draft should be used to facilitate the entrance of volunteers.

During the past few years the enemies of the draft have increased in numbers. Messrs. O'Sullivan and Meckler have listed some of the most notable examples of them as well as of those who disagree with respect to peacetime conscription. Those enemies of the entire institution in peacetime are relatively few today, but if the past is any indication of the future, their numbers will increase as well. Be that as it may, the draft in our country will continue to have a fascinating and tortuous history.

Washington, D.C.   MARK O. HATFIELD
September 19, 1973

Introduction

IF HISTORY can accord an institution the sanction of harmony and consistency with our democratic traditions through long coexistence, the draft is surely not "un-American." The reader of this selection of documents on the history of the draft will find that a military obligation for nearly all males of appropriate age appeared in the statutes of all the British colonies that later became the United States (except Quaker Pennsylvania), that the obligation was enforced for defense against Indians, that during the American Revolution the newly independent states (then including Pennsylvania) perpetuated the obligation, and that the United States recognized the state military service systems in the federal Constitution and promptly adopted the state systems as instruments by which to impose its own military obligations on men between eighteen and forty-five through the Militia Act of 1792.

The reader will learn further that revered leaders of the American Republic have frequently praised a universal military obligation as highly appropriate to the country's ideals—from George Washington, who said, "It must be laid down as a primary position, and the basis of our system, that every Citizen who enjoys the protection of a free Government, owes not only a proportion of his property, but even of his personal services to the defence of it . . . ," to Harry S Truman, who said that universal military training "would provide a democratic and efficient military force. It would be a constant bulwark in support of our ideals of government."

Such endorsement of a universal military obligation owes much to the military circumstances of the European world at the time the American colonies were settled and the United States was founded. The founding fathers held strong antimilitary suspicions inherited from British parliamentary and liberal traditions, but the kind of military force that was most especially suspect in their eyes was a mercenary force of long-term soldiers. Such a career army could readily become isolated from the ideals and sentiments of the rest of a nation and then be turned into a tool of despotism. The founding fathers believed that in contrast to such a force, the needs of military security could be met with relative safety from military despotism by an army of citizen soldiers; the army could not threaten the citizenry because the citizenry themselves would be the army. A general military obligation could provide the desired citizen army.

The writers of the United States Constitution and the Bill of Rights had actually witnessed the overthrow of a threatened military despotism, in the form of the British army in America, by a rising of armed citizens in the Revolution. "With respect to a standing army, I believe there was not a member in the Federal Convention who did not feel indignant at such an institution," James Madison could well say, but the writers of the Second Amendment believed that they provided against the dangers of a standing army the remedy that their own Revolutionary experience had confirmed when they guaranteed that "a well-regulated Militia, being necessary to the security of a free State, the right of the people to keep and bear Arms, shall not be infringed."

This interpretation of a professional army as a likely source of military despotism and of a citizens' army as a truly democratic military force runs through many of the documents reprinted here and has been a consistent theme of debates about the proper form of an American army throughout our history—through the debates about universal military training after World War II and into the still continuing controversy about abandonment of the draft for a volunteer army.

In the nineteenth century, as a professional military officer corps in the full modern sense of the word "professional" developed—officership becoming a profession in the sense that medicine and law are professions—the American professional officers, notably their articulate spokesman General Emory Upton, desired more highly skilled and better-trained soldiers than the United States had generally sent to war, wanted the standing army to be the core of all American military institutions which would determine the characteristics even of much-enlarged wartime armies, and, when America refused to give them a strong standing army, became doubtful that the American democracy could ever compete with the great military powers.

The reply of less intensely professional military men and statesmen, who believed that democracy and military preparedness were by no means incompatible, was that a democratic army must be a citizens' army and that a universal military obligation could enlist, in behalf of military security, the whole vast energies of the American people. In this vein the reader will find General Leonard Wood, a messiah of the 1914–17 preparedness movement, contending that universal military service "is the basic principle upon which truly representative government, or free democracy, rests and must rest if it is successfully to withstand the shock of modern war," and General Hugh L. Scott, chief of staff of the army when the United States entered World War I, saying that "universal military training has been the corner stone upon which has been built every republic in the history of the world, and its abandonment the signal for decline and obliteration." So also in 1945 General George C. Marshall was to call universal military training "a supremely democratic procedure."

The thoughtful student of the history of the draft in the United States and of military history at large will find considerable substantiation for the contention that a citizens' army based on a universal obligation to serve is the most appropriate armed force for a democracy. Yet history also provides disquieting thoughts. Although a universal military obligation existed in theory in the American colonies and the United States from the beginning, and although the theory has frequently been enforced in practice, the draft nevertheless runs against the grain of the values of individualism and free choice that are far more deeply associated with the image of the United States among its own citizens and in the world at large.

Thus, the documents contained in this book will demonstrate that the colonial military obligation began to atrophy very quickly as soon as the Indian menace receded; that while the Revolution gave the obligation something of a revival, the Militia Act of 1792 was without teeth; and that in the early nineteenth century the general military obligation became a theory only, not a fact. The supreme emergency of the Civil War drove both the Confederacy and the United States to conscription, but by that time volunteer armed forces seemed so much the embodiment of the true American military tradition that conscription was much diluted in practice by exemptions in the Confederacy and by commutations and substitutions in the Union, and the conscript was regarded as bearing a stigma.

The two twentieth-century world wars revived the draft because they also seemed to be supreme military emergencies. During the world wars, conscription seemed acceptable also because it operated with relative fairness, since the military services of nearly all eligible young men were required. After World War II, however, the selective service system operated not to draft nearly all eligible men, but, in peacetime and even in the Korean and Vietnam wars, to distinguish the unlucky youths who would have to bear arms from the more numerous lucky ones who would not, and in time the manifest inequity of such a system helped undermine the draft.

As the editors point out, the climate of the Cold War and the inertia that governmental operations tend to acquire kept the draft from being seriously questioned for about twenty years after World War II. But questioning could not be postponed indefinitely, and despite the acquiescence which the draft until very recently was accorded, in the whole span of American history conscription has received general popular acceptance only for relatively brief periods. The basic reason is that despite the historical sanction for a theoretical universal military obligation, Senator Robert A. Taft captured the truth of the matter when in his 1945 speech on post–World War II military training, quoted herein, he spoke of recruiting "by voluntary means" as "in the American tradition." Conscription too much violates the American tradition of individual freedom.

It is not the least disquieting aspect of the historical debates over the draft as the appropriate military system for American democracy that the proponents of the draft so often seem to have felt that to argue convincingly they must resort to arguments less than worthy of themselves—that is, less than honest. This collection offers examples. To avoid some of the difficulties of the Civil War draft, the selective service system of World War I tried to make the process of being drafted lose its old stigma and become patriotic, partly through the sound means of calling upon eligible men to come forward and register rather than sending agents from door to door to hunt them down and partly through more dubious techniques smacking of the incipient trade of the public relations man. In the latter category most notably was Woodrow Wilson's statement that selective service was not "a conscription of the unwilling" but "rather, selection from a nation which has volunteered in mass." Max Eastman, in the editorial from *The Masses* quoted herein, took embarrassingly accurate aim at this pronouncement by saying that Wilson "builds himself up to a height of casuistic complaisance from which the fall may be tragic and terrible." It is similarly embarrassing to find President Truman saying that "Universal Military Training is not conscription" because technically the trainees would not be members of the Army, Navy, or Air Force. Truman also professed to believe that universal military training would serve the moral and spiritual welfare of the trainees, despite Senator Taft's earlier common-sense observation that "the argument that it would improve the morals of our boys has almost been dropped because of its foolishness." Programs that lead otherwise honest men into disingenuousness inevitably raise questions about themselves. (It was at least more honest, but suggestive of the totalitarian implications never far from the surface of even the best-intentioned universal service proposals, that Dwight D. Eisenhower argued for universal military training in 1966 by saying: "I deplore the beatnik dress, the long, unkempt hair, the dirty necks and fingernails now affected by a minority of our boys. If UMT accomplished nothing more than to produce cleanliness and decent grooming, it might be worth the price tag—and I am not altogether jesting when I say this.")

As early as 1775, the Continental Congress noted that "there are some people, who, from religious principles, cannot bear arms in any case" and affirmed that "this Congress intend no violence to their consciences. . . ." But the history of the draft in the United States is a consistent record of the practical impossibility of not violating the consciences of confirmed pacifists while conducting a draft, and the reader of these documents will find conscientious objection one of the most consistently recurring of vexed questions throughout this book. In our own day the question has assumed far more complexity than the Continental Congress perceived in it in 1775; at least it is probably a kind of encouraging evidence that in spite of the recently growing weight of the military-industrial complex, American recognition of the subtle ramifications of freedom has also been growing, and that the country and its courts do appear to perceive with increasing clarity the complexities that may accompany encounters between the individual conscience and war.

Yet the nonpacifist reader is also likely to conclude that the statements of the pacifists printed here express, as usual, a morality that is too good for this world and therefore, in its lack of realism, not good enough. Suggestions that any evil can be countered adequately by nonviolent noncooperation, citing Gandhi's effect on British policy in India, fail to come to grips with such different predicaments as the plight of the Jews under Nazism, for example, whose oppressors had a different moral code from the British in India and were therefore not as responsive. In this world it is likely that some evils still have to be countered by the evil means of war or at least warded off by military preparations. That condition leaves us still with the task of recruiting men for our military forces, and the military responsibilities of the United States remain so large, even if we abandon all efforts to be a world policeman, that finding enough men for our armies by voluntary means will probably be at best a perilously narrow success. There is no easy solution to our military manpower problems; there is no easy solution to the issues raised by the draft. The reader of this volume will find before him all the most important documents, and the perceptive historical summaries and interpretations of the editors, to give him an informed approach to those issues. He will also be reminded that the issues are by no means new, but rather that one gauge of their intractability is that they have persisted unresolved through the whole history of the United States.

RUSSELL F. WEIGLEY

The Draft

and

Its Enemies

1607-1783:
The Birth of the
Citizen Soldier

THE HISTORY of compulsory military service during the colonial period cannot be understood without a comprehension of the colonial militia system, which was derived from the English militia concept. Since the ninth century, England's history had yielded a heritage of a general military obligation on the part of her freemen and the establishment in each county of a fyrd, a mobilization of citizens into a county fighting unit or militia for service to the crown. In 1181 Henry II's issuance of the Assize of Arms enunciated the principle of a compulsory military obligation to the king on the part of every freeman. The Statute of Winchester of 1285 and the Instructions for General Muster of 1572 elaborated and reinforced this principle and strengthened the English militia during the Elizabethan wars against Spain.[1]

Of necessity, the original colonists immediately adopted the heritage of a compulsory military obligation, for early colonization was essentially a military operation. Establishing new settlements while faced with the threat of Indian attacks or the possible encroach-

1. U.S., Selective Service System, *Backgrounds of Selective Service*, Vol. 1, pp. 24–28; Herbert L. Osgood, *The American Colonies in the Seventeenth Century*, 3 vols. (New York, 1904), Vol. 1, p. 499; and Russell F. Weigley, *History of the United States Army*, pp. 3–4.

3

ment of rival colonial powers was a dangerous and oftentimes violent enterprise. Therefore, the colonists relied heavily upon the militia.[2] However, the militiamen were basically farmers and tradesmen who mobilized for local defense; they were therefore loathe to leave their homes and livelihoods for lengthy operations lest social disruptions such as community food shortages or other dangers to their families occur. This attitude, along with the practice of electing officers and the lack of stress upon discipline, resulted in a military system ill suited for any activity except local defense.[3]

As the level of danger facing the early settlements diminished, the militia took on a new character. The progress from a condition of constant alert to one of moderate security resulted in the reduction of prescribed military training days in the various colonies. Militia training seemed unnecessary drudgery to many colonists, and in 1632 Virginia reduced the daily drill requirement to a Sunday obligation. Within ten years, this training time was further reduced to a monthly meeting, and by 1674 it was limited to three meetings each year.[4] Similarly, in Massachusetts training days were decreased to one each month in 1632, and six years later they were set at eight each year. By 1679, four annual drill days were considered sufficient, although officers had the option of adding up to two additional days each year.[5]

Although the idea of a universal military obligation remained fixed throughout the colonial period (over two hundred individual laws defined the principle),[6] the actual requirements of service became continually less onerous. Not only were the numbers of training days continually reduced, but various categories of exemptions were introduced. The Massachusetts militia law of 1647, for example, deferred the following groups from service: members of the General Court, officers, fellows and students of Harvard College, elders and deacons, schoolmasters, physicians and surgeons, masters of vessels over twenty tons' burden, fishermen employed in

2. Quaker influence in Pennsylvania prevented a militia organization from being formed there until 1747. See Daniel J. Boorstin, *The Americans: The Colonial Experience* (New York: Random House, Inc., 1966), pp. 48–54.

3. John Shy, "The American Military Experience: History and Learning," *The Journal of Interdisciplinary History*, Vol. 1 (Winter, 1971), pp. 212–13.

4. John Shy, *Toward Lexington: The Role of the British Army in the Coming of the American Revolution* (Princeton: Princeton University Press, 1965), p. 6.

5. Osgood, *The American Colonies*, p. 506.

6. Selective Service System, *Backgrounds*, Vol. 1, pp. 15–70.

all seasons, and all other individuals with physical problems or other causes excused by a General Court or the Court of Assistants.[7]

The colonial military system had, then, at its base, this "common militia." These units, however, were limited to local defense. The carrying out of any distant or long-term military engagement became the province of the "volunteer militia," which consisted of those men who accepted a larger military responsibility than the defense of their own communities. They devoted more time to military training and were equipped to respond to a call for extended active service. Whenever military necessity required a larger force than the existing volunteer units, the legislature would issue a call for additional volunteers from the common militia. If the requisite numbers were not forthcoming, a draft call would then be issued.

These draft calls frequently met with serious challenge. The foremost example of draft opposition prior to the Revolution occurred in Virginia in 1755, when Governor Robert Dinwiddie attempted to raise a regiment of two thousand volunteers commanded by Colonel George Washington to thwart French military operations in the Ohio Valley. When volunteering failed, Dinwiddie asked the Virginia Assembly to enact draft legislation. Several different draft enactments were tried, each having inequities favoring the higher echelons of society over the lower. These enactments were instrumental in producing a high rate of desertion and what may be called America's first draft riot. The scene was Fredericksburg, where citizens became so irate over draft inequities that a mob stormed the city jail and released draftees who had been jailed as deserters.[8]

Despite the problems posed by such resistance, the volunteer militia had become the first line of colonial defense by the beginning of the Revolutionary period. The manpower which filled its ranks consisted of both volunteers and conscripts, voluntary en-

7. Osgood, *The American Colonies*, p. 506. The question of exemptions bothered Governor Alexander Spotswood of Virginia to such an extent that an unsuccessful attempt to call out the militia during Queen Anne's War in 1713 led him to complain that "no Man of an estate is under any obligation to Muster . . . even the Servants or Overseers of the rich are likewise exempted," and "the whole Burthen lyes upon the poorest sort of people. . . ." (Quoted in Shy, *Toward Lexington*, p. 13.) Spotswood's complaint furnishes one of the earliest examples of a criticism of the draft which became widespread in the 1960's.

8. James Thomas Flexner, *George Washington: The Forge of Experience* (1732–1775) (Boston: Little, Brown & Company, 1965), p. 138.

listments being the ordinary course of procurement, with draft calls
upon the common militia being employed in times of emergency
when larger forces were demanded.

This combination of conscription and voluntarism, then, was
the colonial military tradition. The universal military obligation,
though modified by exemptions, served as the framework for the
common militia. All adult males had a responsible role in local defense, although that service became more symbolic as the threat to
community survival diminished. The larger duty of colonial defense was assumed by the volunteer militia, a force which prided
itself on its voluntary character and which resorted to conscription
only when emergency expansion required it.

Thus, the later colonial experience furnishes a model for the
subsequent American military tradition up through 1940—a reliance on volunteers for the maintenance of a peacetime defense
force for the larger community, with the draft being resorted to in
time of war.

Manpower procurement proved to be one of the biggest problems for the Continental Congress. The difficulty stemmed from
Congress's lack of authority to enforce its decisions. In addition,
when it came to recruiting troops from state militias, the tradition
of local defense took its toll on sustaining the Continental Army.

The Continental Congress authorized a twenty-thousand-man
army for the year 1776. By early January, the recruitment drive
yielded less than one-half of this total, causing General Washington
to rely on short-term militia enlistments. These enlistments ranged
in length from a few days to one year and usually were for no more
than three months' time.

The short-term militia enlistee was the last kind of soldier that
Washington desired. The following remarks in a letter to the president of the Continental Congress in September, 1776, clearly illustrate his feelings:

> To place any dependence upon Militia, is, assuredly, resting upon a
> broken staff. Men just dragged from the tender Scenes of domestick
> life; unaccustomed to the din of Arms; totally unacquainted with
> every kind of Military skill, which being followed by a want of con-
> fidence in themselves, when opposed to Troops regularly train'd,
> disciplined, and appointed, superior in Arms, makes them timid,

and ready to fly from their own shadows. Besides, the sudden change in their manner of living, (particularly in the lodging) brings on sickness in many; impatience in all, and such an unconquerable desire of returning to their respective homes that it not only produces shameful, and scandalous Desertions among themselves, but infuses the like spirit in others. . . . To bring Men to a proper degree of Subordination, is not the work of a day, a Month or even a year; and unhappily for us, and the cause we are Engaged in, the little discipline I have been labouring to establish in the Army under my immediate Command, is in a manner done away by having such a mixture of Troops as have been called together within these few Months.[9]

In order to induce volunteers for long-term service in the Continental Army, bounties were offered. A potential recruit was offered twenty dollars plus one hundred acres for an enlistment for the duration, or ten dollars for signing on for one year. Because of the lack of a centralized recruiting system, the Continental Army was competing against the states, which were recruiting for long-term service in their own militias. This bidding for the same talent reached the point where the Continental Congress offered as much as two hundred dollars for an enlistment for the duration, only to see this offer topped by some states. Washington became bothered enough by this competition for recruits to warn the governor of Rhode Island that if the governor did not stop interfering with Continental Army recruitment the Continental Army would not "bestow any extraordinary attention to the defense" of that state.[10]

As early as 1776 the states, beginning with Massachusetts, adopted compulsory military service. New Hampshire followed one year later, and the remaining states ultimately turned, although unenthusiastically, to the drafting of manpower.[11] Drafts followed similar procedure in each state and were reminiscent of earlier colonial draft practices. The Continental Congress would give a state a quota of men to be delivered to the Continental Army. The state, in turn, divided the quota among various militia regiments, which then appropriated men from the towns or counties within their commands.

9. Walter Millis, ed., *American Military Thought*, pp. 12–13.
10. James Thomas Flexner, *George Washington in the American Revolution* (1775–1783) (Boston: Little, Brown & Company, 1967), p. 193.
11. Don Higginbotham, *The War of American Independence* (New York: The Macmillan Co., 1971), p. 392.

Each state's reaction to these militia drafts depended upon its satisfaction with home defense. The use of the draft in Virginia had serious repercussions on several occasions. Anger at the draft caused mobs to destroy records and papers related to the draft in Augusta and Rockbridge counties. In Accomac County, 150 potential draftees seized a draft officer's papers, causing a postponement of the draft for one week. When the week had passed, the mob returned, seized the courthouse where the draft was to be held, and declared that they would rather die than face the draft.[12] The worst incident of violence against the draft occurred at Northumberland Court House in 1780, when resistance caused rioting in which several people were killed and wounded.[13] In some instances, Congress itself hurt recruitment by adopting resolutions such as the one in 1777 that allowed any two men to be exempted from service if they were able to provide one substitute for three years of service.[14]

If a state actually carried out a draft, the draftee usually had the option of not serving by paying a fine, as in the case of a Joseph Depuy, a New York farmer, who explained his failure to report upon being drafted as "solely owning to these Reasons, Viz.: he having Last Year Met with the Misfortune of loosing his Barn by a Flash of Lightning, and with Much Difficulty and Hard Labour got the Timber for a New Barn which at the time of his being ordered out, wanted four Days work of a Carpenter . . . and said Carpenter Could by No Means Stay Longer with him and if did not imbrace the then oppertunity had Not the Least prospect of Having a Barn this Season and further Says that his Wife was very ill and himself very Subject to Rheumatism. . . ." Depuy was fined fifteen pounds; however, his court record reads that "The Governor Considering the Case of Joseph Depuy and his late Misfortunes remits the Punishment."[15]

In addition to the option of paying a fine to escape the draft, a draftee could, as previously mentioned, hire a substitute. In one case of particular note, Epping, a wealthy New Hampshire town,

12. Isaac Samuel Harrell, *Loyalism in Virginia* (Durham, N.C., 1926; reprint ed., New York: AMS Press, Inc.), pp. 59–61.

13. H. J. Eckenrode, *The Revolution in Virginia* (Hamden, Conn.: The Shoe String Press, 1964), p. 240.

14. Weigley, *United States Army*, p. 41.

15. Paul V. Lutz, "Greetings; or, Do I Feel a Draught?" *American Heritage*, Vol. 17 (Aug., 1966), p. 112.

hired substitutes from other towns, thus sparing her citizens from service.[16]

Desertion also proved to be a problem for the Continental Army. One historian estimates that at least one-half of the militia enrolled in the army during the Revolution deserted.[17] The draft had a significant part to play in desertion, as drafted men were not enthusiastic soldiers. Such was the observation of a Maryland officer who addressed himself to this problem when he advised Governor Thomas Lee that "Draughted men, who are forced out will render very little assistance or rather do no good."[18]

One result of high desertion in Virginia was the vocation of capturing deserters for rewards. At first only a two-pound reward was offered; however, as desertion increased, the reward was raised to sixty pounds. Another enticement that was most appealing to an individual engaged in this pursuit was exemption from a tour of duty in the state militia and from the draft.[19]

In summary, the American Revolution found the Continental Congress resorting to recruiting practices similar to those found in earlier colonial times. Volunteering was preferred, and the inducement of bounties, as in the past, was dangled to entice potential enlistees. The practice of hiring substitutes continued, as did that of paying a fine to escape being drafted, thus favoring the more well-to-do at the expense of the lower echelons of society. Invariably, compulsory military service was resorted to in an attempt to provide the Continental Army with enough soldiers to continue the struggle against the British. Opposition to compulsory military service once again showed itself and was expressed by the reluctance of state legislatures to invoke it as well as by high desertion rates and, in some cases, by mob violence.

However, even with these problems the new American government was able to achieve victory and independence. Despite the militiamen's dislike of serving away from home, and despite their lack of discipline, enough of these oft-maligned citizen-soldiers joined the Continental Army or participated in local militia campaigns, thus carrying on the tradition of a military policy based on a general military obligation.

16. Higginbotham, *American Independence*, p. 393.

17. Arthur J. Alexander, "Desertion and its Punishment in Revolutionary Virginia," *William and Mary Quarterly*, Vol. 3 (July, 1946), p. 387.

18. Higginbotham, *American Independence*, p. 392.

19. Alexander, "Desertion and Punishment," p. 395.

No matter how crude or sluggish the system might have been, and despite General Washington's contempt for the militia itself, most Americans continued to believe that the citizen-soldier ideal was best suited for the new nation. The Articles of Confederation would stress freedom from central authority; problems of defense and manpower procurement would be shelved for another day. A militia which had been glorified by memories of the Minutemen and the exhilaration of victory was not to be lightly cast aside.

1

The American colonies in the seventeenth and eighteenth centuries each passed a series of acts designed to maintain a militia. The first law to provide for compulsory service was enacted in Virginia in 1629, and between then and the Revolution approximately two hundred separate acts were passed in the colonies affirming the principle of compulsion. However, it would be erroneous to assume from this large number of enactments that the colonies were a kind of garrison state. The militia was intended to be a local defensive force, and it was designed to take the place of a professional standing army. Despite the large amount of legislation concerning the militia, its existence seems to have minimized the development of a military tradition: "Militia service, it is true, was required of all able-bodied male colonists, but the exceptions were so numerous and the training days so few that there was little interruption of normal peacetime pursuits."[20]

The following law is representative of militia legislation in the seventeenth century.

New Jersey Militia Legislation, 1675

Forasmuch as it is requisite of necessity amongst all Men to be in a Posture of Defence against Enemies, or Dangers that may accrue, and

Reprinted from *Backgrounds of Selective Service*, Special Monograph No. 1, Vol. 2, Part 8 (Washington, D.C.: U.S. Selective Service System, 1947), p. 5.

20. Arthur A. Ekirch, Jr., *The Civilian and the Military: A History of the American Anti-Militarist Tradition*, p. 6.

especially we being invited hereunto by the Insolence and Outrages of the Heathens in our Neighbouring Colonies, not knowing how soon we may be surprised.

BE IT THEREFORE ENACTED by this Present Assembly that every Male within this Province from Sixteen Years Old, unto Sixty, be provided at his own Cost and Charge with a good sufficient Firelock, Gun, and one Pound of Powder, Twenty four Bullets fitted to the Gun, or four Pound of Pistol Bullets, six Flints, a Worm and priming Wire fit for the said Gun, a good Sword, Bandeleers, Cartridge Box, or Powder Horn to carry the aforesaid Powder, and that every Man be thus furnished within a Fortnight after Publication hereof, upon the Penalty of paying for every default as follows, viz. the first default of a Gun, Two Shillings and Six-pence, the second default Five Shillings, and so to continue; Sword One Shilling, Bandeleers horn or Cartridge box One Shilling, Powder Three Shillings, Bullets Three-pence, Flints Three-pence, Wire Three-pence, Worm Six-pence, and that the Serjeant with the Corporal, do by Order from the Commission Officers, view Arms at least once every quarter, or as often as the said Officers shall see Cause, which said Fines shall be collected by the Clerk of the Band, with Order from the Captain, who shall be assisted by a Serjeant in the Execution thereof, for the use of the Company, and upon refusal of Payment to be taken by distraint. . . .

2

On June 15, 1775, the Continental Congress selected one of its members, George Washington, to command the Continental forces. Washington accepted the command the following day and then departed for Boston to begin the seemingly endless task of developing a stable fighting force. On July 18 Congress passed a resolution recommending the organization of all able-bodied men between the ages of sixteen and fifty into militia units as a complement to the Continental Army. Congress had no authority to order this organization and could only call out such units with the permission of the individual state legislatures. This effort to persuade compliance on the part of the states illustrated a recurring difficulty in developing an effective military force.

Resolution of the Continental Congress, July 18, 1775

Resolved, That it be recommended to the inhabitants of all the united English Colonies in North America, that all able bodied effective men, between sixteen and fifty years of age in each colony, immediately form themselves into regular companies of Militia, to consist of one Captn, two lieutenants, one ensign, four serjeants, four corporals, one clerk, one drummer, one fifer, and about 68 privates.

That the officers of each company be chosen by the respective companies.

That each soldier be furnished with a good musket, that will carry an ounce ball, with a bayonet, steel ramrod, worm, priming wire and brush fitted thereto, a cutting sword or tomhawk, a cartridge-box, that will contain 23 rounds of cartridges, twelve flints and a knapsack.

That the Companies be formed into Regiments or Battalions, officered with a colonel, lieutenant Colonel, two Majors, an Adjutant, and Quarter Master.

That all officers above the Rank of a captain, be appointed by their respective provincial assemblies or conventions, or in their recess, by the committees of safety appointed by said assemblies or conventions. . . .

That all the Militia take proper care to acquire military skill, and be well prepared for defence by being each man provided with one pound of good gun powder, and four pounds of ball, fitted to his gun.

That one fourth part of the Militia in every Colony, be selected for minute men, of such persons as are willing to enter into this necessary service, formed into companies and Battalions, and their officers chosen and commissioned as aforesaid, to be ready on the shortest notice, to march to any place where their assistance may be required, for the defense of their own or a neighbouring colony; And as these minute men may eventually be called to action before the whole body of the militia are sufficiently trained, it is recommended that a more particular and diligent attention be paid to their instruction in military discipline.

That such of the minute men, as desire it, be relieved by new draughts as aforesaid, from the whole body of the Militia, once in four months.

As there are some people, who, from religious principles, cannot bear arms in any case, this Congress intend no violence to their consciences, but earnestly recommend it to them, to contribute liberally in this time of universal calamity, to the relief of their distressed brethren in the several

Reprinted from *Journals of Congress Containing the Proceedings from September 5, 1774 to January 1, 1776*, Vol. 1 (Philadelphia, 1777), pp. 170–71.

colonies, and to do all other services to their oppressed Country, which they can consistently with their religious principles. . . .

3

The following exchange of letters between Thomas Jefferson and John Adams, the beginning of a correspondence which was to last for forty-nine years, reflected their difference of opinion on the draft from the militia. Adams's acceptance of the policy of hiring substitutes provides a striking illustration of the inequity of the drafting procedure.

Jefferson-Adams Correspondence

To John Adams

Williamsburgh May 16, 1777

Dear Sir

Matters in our part of the continent are too much in quiet to send you news from hence. Our battalions for the Continental service were some time ago so far filled as rendered the recommendation of a draught from the militia hardly requisite, and the more so as in this country it was ever the most unpopular and impracticable thing that could be attempted. Our people even under the monarchical government had learnt to consider it as the last of all oppressions. . . .

Th: Jefferson

To Thomas Jefferson

Philadelphia May 26, 1777

My Dear Sir

I had this Morning, the Pleasure of your Favour of the Sixteenth inst, by the Post; and rejoice to learn that your Battalions, were so far fill'd, as to render a Draught from the Militia, unnecessary. It is a dangerous Measure, and only to be adopted in great extremities, even by popular

Reprinted from *The Adams-Jefferson Letters*, Vol. 1, ed. by Lester J. Cappon (Chapel Hill: The University of North Carolina Press, for the Institute of Early American History and Culture, 1959), pp. 4–5, by permission of the publisher.

Governments. Perhaps, in Such Governments Draughts will never be made, but in Cases, when the People themselves see the Necessity of them. Such Draughts are widely different from those made by Monarchs, to carry on Wars, in which the People can see, no Interest of their own nor any other object in View, than the Gratification of the Avarice, Ambition, Caprice, Envy, Revenge, or Vanity of a Single Tyrant. Draughts in the Massachusetts, as they have been there managed, have not been very unpopular, for the Persons draughted are commonly the wealthiest, who become obliged to give large Premiums, to their poorer Neighbours, to take their places. . . .

John Adams

4

The quietude "in our part of the continent" referred to by Thomas Jefferson in his letter to John Adams was eventually to be shattered by open resistance to the draft for the Virginia militia. A series of uprisings occurred in many of the counties of Virginia and reflected the widespread opposition to the draft. The following letter of May 15, 1781, from the tax commissioners of Accomac County to Governor Jefferson reveals the intensity of the resistance.

Letter to Governor Jefferson, 1781

. . . In such a situation were our affairs when a set of Men in the County of Northampton undertook to oppose the Draft, which they effected. From that time if not before a number of People in this County had it in contemplation to oppose the same here and consequently thought it unnecessary to pay the Tax. On the 23d. of April the day appointed to put the Draft Act in execution there assembled at the Court house to the amount of 150 or 200 Men armed with Clubs to oppose it. George Corbin Esqr. who acted as County Lieutenant endeavoured strenuously to appease the people by the most soothing and powerful arguments but could not alter their intentions. Colo. Corbin ordered the Clerk to look on the list for a Class who then appeared and produced to him a Man hired for the War. While the Clerk in the Court house was searching the list and

From *The Papers of Thomas Jefferson, February 1781 to May 1781*, Vol. 5, ed. by Julian P. Boyd (copyright 1952 by Princeton University Press), pp. 652–54. Reprinted by permission of Princeton University Press.

having found the Class laid the list on the table before him, one of the Mob snatch'd up the list, put the same in his pocket, telling the others, who by this time had crowded into the Court house, that if they approved of what was done to signify the same by three Cheers which was accordingly complied with. Colo. Corbin endeavoured to prevail on them to return the list but in vain, and heavy threatnings were denounced by them should any set of Men attempt to draw lots. The Colonel, together with the other Gentlemen who presided over the business, having held a consultation and thinking it impossible to carry the law into execution that day but supposing they might do it at some future opportunity when men had time to reflect again on the consequences of opposing the laws of their Country, they thought it most prudent to postpone the same until the Thursday following, the Clerk having taken care to preserve a duplicate of the list which the mob had deprived him of. Thursday the same set of Men appeared (some few excepted who pretended they were convinced by the Gentlemens arguments and being men of property did not apparently head the Mob but were generally believed to act behind the Scene) armed with Clubs swords guns and pistols and took possession of the Court house at the door of which they placed a sentinel with his Musket. Colo. Corbin went and talk'd to them moderately endeavouring to diswade them from such an unlawful act, but they all unanimously declared they were determined to oppose the Draft at the hazard of their lives and that it was in vain for him to attempt to alter their resolution. The Colonel told them he should be oblig'd to take an account of their names and ordered the Clerk who stood by him to note them down accordingly. This did not at all intimidate them neither was it possible to carry the Law into execution. Next day a Court Martial was summoned and held at Onancock where those who appeared to the said Court Martiall the most culpable were deemed Soldiers for the time prescribed by Law whose names will doubtless be transmitted to your Excellency officially by Colo. Corbin.

These lawless proceedings have thrown the County into the greatest confusion imaginable. People begin to publish, propagate and avow the most dangerous doctrines, sentiments and opinions. . . .

5

The inability of the Continental Congress to develop a stable army plagued Washington's efforts throughout the war. The Continental

Army fluctuated from 47,000 to as low as 2,000 men at one point, with the average complement being from 5,000 to 9,000 men. General Washington was forced, therefore, to be constantly involved in the process of creating an army, continually training replacements for the numbers departing from the Continental Army.

The militia proved to be an ever greater source of difficulty for Washington: "It is needless to add that short Inlistments, and a mistaken dependence upon Militia, have been the Origin of all our Misfortunes and the great accumulation of our Debt."[21] The following letter to the president of the Continental Congress illustrates Washington's growing despair during the second year of the war. He alludes to the competition in bounties that was going on between Congress and the state governments and the difficult situation it has created, yet he refuses to recommend a draft—"to force them into the Service would answer no valuable purpose."

Washington to the Continental Congress, 1776

To The President of Congress

Colonel Morris's, on the Heights of Harlem,
September 24, 1776

. . . We are now as it were, upon the eve of another dissolution of our Army; the remembrance of the difficulties which happened upon that occasion last year, the consequences which might have followed the change, if proper advantages had been taken by the Enemy; added to a knowledge of the present temper and Situation of the Troops, reflect but a very gloomy prospect upon the appearance of things now, and satisfie me, beyond the possibility of doubt, that unless some speedy, and effectual measures are adopted by Congress, our cause will be lost.

It is vain to expect, that any (or more than a trifling) part of this Army will again engage in the Service on the encouragement offered by Congress. When Men find that their Townsmen and Companions are receiving 20, 30, and more Dollars, for a few Months Service, (which is truely the case) it cannot be expected; without using compulsion; and to force them into the Service would answer no valuable purpose. When Men are irritated, and the Passions inflamed, they fly hastely and chearfully to Arms; but after the first emotions are over, to expect, among such

Reprinted from *The Writings of George Washington*, Vol. 6, ed. by John C. Fitzpatrick (Washington, D.C., 1931–44), pp. 106–12.

21. Fitzpatrick, *The Writings of George Washington*, Vol. 6, p. 402.

People, as compose the bulk of an Army, that they are influenced by any other principles than those of Interest, is to look for what never did, and I fear never will happen; the Congress will deceive themselves therefore if they expect it. . . .

With respect to the Men, nothing but a good bounty can obtain them upon a permanent establishment; and for no shorter time than the continuance of the War, ought they to be engaged; as Facts incontestibly prove, that the difficulty, and cost of Inlistments, increase with time. . . .

These Sir, Congress may be assured, are but a small part of the Inconveniences which might be enumerated and attributed to Militia; but there is one that merits particular attention, and that is the expence. Certain I am, that it would be cheaper to keep 50, or 100,000 Men in constant pay than to depend upon half the number, and supply the other half occasionally by Militia. The time the latter is in pay before and after they are in Camp, assembling and Marching; the waste of Ammunition; the consumption of Stores, which in spite of every Resolution, and requisition of Congress they must be furnished with, or sent home, added to other incidental expences consequent upon their coming, and conduct in Camp, surpasses all Idea, and destroys every kind of regularity and oeconomy which you could establish among fixed and Settled Troops; and will, in my opinion prove (if the scheme is adhered to) the Ruin of our Cause.

The Jealousies of a standing Army, and the Evils to be apprehended from one, are remote; and in my judgment, situated and circumstanced as we are, not at all to be dreaded; but the consequence of wanting one, according to my Ideas, formed from the present view of things, is certain, and inevitable Ruin; for if I was called upon to declare upon Oath, whether the Militia have been most serviceable or hurtful upon the whole; I should subscribe to the latter. I do not mean by this however to arraign the Conduct of Congress, in so doing I should equally condemn my own measures, (if I did not my judgment); but experience, which is the best criterion to work by, so fully, clearly, and decisively reprobates the practice of trusting to Militia, that no Man who regards order, regularity, and oeconomy; or who has any regard for his own honour, Character, or peace of Mind, will risk them upon this Issue. . . .

6

Washington's hesitancy over advocating compulsory military service in the Continental Army had ended by January, 1778. He recommended to the Continental Congress that the states fill their quotas in the Continental Army by a draft from the militia. For Washington it was a "disagreeable alternative" but an "unavoidable" one. A congressional delegation visited the army at Valley Forge soon after that date and in their report to Congress supported Washington's suggestion. A resolution was then passed by Congress providing that the states, except in cases where they were under invasion, should draft from their militia to fulfill their responsibilities to the Continental Army. All draftees were to serve for nine months but would be released sooner if replaced by volunteers from the respective states. The plan met with a great deal of hostility and opposition and achieved very little success.

Washington to the Continental Congress, 1778

Of Completing the Regiments and Altering Their Establishment

The necessity of the first, in the most expeditious manner possible, is too self evident to need illustration or proof, and I shall therefore only beg leave to offer some reflections on the mode. Voluntary inlistments seem to be totally out of the question; all the allurements of the most exorbitant bounties and every other inducement, that could be thought of, have been tried in vain, and seem to have had little other effect than to increase the rapacity and raise the demands of those to whom they were held out. We may fairly infer, that the country has been already pretty well drained of that class of Men, whose tempers, attachments and circumstances disposed them to enter permanently, or for a length of time, into the army; and that the residue of such men, who from different motives, have kept out of the army, if collected, would not augment our general strength in any proportion to what we require. If experience has demonstrated, that little more can be done by voluntary inlistments, some other mode must be concerted, and no other presents itself, than that of filling the Regiments by drafts from the Militia. This is a disagreeable alternative, but it is an unavoidable one.

As drafting for the war, or for a term of years, would probably be disgusting and dangerous, perhaps impracticable, I would propose an annual draft of men, without officers, to serve 'till the first day of January, in each year; That on or before the first day of October preceding,

Reprinted from The Writings of George Washington, Vol. 10, ed. by John C. Fitzpatrick (Washington, D.C., 1931–44), pp. 365–67.

these drafted Men should be called upon to reinlist for the succeeding year; and as an incitement to doing it, those being much better and less expensive than raw recruits, a bounty of twenty five dollars should be offered: That, upon ascertaining, at this period, the number of men, willing to re-engage, exact returns should be made to the Congress of the deficiency in each regiment, and transmitted by them to the respective states, in order that they may have their several quotas immediately furnished, and sent on to Camp, for the service of the ensuing year, so as to arrive by, or before, the first day of January.

This method, though not so good as that of obtaining Men for the war, is perhaps the best our circumstances will allow; and as we shall always have an established corps of experienced officers, may answer tolerably well. It is the only mode, I can think of, for completing our battalions in time, that promises the least prospect of success; the accomplishment of which is an object of the last importance; and it has this advantage, that the minds of the people being once reconciled to the experiment, it would prove a source of continual supplies hereafter.

Men drafted in this manner should not, in the first instance, receive any bounty from the public; which being solemnly enjoined upon each state, and a stop put to the militia substitution laws, would probably be attended with very happy consequences. A number of idle, mercenary fellows would be thrown out of employment, precluded from their excessive wages, as substitutes for a few weeks or months; and constrained to inlist in the Continental army. In speaking of abolishing the militia substitution laws, it is not meant to hinder a person, who might be drafted in the annual allotments, from procuring a substitute in his stead, himself in consequence being excused. This indulgence would be admissible, and considering all things, necessary, as there are many individuals, whose dispositions and private affairs would make them irreconcilably averse to giving their personal services, for so long a duration; and with whom it would be impolitic to use compulsion. The allowance of substitution, upon a smaller scale, in the occasional coming out of the militia, for a few Weeks, a month or two, is the thing meant to be reprobated. It is highly productive of the double disadvantage of preventing the growth of the Army, and depreciating our currency. . . .

1783-1861:
Reliance on the
Militia

THE ISSUE of compulsory military service asserted itself on several occasions during the period from the end of the Revolutionary War up until the beginning of the Civil War. The nation's military defense was an important consideration for the founding fathers, and it proved a continuing concern during the early years of the Republic. The outbreak of war in 1812 and again in 1846 brought renewed attention to the question of manpower procurement. Despite these periodic surges of interest, the federal government failed to develop its own workable program to provide a large military force when needed. It retained its dependence upon the states for that service, moving beyond that arrangement only when it proved inadequate for the waging of the Civil War.

Soon after the achievement of independence, the Continental Army was disbanded. Many of the nation's leaders held deep-seated fears about the dangers of a standing army. After all, had not a war just been fought to rid the nation of such a force? Indeed, this antagonism can be traced back to seventeenth-century England and the Great Rebellion, when the various participants abused the populace by quartering troops with the citizenry, suspending civil process, and declaring martial law. The writings of Cicero, Aristotle, Montesquieu, Coke, and Blackstone, among others, offered the founding fathers a recurring warning of the potential tyranny associated with a standing army.[1] Thomas Jefferson incorporated the colonists' intense dislike of British troops into the grievances directed against King George III in the Declaration of Independence: "He has kept among us, in Times of Peace, Standing Armies without the consent of our Legislatures. He has affected to render the Military independent of and superior to the Civil Power."

Therefore, it is easy to understand why the military powers of Congress during the Confederation period were not expanded over those of the Continental Congress; that is, Congress could declare war, but it could only ask for troops and money from the states. Thus, when there were Indian problems in the West or domestic uprisings such as Shays's Rebellion in Massachusetts, Congress could call for militia quotas, but it could only attempt to enlist volunteers in a national force or wait upon the states to raise troops.

These conditions, however, did not prevent Congress in 1783 from appointing a committee to study the question of a proper defense posture for the United States. One document resulting from this study was General George Washington's "Sentiments on a Peace Establishment." Dismissing the idea of a large standing army as anathema to the American people, Washington proposed instead the adoption of a small professional force backed by a national militia. His theory of a universal military obligation was the key to a national militia: "It may be laid down as a primary position, and the basis of our system," he stated, "that every Citizen who enjoys the protection of a free Government owes . . . his personal services to the defence of it."[2] Washington's proposal, along with several others, was discussed, but no action was taken, and the ultimate responsibility for defense still rested in the hands of the states.

When the Constitutional Convention assembled in 1787, the delegates addressed themselves to the question of national defense; indeed, they examined this question in greater detail than that of any other governmental function.[3] The constitution they drew up provided for civilian supremacy over the military, a president as civilian commander in chief responsible in turn to Congress, and

1. Gordon B. Turner, ed., *A History of Military Affairs in Western Society since the Eighteenth Century* (New York: Harcourt, Brace and Co., 1953), p. 33.

2. U.S., Selective Service System, *Backgrounds of Selective Service*, Vol. 1, p. 56.

3. Leon Friedman, "Conscription and the Constitution: The Original Understanding," *Michigan Law Review*, Vol. 67 (June, 1969), p. 1493.

reliance on a professional army reinforced by the state militias.

There is little doubt that many of the delegates were opposed to the proposition of a standing army. James Monroe asserted that "with respect to a standing army, I believe there was not a member in the Federal Convention who did not feel indignant at such an institution."[4] Elbridge Gerry of Massachusetts sought to limit the size of the national army to two thousand or, at most, three thousand men.[5] Despite stern opposition, the national government was given the power, along with certain restrictions, to maintain a small standing army. To provide for the defense of the nation, the government was allowed to "raise and support armies," a principle that became the basis for federal draft legislation throughout later American history. Moreover, the states retained control of their militias (which were considered the first lines of defense), and the people were guaranteed the right to bear arms, which "preserved their final power over both national and state governing authorities."[6]

The state conventions and the debates that followed produced many arguments relating to military matters. Ten states debated the military clauses, and five asked for amendments to mitigate against the possibility of military despotism.[7] The Rhode Island convention, for example, proposed an amendment to the Constitution providing "that no person shall be compelled to do military service otherwise than by voluntary enlistment, except in cases of general invasion, anything in the second paragraph of the Sixth Article of the Constitution or any law made under the Constitution to the contrary notwithstanding."[8] Additionally, the *Federalist Papers* examined the military clauses, with eight of the papers (4, 23, 24, 25, 26, 27, 28, and 29) emphasizing military matters.

As the 1790's approached, the militia, although guaranteed in the Constitution, had yet to receive organizational guidelines. In a message to Congress in August, 1789, President Washington urged passage of legislation to regulate the militia. Secretary of War Knox presented a plan calling for a "tightly controlled national militia system" to be maintained by a universal military obligation

4. Turner, *Military Affairs*, p. 31.
5. *Ibid.*, p. 32
6. Walter Millis, *Arms and Men*, p. 23.
7. Marcus Cunliffe, *Soldiers and Civilians*, p. 44.
8. Edward A. Fitzpatrick, *Universal Military Training* (New York, 1945), p. 343.

on all able-bodied men.[9] Congress rejected Knox's plan as too restrictive on the states and adopted instead the Militia Act of 1792.

This legislation required that all able-bodied male citizens (excluding blacks) between the ages of eighteen and forty-five be enrolled in the militia of their states. The drawback to the legislation was that the federal supervision of the state militias, which both Washington and Knox had recommended, was lacking. Historical hindsight might view this as an apparent oversight; however, recent independence and an inflated impression of the militia's excellence in previous conflicts persuaded the national legislators that federal control was both unnecessary and dangerous. In any case, this situation, and the fact that citizens were to provide their own equipment, made for an ineffective and lackadaisical militia. Finally, no penalties were stipulated for nonparticipation by enrollees.[10]

Thus, the states retained control of the militia. The tradition of uncooperative colonial militias still prevailed and continued to persist through the War of 1812 and into the Mexican War, when several New England states refused to commit their militias. The idea of a national militia, as outlined by Washington, never came to fruition. "The basic difficulty," Marcus Cunliffe wrote, "was that a casually administered, voluntary militia was militarily useless, while a well-trained, obligatory system was politically unattainable. In peacetime Americans would give only the most grudging, perfunctory assent to Washington's dictum of 1783 that 'every Citizen who enjoys the protection of a free Government, owes . . . his personal services to the defence of it.' "[11]

The development of organized militia units resulted from the poorly conceived 1792 legislation. These units were volunteer organizations, not unlike the volunteer militia of colonial times, composed of enrolled militiamen who were willing to drill on a regular

9. Millis, *Arms and Men*, p. 50.
10. Emory Upton, *The Military Policy of the United States*, p. 82; Russell F. Weigley, *Towards an American Army*, p. 20; and T. Harry Williams, *Americans at War: The Development of the American Military System* (Baton Rouge: Louisiana State University Press, 1960), p. 19. Jim Dan Hill argues that this legislation was merely an arrangement of American manpower similar to the function of registering with a local draft board in contemporary America and therefore should not be condemned for a lack of controls. By 1811 the legislation was responsible for enrolling 719,499 men. See Jim Dan Hill, *The Minute Man in Peace and War: A History of the National Guard* (Harrisburg, Pa.: Stackpole Co., 1964), pp. 10–11.
11. Cunliffe, *Soldiers and Civilians*, pp. 185–86.

basis. States urged the development of organized militia units to make up for their neglect of the enrolled militia. Tax exemptions for volunteers, fines for negligent enrollees, and contributions on the part of volunteers helped to arm and provide uniforms for these units.

The organized militia assured a governor of several units of trained fighting men if his state were ordered to produce a quota of troops for national defense. Should additional troops be required, the governor could resort to the unorganized or enrolled militia. These troops would either volunteer or be compelled by state draft laws to serve. Thus, a general military obligation was recognized, but only a portion of the population participated.

As the War of 1812 approached, a small regular army and the organized militia, backed by the enrolled militia, became America's basic manpower sources. The enrolled militia provided thousands of troops for that war. The majority served for short terms of one to twelve weeks for defense against Indian raids inland and in local campaigns, such as the inept defense of the nation's capital. The day-to-day fighting was performed by the regular army and volunteer organized militiamen and units who served for varying terms of duty. As these terms of duty ended, bounties (both money and land) were offered to induce organized militiamen to enter the regular army for additional duty.[12]

Federal conscription was not employed during the War of 1812, although it came very close to being adopted. Facing manpower procurement problems, Secretary of War John Armstrong suggested the use of a federal draft early in the conflict.[13] However, his proposal met with such negative response that it was soon shelved. Later, the fall of Washington, D.C., and continuing recruitment problems spurred the new secretary of war, James Monroe, to propose a comprehensive draft law. This was followed by a Senate version of Monroe's bill that called for the drafting of eighty thousand militiamen for two years' service.

The debate in the House on the bill precipitated some of the most

12. The decision to increase the size of the regular army rather than to recruit complete, organized militia units was based on the questionable constitutionality of having militia serve outside the territorial United States (for example, in Canada). This question, partially settled by an 1827 Supreme Court decision (*Martin* v. *Mott*, 12 Wheaton 19) ruling in favor of the federal government, continued to be a point of controversy until passage of the National Defense Act of 1916.

13. The successful use of the *levée en masse* by Napoleon was influential in the suggestion of a draft at this time.

heated exchanges ever heard in that chamber. Opposition forces led by Congressman Daniel Webster of Massachusetts fiercely denounced such a draft as unconstitutional. On December 8, 1814, Congressman Morris Miller of New York exclaimed: "The plan which gentlemen wish adopted is conscription! They call it classification and penalty—classification and draught. Sir, there is poison in the dish; garnish it as you please there is poison still. . . . The times demand that things should be called by their right names— this is conscription, and with features more hideous, than are to be found in the exploded system of our unfortunate cousin of Elba." [14] The draft bill was between Senate and House conferences when a turn in American military fortunes allowed the bill to die. America's first federal draft law would thus be delayed for another fifty years.

One of the by-products of the return to peacetime concerns in the aftermath of the War of 1812 was the complete demise of the enrolled militia. For example, in 1840 Massachusetts passed legislation that allowed all white males between the ages of eighteen and forty-five to enroll in the militia. However, enrollees would not have to drill or supply weapons as stipulated by the Militia Act of 1792. The law further stated that the organized militia would now become the recognized militia of the state. Thus, the enrolled militia, which had already been replaced physically, was now replaced legally as well. [15] In actuality, Massachusetts was finally recognizing the true condition of the militia.

This period of relative calm was also marked by innovative proposals on the part of two secretaries of war: John C. Calhoun (1817–25) and Joel R. Poinsett (1837–41). Each proposal sought to strengthen the inherent weaknesses in the manpower defense posture of the United States. Calhoun, in his "Report on the Reduction of the Army" in 1820, opted for elevating the regular army and disregarding the importance of the militia. Later, Poinsett theorized that by trimming down the enrolled militia, the United States could develop greater effectiveness through selectivity and intensive training. However, in the absence of any impending military threat, both plans were rejected without serious consideration.

The Mexican War found the United States relying on the regular army and on the organized militia, who, when offered the option of volunteering for twelve months' service or for the duration of the war, chose the former. This policy resulted in volunteers, in

14. U.S., House, *Annals of Congress*, 13th Cong., 3d sess., pp. 775–76
15. Cunliffe, *Soldiers and Civilians*, p. 222.

some instances, resigning at crucial times; in fact, General Winfield
Scott was forced to part with seven of his eleven regiments when
he was only three days' march from Mexico City. After February,
1847, no enlistment was permitted for less than the duration.[16]

The organized militia contributed mightily to the Mexican War
effort. Both short-term and duration enlistments accounted for approximately 75,000 out of the nearly 100,000 men who served.[17] In
a technical sense, the militia (that is, the enrolled militia), as de-
picted by the Militia Act of 1792, did not serve in the Mexican
War. The militia that did serve came predominantly from the volunteer organized militia units placed on active duty by the president. These units were mobilized by calls made to the governors
from the president in a way similar to the calling up of the National
Guard today.

After the Mexican War, the United States reverted to a small
regular army and organized militia units in each state.[18] The fighting ability of these units varied from state to state. Thus, situations
developed such as that in New York, in which the infantry, artillery
and cavalry units of the organized militia contained greater strength
than the United States Army itself. Furthermore, this power was
enhanced by the states' geographical concentration of the troops,
whereas the regular army, which never exceeded 17,500 men, was
dispersed throughout the United States.

The Civil War would create a need for vast armies requiring a
continuous supply of soldiers. This insatiable appetite for manpower would ultimately force a recognition that reliance upon a
small regular army backed by volunteers was not viable for prosecuting such a wide-ranging conflict. Thus, conditions totally new
to the American military experience would force the adoption of
the first American federal draft law.

7

In April, 1783, the Continental Congress established a Committee on the Peace Establishment chaired by Alexander Hamilton.
Hamilton solicited General Washington's views on the question of

16. Russell F. Weigley, *History of the United States Army*, p. 183.
17. Hill, *The Minute Man*, p. 23.
18. The organized militia was made up of approximately 130,000 men in 1860.
See *ibid.*, p. 51.

a peacetime army, and Washington responded on May 2 with his "Sentiments on a Peace Establishment." The basis of our national defense, according to Washington, should be a small regular army, less than three thousand men, for frontier duty backed up by a well-regulated militia composed of all of the able-bodied males between the ages of eighteen and fifty. Washington repeated his recommendations in an appearance before the Congress and in a circular letter to the governors, but no action was taken on his proposals.

Washington's "Sentiments on a Peace Establishment," 1783

... Altho' a *large* standing Army in time of Peace hath ever been considered dangerous to the liberties of a Country, yet a few Troops, under certain circumstances, are not only safe, but indispensably necessary. Fortunately for us our relative situation requires but few. The same circumstances which so effectually retarded, and in the end conspired to defeat the attempts of Britain to subdue us, will now powerfully tend to render us secure. Our *distance* from the European States in a great degree frees us of apprehension, from their numerous regular forces and the Insults and dangers which are to be dreaded from their Ambition. ...

I come next in the order I have prescribed myself, to treat of the Arrangements necessary for placing the Militia of the Continent on a respectable footing ... being persuaded, that the immediate safety and future tranquility of this extensive Continent depend in a great measure upon the peace Establishment now in contemplation; and being convinced at the same time, that the only probable means of preventing insult or hostility for any length of time and from being exempted from the consequent calamities of War, is to put the National Militia in such a condition as that they may appear truly respectable in the Eyes of our Friends and formidable to those who would otherwise become our enemies. ...

It may be laid down as a primary position, and the basis of our system, that every Citizen who enjoys the protection of a free Government, owes not only a proportion of his property, but even of his personal services to the defence of it, and consequently that the Citizens of America (with a few legal and official exceptions) from 18 to 50 Years of Age should be borne on the Militia Rolls, provided with uniform Arms, and so far accustomed to the use of them, that the Total strength of the Country might

Reprinted from *The Writings of George Washington,* Vol. 26, ed. by John C. Fitzpatrick (Washington, D.C., 1931–44), pp. 374–91.

be called forth at a Short Notice on any very interesting Emergency, for these purposes they ought to be duly organized into Commands of the same formation; (it is not of *very* great importance, whether the Regiments are large or small, provided a sameness prevails in the strength and composition of them and I do not know that a better establishment, than that under which the Continental Troops now are, can be adopted. They ought to be regularly Mustered and trained, and to have their Arms and Accoutrements inspected at certain appointed times, not less than once or twice in the course of every [year] but as it is obvious, amongst such a Multitude of People (who may indeed be useful for temporary service) there must be a great number, who from domestic Circumstances, bodily defects, natural awkwardness or disinclination, can never acquire the habits of Soldiers; but on the contrary will injure the appearance of any body of Troops to which they are attached, and as there are a sufficient proportion of able bodied young Men, between the Age of 18 and 25, who, from a natural fondness for Military parade (which passion is almost ever prevalent at that period of life) might easily be enlisted or drafted to form a Corps in every State, capable of resisting any sudden impression which might be attempted by a foreign Enemy, while the remainder of the National forces would have time to Assemble and make preparation for the Field. I would wish therefore, that the former, being considered as a *denier resort* reserved for some great occasion, a judicious system might be adopted for the forming and the placing the latter on the best possible Establishment. And while the Men of this description shall be viewed as the Van and flower of the American Forces, ever ready for Action and zealous to be employed whenever it may become necessary in the service of their Country; they should meet with such exemptions, privileges or distinctions, as might tend to keep alive a true Military pride, a nice sense of honour, and a patriotic regard for the public. Such sentiments, indeed, ought to be instilled into our Youth, with their earliest years, to be cherished and inculcated as frequently and forcibly as possible. . . .

8

Secretary of War Henry Knox published a pamphlet in 1786 entitled "A Plan for the General Arrangement of the Militia of the United States," and this program, with certain revisions suggested by General Washington, was submitted to Congress on January 21,

1790. The plan was essentially one of universal military training, with the male population between the ages of eighteen and sixty being formed into advanced corps, main corps, and reserved corps. The plan was not well received by Congress, and no action was taken on it, nor on a weakened version the following year.[19]

Knox Militia Plan, 1786

That a well constituted Republic is more favorable to the liberties of society, and that its principles give a higher elevation to the human mind than any other form of Government, has generally been acknowledged by the unprejudiced and enlightened part of mankind.

But it is at the same time acknowledged, that, unless a Republic prepares itself by proper arrangements to meet those exigencies to which all States are in a degree liable, that its peace and existence are more precarious than the forms of Government in which the will of one directs the conduct of the whole, for the defence of the nation.

A Government, whose measures must be the result of multiplied deliberations, is seldom in a situation to produce instantly those exertions which the occasion may demand; therefore, it ought to possess such energetic establishments as should enable it, by the vigor of its own citizens, to control events as they arise, instead of being convulsed or subverted by them. . . .

It is the intention of the present attempt to suggest the most efficient system of defence which may be compatible with the interests of a free people—a system which shall not only produce the expected effect, but which, in its operations, shall also produce those habits and manners which will impart strength and durability to the whole Government.

The modern practice of Europe, with respect to the employment of standing armies, has created such a mass of opinion in their favor, that even philosophers, and the advocates of liberty, have frequently confessed their use and necessity in certain cases.

But whoever seriously and candidly estimates the power of discipline, and the tendency of military habits, will be constrained to confess that, whatever may be the efficacy of a standing army in war, it cannot in peace

Reprinted from *Annals of Congress*, 1st Cong., Vol. II, pp. 2088–2107.

19. William Maclay, senator from Pennsylvania, expressed the thoughts of many congressmen when he said, "Give Knox his army, and he will soon have a war on hand; indeed, I am clearly of opinion that he is aiming at this even now. . . ." (Charles Beard, ed., *The Journal of William Maclay* [New York, 1927], p. 233.)

be considered as friendly to the rights of human nature. The recent instance in France cannot with propriety be brought to overturn the general principle, built upon the uniform experience of mankind.

It may be found, on examining the causes that appear to have influenced the military of France, that, while the springs of power were wound up in the nation to the highest pitch, the discipline of the army was proportionately relaxed. But any argument on this head may be considered as unnecessary to the enlightened citizens of the United States.

A small corps of well disciplined and well informed artillerists and engineers, and a legion for the protection of the frontiers, and the magazines and arsenals, are all the military establishment which may be required for the present use of the United States. The privates of the corps to be enlisted for a certain period, and after the expiration of which, to return to the mass of the citizens.

An energetic national militia is to be regarded as the capital security of a free Republic; and not a standing army, forming a distinct class in the community.

It is the introduction and diffusion of vice and corruption of manners into the mass of the people that render a standing army necessary. It is when public spirit is despised, and avarice, indolence, and effeminacy of manners predominate, and prevent the establishment of institutions which would elevate the minds of youth in the paths of virtue and honor, that a standing army is formed and riveted forever.

While the human character remains unchanged, and societies and governments of considerable extent are formed, a principle ever ready to execute the laws and defend the State must constantly exist. Without this vital principle, the Government would be invaded or overturned, and trampled upon by the bold and ambitious. No community can be long held together, unless its arrangements are adequate to its probable exigencies.

If it should be decided to reject a standing army for the military branch of the Government of the United States, as possessing too fierce an aspect, and being hostile to the principles of liberty, it will follow that a well constituted militia ought to be established.

A consideration of the subject will show the impracticability of disciplining at once the mass of the people. All discussions on the subject of a powerful militia will result in one or other of the following principles:

First. Either efficient institutions must be established for the military education of youth, and that the knowledge acquired therein shall be diffused throughout the community, by the means of rotation; or,

Secondly. That the militia must be formed of substitutes, after the manner of the militia of Great Britain.

If the United States possess the vigor of mind to establish the first institution, it may reasonably be expected to produce the most un-equivocal advantages. A glorious national spirit will be introduced, with its extensive train of political consequences. The youth will imbibe a love of their country; reverence and obedience to its laws; courage and elevation of mind; openness and liberality of character; accompanied by a just spirit of honor; in addition to which their bodies will acquire a robustness, greatly conducive to their personal happiness, as well as the defence of their country; while habit, with its silent but efficacious operations, will durably cement the system. Habit, that powerful and universal law, incessantly acting on the human race, well deserves the attention of legislators—formed at first in individuals, by separate and almost imperceptible impulses, until at length it acquires a force which controls with irresistible sway. The effects of salutary or pernicious habits, operating on a whole nation, are immense, and decide its rank and character in the world.

Hence the science of legislation teaches to scrutinize every national institution, as it may introduce proper or improper habits; to adopt with religious zeal the former, and reject with horror the latter.

A Republic, constructed on the principles herein stated, would be uninjured by events, sufficient to overturn a Government supported solely by the uncertain power of a standing army.

The well-informed members of the community, actuated by the highest motives of self-love, would form the real defence of the coun-try. Rebellions would be prevented, or suppressed with ease. Invasions of such a government would be undertaken only by madmen; and the virtues and knowledge of the people would effectually oppose the introduction of tyranny.

But the second principle, a militia of substitutes, is pregnant, in a degree, with the mischiefs of a standing army; as it is highly probable the substitutes, from time to time, will be nearly the same men, and the most idle and worthless part of the community. Wealthy families, proud of distinctions which riches may confer, will prevent their sons from serving in the militia of substitutes; the plan will generate into habitual contempt; a standing army will be introduced, and the liberties of the people subjected to all the contingencies of events.

strongly urged as an objection to the institution. But it is to be remem-

The expense attending an energetic establishment of militia may be

bered that this objection is levelled at both systems, whether by rotation or by substitutes; for, if the numbers are equal, the expense will also be equal. The estimate of the expense will show its unimportance, when compared with the magnitude and beneficial effects of the institution.

But the people of the United States will cheerfully consent to the expenses of a measure calculated to serve as a perpetual barrier to their liberties; especially as they well know that the disbursements will be made among the members of the same community, and therefore cannot be injurious.

Every intelligent mind would rejoice in the establishment of an institution, under whose auspices the youth and vigor of the constitution would be renewed with each successive generation, and which would appear to secure the great principles of freedom and happiness against the injuries of time and events.

The following plan is formed on these general principles:

First. That it is the indispensable duty of every nation to establish all necessary institutions for its own perfection and defence.

Secondly. That it is a capital security to a free State for the great body of the people to possess a competent knowledge of the military art.

Thirdly. That this knowledge cannot be attained in the present state of society, but by establishing adequate institutions for the military education of youth; and that the knowledge acquired therein should be diffused throughout the community by the principles of rotation.

Fourthly. That every man of the proper age and ability of body, is firmly bound by the social compact to perform, personally, his proportion of military duty for the defence of the State.

Fifthly. That all men, of the legal military age should be armed, enrolled, and held responsible for different degrees of military service. And,

Sixthly. That, agreeably to the Constitution, the United States are to provide for organizing, arming, and disciplining the militia; and for governing such a part of them as may be employed in the service of the United States; reserving to the States, respectively, the appointment of the officers, and the authority of training the militia, according to the discipline prescribed by Congress.

THE PLAN

The period of life, in which military service shall be required of the citizens of the United States, to commence at eighteen, and terminate at the age of sixty years.

The men comprehended by this description, exclusive of such exceptions as the Legislatures of the respective States may think proper to make, and all actual mariners, shall be enrolled for different degrees of military duty, and divided into three distinct classes.

The first class shall comprehend the youth of eighteen, nineteen, and twenty years of age; to be denominated the advanced corps.

The second class shall include the men from twenty-one to forty-five years of age; to be denominated the main corps.

The third class shall comprehend, inclusively, the men from forty-six to sixty years of age; to be denominated the reserved corps. . . .

OF THE ADVANCED CORPS

The advanced corps are designed not only as a school in which the youth of the United States are to be instructed in the art of war, but they are, in all cases of exigence, to serve as an actual defence to the community.

The whole of the armed corps shall be clothed according to the manner hereafter directed, armed and subsisted at the expense of the United States; and all the youth of the said corps, in each State, shall be encamped together, if practicable, or by legions; which encampments shall be denominated the annual camps of discipline.

The youth of eighteen and nineteen years shall be disciplined for thirty days successively in each year; and those of twenty years shall be disciplined only for ten days in each year, which shall be the last ten days of the annual encampments. . . .

OF THE MAIN CORPS

. . . The main corps will be perfectly armed, in the first instance, and will practise the exercise and manoeuvres four days in each year, and will assemble in their respective districts, by companies, battalions, regiments, or legions, as shall be directed by the legionary general; but it must be a fixed rule, that in the populous parts of the States, the regiments must assemble once annually, and the legions once in three years.

Although the main corps cannot acquire a great degree of military knowledge in the few days prescribed for its annual exercise, yet by the constant accession of the youth from the advanced corps it will soon command respect for its discipline as well as its numbers. . . .

Of the Reserved Corps

The reserved corps will assemble only twice annually for the inspection of arms, by companies, battalions, or regiments, as shall be directed by each State. It will assemble by legions, whenever the defence of the State may render the measure necessary.

Such are the propositions of the plan: to which it may be necessary to add some explanations.

Although the substantial political maxim, which requires personal service of all the members of the community for the defence of the State, is obligatory under all forms of society, and is the main pillar of a free Government, yet the degrees thereof may vary at the different periods of life, consistently with the general welfare. The public convenience may also dictate a relaxation of the general obligation as it respects the principal magistrates, and the ministers of justice and religion, and perhaps some religious sects. But it ought to be remembered that measures of national importance never should be frustrated for the accommodation of individuals.

The military age has generally commenced at sixteen, and terminated at the age of sixty years; but the youth of sixteen do not commonly attain such a degree of robust strength as to enable them to sustain without injury the hardships incident to the field; therefore the commencement of military service is herein fixed at eighteen, and the termination, as usual, at sixty years of age.

As the plan proposes that the militia shall be divided into three capital classes, and that each class shall be formed into legions, the reasons for which shall be given in succession.

The advanced corps and annual camps of discipline are instituted in order to introduce an operative military spirit in the community. To establish a course of honorable military service which will, at the same time, mould the minds of the young men to a due obedience of the laws, instruct them in the art of war, and by the manly exercises of the field form a race of hardy citizens, equal to the dignified task of defending their country. . . .

Youth is the time for the State to avail itself of those services which it has a right to demand and by which it is to be invigorated and preserved; in this season, the passions and affections are strongly influenced by the splendor of military parade. The impressions the mind receives will be retained through life. The young man will repair with pride and pleasure to the field of exercise; while the head of a family, anxious for its general welfare, and perhaps its immediate subsistence, will reluctantly quit his domestic duties for any length of time.

The habits of industry will be rather strengthened than relaxed by the establishment of the annual camps of discipline, as all the time will be occupied by the various military duties. Idleness and dissipation will be regarded as disgraceful and punished accordingly. As soon as the youth attain the age of manhood, a natural solicitude to establish themselves in society will occur in its full force. The public claims for military service will be too inconsiderable to injure their industry. It will be sufficiently stimulated to proper exertions by the prospects of opulence attending on the cultivation of a fertile soil, or the pursuits of a productive commerce.

It is presumed that thirty days annually during the eighteenth and nineteenth, and ten days during the twentieth year, is the least time that ought to be appropriated by the youth to the acquisition of the military art. The same number of days might be added during the twentieth as during the two preceding years, were not the expense an objection.

Every means will be provided by the public to facilitate the military education of the youth, which it is proposed shall be an indispensable qualification of a free citizen, therefore they will not be entitled to any pay. But the officers being of the main corps are in a different predicament; they are supposed to have passed through the course of discipline required by the laws, and to be competent to instruct others in the military art. As the public will have but small claims for personal services on them, and as they must incur considerable expenses to prepare themselves to execute properly their respective offices, they ought to be paid while on actual duty.

As soon as the service of the youth expires in the advanced corps they are to be enrolled in the main corps. On this occasion the Republic receives disciplined and free citizens, who understand their public rights, and are prepared to defend them.

The main corps is instituted to preserve and circulate throughout the community the military discipline acquired in the advanced corps; to arm the people, and fix firmly, by practice and habit, those forms and maxims which are essential to the life and energy of a free Government.

The reserved corps is instituted to prevent men being sent to the field whose strength is unequal to sustain the severities of an active campaign. But by organizing and rendering them eligible for domestic service, a greater proportion of the younger and robust part of the community may be enabled, in cases of necessity, to encounter the more urgent duties of war. . . .

The vigor and importance of the proposed plan will entirely depend on the laws relative thereto. Unless the laws shall be equal to the object, and rigidly enforced, no energetic national militia can be established.

If wealth be admitted as a principle of exemption the plan cannot be executed. It is the wisdom of political establishments to make the wealth of individuals subservient to the general good, and not to suffer it to corrupt or attain undue indulgence.

It is conceded that people, solicitous to be exonerated from their proportion of public duty, may exclaim against the proposed arrangement as an intolerable hardship; but it ought to be strongly impressed, that, while society has its charms, it also has its indispensable obligations; that to attempt such a degree of refinement, as to exonerate the members of the community from all personal service, is to render them incapable of the exercise and unworthy of the characters of freemen.

Every State possesses, not only the right of personal service from its members, but the right to regulate the service on principles of equality for the general defence. All being bound, none can complain of injustice on being obliged to perform his equal proportion. Therefore, it ought to be a permanent rule, that those who in youth decline, or refuse to subject themselves to the course of military education, established by the laws, should be considered as unworthy of public trust, or public honors, and be excluded therefrom accordingly.

If the majesty of the laws should be preserved inviolate in this respect, the operations of the proposed plan would foster a glorious public spirit, infuse the principles of energy and stability into the body politic and give a high degree of political splendor to the national character.

9

The Knox plan of 1786 became, in an "eviscerated" form,[20] the Militia Act of 1792. This act, which was to remain on the books for over a century, gave sanction to many of the procedures which had rendered Washington's task so difficult during the Revolutionary War. The individual states were left to their own discretion on questions of training, leadership, and deferments, and the individual militiaman was held responsible for providing his own firearm, with no penalty assessed for noncompliance. The national militia repeatedly sought by Washington and Knox was now re-

20. Millis, *Arms and Men*, p. 45.

placed by a "phantom citizen army"[21]—or, rather, thirteen largely paper armies, since the states did not make any strenuous efforts to keep their militias viable.

Militia Act of 1792

Section 1. *Be it enacted by the Senate and House of Representatives of the United States of America in Congress assembled,* That each and every free able-bodied white male citizen of the respective states, resident therein, who is or shall be of the age of eighteen years, and under the age of forty-five years (except as is herein after excepted) shall severally and respectively be enrolled in the militia by the captain or commanding officer of the company, within whose bounds such citizen shall reside, and that within twelve months after the passing of this act. And it shall at all times hereafter be the duty of every such captain or commanding officer of a company to enrol every such citizen, as aforesaid, and also those who shall, from time to time, arrive at the age of eighteen years, or being of the age of eighteen years and under the age of forty-five years (except as being excepted) shall come to reside within his bounds; and shall without delay notify such citizen of the said enrolment, by a proper non-commissioned officer of the company, by whom such notice may be proved. That every citizen so enrolled and notified, shall, within six months thereafter, provide himself with a good musket or firelock, a sufficient bayonet and belt, two spare flints, and a knapsack, a pouch with a box therein to contain not less than twenty-four cartridges, suited to the bore of his musket or firelock, each cartridge to contain a proper quantity of powder and ball: or with a good rifle, knapsack, shot-pouch and powder-horn, twenty balls suited to the bore of his rifle, and a quarter of a pound of powder; and shall appear, so armed, accoutred and provided, when called out to exercise, or into service, except that when called out on company days to exercise only, he may appear without a knapsack. . . .

Section 2. *And be it further enacted,* That the Vice President of the United States; the officers judicial and executive of the government of the United States; the members of both Houses of Congress, and their respective officers; all custom-house officers with their clerks; all post-

Reprinted from *Statutes at Large,* 2d Cong., 1st sess., Vol. 1, pp. 271–74.

21. Williams, *Americans at War,* p. 27.

officers, and stage drivers, who are employed in the care and conveyance
of the mail of the post-office of the United States; all ferrymen employed
at any ferry on the post road; all inspectors of exports; all pilots; all
mariners actually employed in the sea service of any citizen or merchant
within the United States; and all persons who now are or may hereafter
be exempted by the laws of the respective states, shall be, and are hereby
exempted from militia duty, notwithstanding their being above the age
of eighteen, and under the age of forty-five years.

Section 3. *And be it further enacted,* That within one year after passing of this act, the militia of the respective states shall be arranged into
divisions, brigades, regiments, battalions and companies, as the legislature of each state shall direct; and each division, brigade and regiment,
shall be numbered at the formation thereof; and a record made of such
numbers in the adjutant-general's office in the state; and when in the
field, or in service in the state, each division, brigade and regiment shall
respectively take rank according to their numbers, reckoning the first or
lowest number highest in rank. That if the same be convenient, each
brigade shall consist of four regiments; each regiment of two battalions,
each battalion of five companies, each company of sixty-four privates.
That the said militia shall be offered by the respective states, as follows:
To each division, one major-general and two aids-de-camp, with the
rank of major; to each brigade, one brigadier-general, with one brigade
inspector, to serve also as brigade-major, with the rank of a major; to
each regiment, one lieutenant-colonel commandant; and to each battalion one major; to each company one captain, one lieutenant; one
ensign, four sergeants, four corporals, one drummer and one fifer or
bugler. That there shall be a regimental staff, to consist of one adjutant
and one quartermaster, to rank as lieutenants; one paymaster; one surgeon, and one surgeon's mate; one sergeant-major; one drum-major, and
one fife-major. . . .

Section 6. *And be it further enacted,* That there shall be an adjutant-
general appointed in each state, whose duty it shall be to distribute all
orders from the commander-in-chief of the state to the several corps; to
attend all public reviews when the commander-in-chief of the state shall
review the militia, or any part thereof; to obey all orders from him relative to carrying into execution and perfecting the system of military
discipline established by this act; to furnish blank forms of different
returns that may be required, and to explain the principles on which
they should be made; to receive from the several officers of the different
corps throughout the state, returns of the militia under their command,

reporting the actual situation of their arms, accoutrements, and ammunition, their delinquencies, and every other thing which relates to the general advancement of good order and discipline: all which the several officers of the divisions, brigades, regiments, and battalions, are hereby required to make in the usual manner, so that the said adjutant-general may be duly furnished therewith: from all which returns he shall make proper abstracts, and lay the same annually before the commander-in-chief of the state.

Section 7. *And be it further enacted*, That the rules of discipline, approved and established by Congress in their resolution of the twenty-ninth of March, one thousand seven hundred and seventy-nine, shall be the rules of discipline to be observed by the militia throughout the United States, except such deviations from the said rules as may be rendered necessary by the requisitions of this act, or by some other unavoidable circumstances. It shall be the duty of the commanding officer at every muster, whether by battalion, regiment, or single company, to cause the militia to be exercised and trained agreeable to the said rules of discipline. . . .

Section 9. *And be it further enacted*, That if any person, whether officer or soldier, belonging to the militia of any state, and called out into the service of the United States, be wounded or disabled while in actual service, he shall be taken care of and provided for at the public expense.

Section 10. *And be it further enacted*, That it shall be the duty of the brigade-inspector to attend the regimental and battalion meetings of the militia composing their several brigades, during the time of their being under arms, to inspect their arms, ammunition, and accoutrements; superintend their exercise and manoeuvres, and introduce the system of military discipline before described throughout the brigade, agreeable to law, and such orders as they shall from time to time receive from the commander-in-chief of the state; to make returns to the adjutant-general of the state, at least once in every year, of the militia of the brigade to which he belongs, reporting therein the actual situation of the arms, accoutrements, and ammunition of the several corps, and every other thing which, in his judgement, may relate to their government and the general advancement of good order and military discipline; and the adjutant-general shall make a return of all the militia of the state to the commander-in-chief of the said state, and a duplicate of the same to the President of the United States. . . .

Approved, May 8, 1792.

10

The same difficulties in systematic manpower procurement that had damaged the American effort in the Revolutionary War recurred during the War of 1812. At the outbreak of the war, the United States Army was at only 20 percent of its authorized strength, and it proved increasingly difficult to remedy that situation because of the widespread opposition to the war. Several of the New England states refused to supply the militia requested by the president on the grounds that since there was no insurrection or invasion the president lacked the authority to call for the state militia. This legal point was not resolved until long after the war had ended, with the Supreme Court deciding that the power was exclusively the president's to determine whether the conditions allowing a militia call were in existence.[22]

It was in the face of these difficulties that Secretary of War James Monroe, on October 17, 1814, submitted a program to the chairmen of the committees on military affairs. His recommendations presented four possible plans to improve and strengthen the army, the first of which, according to Monroe, would be the most successful.

Monroe's First Plan to Strengthen the Army, 1814

EXPLANATORY OBSERVATIONS

... A nation contending for its existence against an enemy powerful by land and sea, favored in a peculiar manner, by extraordinary events, must make great exertions, and suffer great sacrifices. Forced to contend again for our liberties and independence, we are called on for a display of all the patriotism which distinguished our fellow-citizens in the first great struggle. It may be fairly concluded that if the United States sacrifice any right, or make any dishonorable concession to the demands of the British Government, the spirit of the nation will be broken, and the foundations of their union and independence shaken. The United States must relinquish no right, or perish in the struggle. ...

It follows, from this view of the subject, that it will be necessary to bring into the field, next campaign, not less than one hundred thousand

Reprinted from *American State Papers*, Class V, *Military Affairs*, Vol. 1, pp. 514–17.

22. *Martin* v. *Mott*, 12 Wheaton 19 (1827).

regular troops. Such a force, aided, in extraordinary emergencies, by volunteers and the militia, will place us above all inquietude as to the final result of this contest. It will fix on a solid and imperishable foundation, our union and independence, on which the liberties and happiness of our fellow-citizens so essentially depend. It will secure to the United States an early and advantageous peace. It will arrest, in the further prosecution of the war, the desolation of our cities and our coast, by enabling us to retort on the enemy, those calamities which our citizens have been already doomed to suffer—a resort which self defence alone, and a sacred regard for the rights and honor of the nation, could induce the United States to adopt.

The return of the regular force now in service, laid before you, will show how many men will be necessary to fill the present corps; and the return of the numerical force of the present military establishment will show how many are required to complete it to the number proposed. The next part and most important inquiry is, how shall these men be raised? Under existing circumstances, it is evident that the most prompt and efficient mode that can be devised, consistent with the equal rights of every citizen, ought to be adopted. The following plans are respectfully submitted to the consideration of the committee. Being distinct in their nature, I will present each separately, with the considerations applicable to it.

FIRST PLAN

Let the free male population of the United States, between eighteen and forty-five years, be formed into classes of one hundred men each, and let each furnish four men for the war, within thirty days after the classification, and replace them in the event of casualty.

The classification to be formed with a view to the equal distribution of property among the several classes.

If any class fails to provide the men required of it, within the time specified, they shall be raised by draught on the whole class, any person thus draughted, being allowed to furnish a substitute. . . .

That this plan will be efficient cannot be doubted. It is evident that the men contemplated may soon be raised by it. Three modes occur by which it may be carried into effect: first, By placing the execution of it in the hands of the county courts throughout the United States; second, By relying on the militia officers in each county; third, By appointing particular persons for that purpose in every county. It is believed that either of these modes would be found inadequate.

Nor does there appear to be any well founded objection to the right in Congress to adopt this plan, or to its equality in its application to our fellow-citizens individually. Congress have a right, by the constitution, to raise regular armies, and no restraint is imposed on the exercise of it, except in the provisions which are intended to guard generally against the abuse of power, with none of which does this plan interfere. It is proposed that it shall operate on all alike; that none shall be exempted from it except the Chief Magistrate of the United States, and the Governors of the several States.

I would be absurd to suppose that Congress could not carry this power into effect, otherwise than by accepting the voluntary service of individuals. It might happen that an army could not be raised in that mode, whence the power would have been granted in vain. The safety of the State might depend on such an army. Long continued invasions, conducted by regular, well disciplined troops, can best be repelled by troops kept constantly in the field, and equally well disciplined. Courage in an army, is, in a great measure, mechanical. A small body, well trained, accustomed to action, gallantly led on, often breaks three or four times the number of more respectable and more brave, but raw and undisciplined troops. The sense of danger is diminished by frequent exposure to it, without harm; and confidence, even in the timid, is inspired by a knowledge that reliance may be placed on others, which can grow up only by service together. The grant to Congress to raise armies, was made with a knowledge of all these circumstances, and with an intention that it should take effect. The framers of the constitution, and the States who ratified it, knew the advantage which an enemy might have over us, by regular forces, and intended to place their country on an equal footing.

The idea that the United States cannot raise a regular army in any other mode than by accepting the voluntary service of individuals, is believed to be repugnant to the uniform construction of all grants of power, and equally so to the first principles and leading objects of the federal compact. An unqualified grant of power gives the means necessary to carry it into effect. This is an universal maxim, which admits of no exception. Equally true is it, that the conservation of the State is a duty paramount to all others. The commonwealth has a right to the service of all its citizens; or rather, the citizens composing the commonwealth have a right, collectively and individually, to the service of each other, to repel any danger which may be menaced. The manner in which the service is to be apportioned among the citizens, and rendered by them, are objects of legislation. All that is to be dreaded in such case, is, the abuse of powers; and, happily, our constitution has provided ample security against that evil.

In support of this right in Congress, the militia service affords a conclusive proof and striking example. The organization of the militia is an act of public authority, not a voluntary association. The service required must be performed by all, under penalties, which delinquents pay. The generous and patriotic perform them cheerfully. In the alacrity with which the call of the Government has been obeyed, and the cheerfulness with which the service has been performed throughout the United States, by the great body of the militia, there is abundant cause to rejoice in the strength of our republican institutions, and in the virtue of the people.

The plan proposed is not more compulsive than the militia service, while it is free from most of the objections to it. The militia service calls from home, for long terms, whole districts of country. None can elude the call. Few can avoid the service; and those who do are compelled to pay great sums for substitutes. This plan fixes on no one personally, and opens to all who choose it a chance of declining the service. It is a principal object of this plan to engage in the defence of the State the unmarried and youthful, who can best defend it, and best be spared, and to secure to those who render this important service an adequate compensation from the voluntary contributions of the more wealthy, in every class. Great confidence is entertained that such contribution will be made in time to avoid a draught. Indeed, it is believed to be the necessary and inevitable tendency of this plan to produce that effect.

The limited powers which the United States have in organizing the militia may be urged as an argument against their right to raise regular troops in the mode proposed. If any argument could be drawn from that circumstance, I should suppose that it would be in favor of an opposite conclusion. The power of the United States over the militia has been limited, and that for raising regular armies granted without limitation. There was doubtless some object in this arrangement. The fair inference seems to be, that it was made on great consideration; that the limitation, in the first instance, was intentional, the consequence of the unqualified grant in the second. But it is said, that, by drawing the men from the militia service into the regular army, and putting them under regular officers, you violate a principle of the constitution, which provides that the militia shall be commanded by their own officers. If this was the fact, the conclusion would follow. But it is not fact. The men are not drawn from the militia, but from the population of the country. When they enlist voluntarily, it is not as militia men they act, but as citizens. If they are draughted, it must be in the same sense. In both instances, they are enrolled in the militia corps; but that, as is presumed, cannot prevent the voluntary act in the one instance or the compulsive in the other. The whole population of the United States, within certain ages, belong to these corps. If the United States could not form regular armies from them, they could raise none.

In proposing a draught as one of the modes of raising men, in case of actual necessity, in the present great emergency of the country, I have thought it my duty to examine such objections to it as occurred, particularly those of a constitutional nature. It is from my sacred regard for the principles of our constitution, that I have ventured to trouble the committee with any remarks on this part of the subject. . . .

11

The Monroe proposal passed in the Senate and, in an amended version, in the House despite the fact that twenty-nine out of thirty New England congressmen voted against it. The bill then passed to a conference committee of both houses, where the discrepancies in the two versions were to be resolved, but the war ended before the committee acted.

Without question, the most telling assault on the draft bill was made by Daniel Webster, who had been elected to the House from Massachusetts two years previously as an antiwar candidate. Webster rose on December 9, 1814, and delivered what has become a classic statement of opposition to conscription in a free society.

Webster's Anticonscription Speech

Dec. 9, 1814

Mr. Chairman,

After the best reflection which I have been able to bestow on the subject of the bill before you, I am of opinion that its principles are not warranted by any provision of the constitution. . . .

This bill indeed is less undisguised in its object, and less direct in its means, than some of the measures proposed. It is an attempt to exercise

Reprinted from C. H. Van Tyne, *The Letters of Daniel Webster* (New York, 1902), pp. 56–68.

the power of forcing the free men of this country into the ranks of an army, for the general purposes of war, under color of a military service. To this end it commences with a *classification*, which is no way connected with the general organization of the Militia, nor, to my apprehension, included within any of the powers which Congress possesses over them. All the authority which this Government has over the Militia, until actually called into its service, is to enact laws for their organization and discipline. This power it has exercised. It now possesses the further power of calling into its service any portion of the Militia of the States, in the particular exigencies for which the Constitution provides, and of governing them during the continuance of such service. Here its authority ceases. The classification of the whole body of the Militia, according to the provisions of this bill, is not a measure which respects either their general organization or their discipline. It is a distinct system, introduced for new purposes, and not connected with any power, which the Constitution has conferred on Congress.

But, Sir, there is another consideration. The services of the men to be raised under this act are not limited to those cases in which alone this Government is entitled to the aid of the militia of the States. These cases are particularly stated in the Constitution—"to repel invasion, suppress insurrection, or execute the laws." But this bill has no limitation in this respect. The usual mode of legislating on the subject is abandoned. The only section which would have confined the service of the Militia, proposed to be raised, within the United States has been stricken out; and if the President should not march them into the Provinces of England at the North, or of Spain at the South, it will not be because he is prohibited by any provision in this act.

This, then, Sir, is a bill for calling out the Militia, not according to its existing organization, but by draft from new created classes;—not merely for the purpose of "repelling invasion, suppressing insurrection, or executing the laws," but for the general objects of war—for defending ourselves, or invading others, as may be thought expedient;—not for a sudden emergency, or for a short time, but for long stated periods; for two years, if the proposition of the Senate should finally prevail; for one year, if the amendment of the House should be adopted. What is this, Sir, but raising a standing army out of the Militia by draft, and to be recruited by draft, in like manner, as often as occasion may require?

This bill, then is not different in principle from the other bills, plans, and resolutions, which I have mentioned. The present discussion is properly and necessarily common to them all. It is a discussion, Sir, of the last importance. That measures of this nature should be debated at all, in the councils of a free Government, is cause of dismay. The question is nothing less, than whether the most essential rights of personal liberty shall be surrendered, and despotism embraced in its worst form.

I have risen, on this occasion, with anxious and painful emotions, to add my admonition to what has been said by others. Admonition and remonstrance, I am aware, are not acceptable strains. They are duties of unpleasant performance. But they are, in my judgment, the duties which the condition of a falling state imposes. They are duties which sink deep in his conscience, who believes it probable that they may be the last services, which he may be able to render to the Government of his Country. On the issue of this discussion, I believe the fate of this Government may rest. Its duration is incompatible, in my opinion, with the existence of the measures in contemplation. A crisis has at last arrived, to which the course of things has long tended, and which may be decisive upon the happiness of present and of future generations. If there be anything important in the concerns of men, the considerations which fill the present hour are important. I am anxious, above all things, to stand acquitted before God, and my own conscience, and in the public judgments, of all participations in the Counsels, which have brought us to our present condition, and which now threaten the dissolution of the Government. When the present generation of men shall be swept away, and that this Government ever existed shall be a matter of history only, I desire that it may then be known, that you have not proceeded in your course unadmonished and unforewarned. Let it then be known, that there were those, who would have stopped you, in the career of your measures, and held you back, as by the skirts of your garments, from the precipice, over which you are plunging, and drawing after you the Governor of your Country. . . .

Let us examine the nature and extent of the power, which is assumed by the various military measures before us. In the present want of men and money, the Secretary of War has proposed to Congress a Military Conscription. For the conquest of Canada, the people will not enlist; and if they would, the Treasury is exhausted, and they could not be paid. Conscription is chosen as the most promising instrument, both of overcoming reluctance to the Service, and of subduing the difficulties which arise from the deficiencies of the Exchequer. The administration asserts the right to fill the ranks of the regular army by compulsion. It contends that it may now take one out of every twenty-five men, and any part or the whole of the rest, whenever its occasions require. Persons thus taken by force, and put into an army, may be compelled to serve there, during the war, or for life. They may be put on any service, at home or abroad, for defense or for invasion, according to the will and pleasure of Government. This power does not grow out of any invasion of the country, or even out of a state of war. It belongs to Government at all times, in peace as well as in war, and is to be exercised under all circumstances, according to its mere discretion. This, Sir, is the amount of the principle contended for by the Secretary of War.

Is this, Sir, consistent with the character of a free Government? Is this civil liberty? Is this the real character of our Constitution? No, Sir, indeed it is not. The Constitution is libelled, foully libelled. The people of this country have not established for themselves such a fabric of despotism. They have not purchased at a vast expense of their own treasure and their own blood a Magna Charta to be slaves. Where is it written in the Constitution, in what article or section is it contained, that you may take children from their parents, and parents from their children, and compel them to fight the battles of any war, in which the folly or the wickedness of Government may engage it? Under what concealment has this power lain hidden, which now for the first time comes forth, with a tremendous and baleful aspect, to trample down and destroy the dearest rights of personal liberty? Who will show me any constitutional injunction, which makes it the duty of the American people to surrender every thing valuable in life, and even life itself, not when the safety of their country and its liberties may demand the sacrifice, but whenever the purposes of an ambitious and mischievous Government may require it? Sir, I almost disdain to go to quotations and references to prove that such an abominable doctrine has no foundation in the Constitution of the country. It is enough to know that that instrument was intended as the basis of a free Government, and that the power contended for is incompatible with any notion of personal liberty. An attempt to maintain this doctrine upon the provisions of the Constitution is an exercise of perverse ingenuity to extract slavery from the substance of a free Government. It is an attempt to show, by proof and argument, that we ourselves are subjects of despotism, and that we have a right to chains and bondage, firmly secured to us and our children, by the provisions of our Government. It has been the labor of other men, at other times, to mitigate and reform the powers of Government by construction; to support the rights of personal security by every species of favorable and benign interpretation, and thus to infuse a free spirit into Governments, not friendly in their general structure and formation to public liberty.

The supporters of the measures before us act on the opposite principle. It is their task to raise arbitrary powers, by construction, out of a plain written charter of National Liberty. It is their pleasing duty to free

us of the delusion, which we have fondly cherished, that we are the
subjects of a mild, free and limited Government, and to demonstrate by
a regular chain of premises and conclusions, that Government possesses
over us a power more tyrannical, more arbitrary, more dangerous, more
allied to blood and murder, more full of every form of mischief, more
productive of every sort and degree of misery, than has been exercised
by any civilized Government, with a single exception, in modern times.

The Secretary of War has favored us with an argument on the constitutionality of this power. Those who lament that such doctrines
should be supported by the opinion of a high officer of Government,
may a little abate their regret, when they remember that the same
officer, in his last letter of instructions to our ministers abroad, maintained the contrary. In that letter, he declares, that even the impressment of seamen, for which many more plausible reasons may be given
than for the impressment of soldiers, is repugnant to our Constitution. . . .

Congress having, by the Constitution a power to raise armies, the
Secretary contends that no restraint is to be imposed on the exercise of
this power, except such as is expressly stated in the written letter of the
instrument. In other words, that Congress may execute its powers, by
any means it chooses, unless such means are particularly prohibited. But
the general nature and object of the Constitution impose as rigid a
restriction on the means of exercising power, as could be done by the
most explicit injunctions. It is the first principle applicable to such a
case, that no construction shall be admitted which impairs the general
nature and character of the instrument. A free constitution of Government is to be construed upon free principles, and every branch of its
provisions is to receive such an interpretation as is full of its general
spirit. No means are to be taken by implication, which would strike us
absurdly, if expressed. And what would have been more absurd, than
for this Constitution to have said, that to secure the great blessings of
liberty it gave to Government an uncontrolled power of military conscription? Yet such is the absurdity which it is made to exhibit, under
the commentary of the Secretary of War. . . .

If the Secretary of War has proved the right of Congress to enact a
law enforcing a draft of men out of the Militia into the regular army, he
will at any time be able to prove, quite as clearly, that Congress has
power to create a Dictator. The arguments which have helped him in
one case, will equally aid him in the other. The same reason of a supposed or possible state necessity, which is urged now, may be repeated
then, with equal pertinency and effect.

Sir, in granting Congress the power to raise armies, the People have granted all the means which are ordinary and usual, and which are consistent with the liberties and security of the People themselves; and they have granted no others. To talk about the unlimited power of the Government over the means to execute its authority, is to hold a language which is true only in regard to despotism. The tyranny of Arbitrary Government consists as much in its means as in its ends; and it would be a ridiculous and absurd constitution which should be less cautious to guard against abuses in the one case than in the other. All the means and instruments which a free Government exercises, as well as the ends and objects which it pursues, are to partake of its own essential character, and to be conformed to its genuine spirit. A free Government with arbitrary means to administer it is a contradiction; a free Government without adequate provision for personal security is an absurdity; a free Government, with an uncontrolled power of military conscription, is a solecism, at once the most ridiculous and abominable that ever entered into the head of man.

Sir, I invite the supporters of the measures before you to look to their actual operation. Let the men who have so often pledged their own fortunes and their own lives to the support of this war, look to the wanton sacrifice which they are about to make of their lives and fortunes. They may talk as they will about substitutes, and compensations, and exemptions. It must come to the draft at last. If the Government cannot hire men voluntarily to fight its battles, neither can individuals. If the war should continue, there will be no escape, and every man's fate, and every man's life will come to depend on the issue of the military draught. Who shall describe to you the horror which your orders of Conscription shall create in the once happy villages of this country? Who shall describe the distress and anguish which they will spread over those hills and valleys, where men have heretofore been accustomed to labor, and to rest in security and happiness. Anticipate the scene, Sir, when the class shall assemble to stand its draft, and to throw the dice for blood. What a group of wives and mothers, and sisters, of helpless age and helpless infancy, shall gather round the theatre of this horrible lottery, as if the stroke of death were to fall from heaven before their eyes, on a father, a brother, a son or an husband. And in a majority of cases, Sir, it will be the stroke of death. . . .

In my opinion, Sir, the sentiments of the free population of this country are greatly mistaken here. The nation is not yet in a temper to submit to conscription. The people have too fresh and strong a feeling of the blessings of civil liberty to be willing thus to surrender it. You may talk to them as much as you please, of the victory and glory to be obtained in the Enemy's Provinces; they will hold those objects in light estimation, if the means be a forced military service. You may sing to them the song of Canada Conquests in all its variety, but they will not be charmed out of the remembrance of their substantial interests, and true happiness. Similar pretences, they know, are the graves in which the liberties of other nations have been buried, and they will take warning.

Laws, Sir, of this nature can create nothing but opposition. If you scatter them abroad, like the fabled serpents' teeth, they will spring up into armed men. A military force cannot be raised, in this manner, but by the means of a military force. If administration has found that it can not form an army without conscription, it will find, if it venture on these experiments, that it can not enforce conscription without an army. The Government was not constituted for such purposes. Framed in the spirit of liberty, and in the love of peace, it has no powers which render it able to enforce such laws. The attempt, if we rashly make it, will fall; and having already thrown away our peace, we may thereby throw away our Government.

12

John C. Calhoun was the first man to bring distinction to the office of secretary of war. During his tenure, which ran from 1817 to 1825, Calhoun performed the dual function of keeping the Congress aware of the needs of the military while, through the publication of his reports to the Congress, informing and educating the public as to the role of the army in American life. His biographer, Charles M. Wiltse, has aptly summarized Calhoun's achievement as secretary of war: "The organization of the War Department was given a form so nearly definitive that no essential changes were needed, even to cope with the shock of Civil War forty years later, and it long served as the model after which other departments were patterned.[23]

The following excerpt is from a speech delivered in the House on January 31, 1816, a year before he moved into the War Department. In it, Calhoun offers support for a "regular draft from the body of the people."

23. Charles M. Wiltse, *John C. Calhoun, Nationalist* (Indianapolis: Bobbs-Merrill Co., Inc., 1944), p. 297.

Calhoun's Speech in Support of the Draft, 1816

In regard to our present military establishment, Mr. C. said, it was small enough. That point the honorable Speaker had fully demonstrated: it was not sufficiently large at present to occupy all our fortresses. Gentlemen had spoken in favor of the militia, and against the army. In regard to the militia, said Mr. C., I would go as far as any gentleman, and considerably further than those would who are so violently opposed to our small army. I would not only arm the militia, but I would extend their term of service, and make them efficient. To talk about the efficiency of militia called into service for six months only, is to impose on the people; it is to ruin them with false hopes. I know the danger of large standing armies, said Mr. C. I know the militia are the true force; that no nation can be safe at home and abroad which has not an efficient militia; but the time of service ought to be enlarged, to enable them to acquire a knowledge of the duties of the camp, to let the habits of civil life be broken. For though militia, freshly drawn from their homes, may in a moment of enthusiasm do great service, as at New Orleans, in general they are not calculated for service in the field, until time is allowed for them to acquire habits of discipline and subordination. Your defence ought to depend on the land, on a regular draft from the body of the people. It is thus in time of war the business of recruiting will be dispensed with; a mode of defending the country every way uncongenial with our republican institutions; uncertain, slow in its operations and expensive, it draws from society its worse materials, introducing into our army, of necessity, all the severities, which are exercised in that of the most despotic government. Thus compounded, our army in a great degree, lose that enthusiasm which citizen-soldiers, conscious of liberty, and fighting in defence of their country, have ever been animated.

All free nations of antiquity entrusted the defence of the country, not to the dregs of society, but to the body of citizens; hence that heroism which modern times may admire but cannot equal. I know that I utter truths unpleasant to those who wish to enjoy liberty without making the efforts necessary to secure it. Her favor is never won by the cowardly, the vicious or indolent. It has been said by some physicians that life is a forced state; the same may be said of freedom. It requires efforts; it presupposes mental and moral qualities of a high order to be generally

From *The Papers of John Calhoun*, Vol. 1, *1801–1817*, ed. by Robert L. Meriwether (Columbia: The University of South Carolina Press, 1959), pp. 324–25. Copyright © 1959 by the South Carolina Archives Department; reproduced by permission of the University of South Carolina Press.

diffused in the society where it exists. It mainly stands on the faithful discharge of two great duties which every citizen of proper age owes the republic; a wise and virtuous exercise of the right of suffrage; and a prompt and brave defence of the country in the hour of danger. The first symptom of decay has ever appeared in the backward and negligent discharge of the latter duty. Those who are acquainted with the historians and orators of antiquity know the truth of this assertion. The least decay of patriotism, the least verging towards pleasure, and luxury will there immediately discover itself. Large standing and mercenary armies then become necessary; and those who are not willing to render the military service essential to the defence of their rights, soon find, as they ought to do, a master. It is the order of nature and cannot be reversed. . . .

1861-1900:
The Beginning of Federal Conscription

As THE CIVIL WAR became imminent, neither the North nor the South made any detailed plans for manpower procurement. The traditional methods that had been used in previous conflicts seemed adequate for the coming battles—that is, a reliance upon the organized militia, individual volunteers from the states, and whatever troops could be garnered from the small regular army. It was universally felt that the war would be short; never did the leaders think that the greatest conflict in the history of the western hemisphere was about to explode.

Draft laws were adopted in the North and South as it became clear that the traditional methods of raising troops were not satisfactory to meet the insatiable demands of a total war. Volunteers were enthusiastic at the outbreak of the hostilities; however, high casualties and the ever-widening conflict soon necessitated new ways of raising troops. In Europe, the use of a national draft had been well accepted since the Napoleonic wars. With this model, the Confederacy, soon followed by the Union, adopted the first federal draft laws in America.

The draft became a reality in the South on April 16, 1862. The law put all existing military units in service to the central government. The official limits on draft ages were eighteen to thirty-five. The administration of the draft was directed from Richmond; however, a smooth operation depended upon cooperation from each state. At once, the law kept in arms those volunteers whose one-year terms of service were due to end. More importantly, however, this legislation marked the first time in American history that individuals owed their militia allegiance directly to the central government.[1] It is ironic that the Southern states were the first to give such an allegiance, since secession had been based on the theory of state supremacy.

For the North, the Southern action paved the way for the eventual adoption of a federal draft on March 3, 1863. Prior to passage however, Congress moved halfway toward a federal draft act by passing the Militia Act of July 17, 1862. This act reiterated the militia obligation of all men between the ages of eighteen and forty-five and permitted the president to establish the term of service (up to nine months). Those states that lacked regulations for the call-up of militiamen to meet federal quotas would be subjected to direct presidential intervention in order to provide for the enrollment and procurement of militia. This legislation was only a stopgap measure, for the governors of the Union states refused to cooperate. The Enrollment Act of March 3, 1863, created a three-year military obligation for citizens between the ages of twenty and forty-five. The militia clauses of the Constitution were thereby bypassed—the act was based upon the government's power to "raise and support armies" and on the need "for the maintenance of the Constitution and Union, and the consequent preservation of free government."[2]

The Union draft worked in the following manner. Each State was divided into draft districts coinciding with the congressional districts. The enrollment procedure was under the control of the Washington office of the provost marshal general, Colonel James B. Fry, who in turn was supervised by the secretary of war. Districts were administered by assistant provosts, who were in charge of enrolling officers to go from door to door in an effort to enroll eligibles. This enrollment method was one of the most antagonistic features

1. Jim Dan Hill, *The Minute Man in Peace and War*, p. 68; and Russell F. Weigley, *History of the United States Army*, p. 206.
2. Fred Albert Shannon, *The Organization and Administration of the Union Army*, 2 vols. (Cleveland, 1928; reprint ed., Gloucester, Mass.: Peter Smith, 1965), Vol. 1, p. 304.

of the draft for most citizens, since it took the initiative for registration away from the citizen and symbolized a loss of personal freedom. Many detested the enrolling officer and made his task as difficult, and often as dangerous, as possible.

In an effort to evade the enrollment procedure, thousands of eligible young men moved from one locality to another. The situation became so critical that the president ordered that any persons participating in draft resistance or encouraging such activity would be subject to martial law and court-martial. Lincoln proclaimed on September 15, 1863, that the privileges of the writ of habeas corpus would be suspended in cases of encouraging draft resistance as well as other offenses such as spying and aiding the enemy or deserters.[3] Not even the press was safe, for the editors of the *Bangor Republican Journal*, the *Newark Evening Journal*, and the *New York Metropolitan Record* were eventually prosecuted for attacking the draft.[4]

Protest against the draft took another form—that of violent opposition. Full-scale rioting broke out as the draft got under way in New York City, and it caused widespread havoc as it raged from July 13 to 16, 1863. The draft, with its built-in inequities, served as the catalyst among other grievances to spark what proved to be the most violent episode of civil insurrection in American history.[5] Somewhere between two hundred and five hundred lives were lost, with property damage running into the millions of dollars.[6] Federal troops were eventually dispatched from the Gettysburg battlefield to help restore order.

Although not nearly as costly or dramatic as those in New York City, riots related to the draft occured in practically every state in the Union. The havoc attendant upon these disorders prompted General Henry W. Halleck to observe, in a letter to General William T. Sherman, that "your ranks cannot be filled by the present

3. *Ibid.*, p. 286. For an excellent contemporary view of the suspension of the writ of habeas corpus, see Frank Freidel, ed., *Union Pamphlets of the Civil War 1861–1865* (Cambridge, Mass.: Harvard University Press, 1967), Vol. 1, pp. 199–252. The South also suspended the writ of habeas corpus by means of a law of February 27, 1862. See James G. Randall and David Donald, *The Civil War and Reconstruction* (Boston: D. C. Heath and Co., 1961), p. 269.

4. Allan Nevins, *The War for the Union*, Vol. 4: *The Organized War to Victory, 1864–1865* (New York: Charles Scribner's Sons, 1971), p. 128.

5. Richard Hofstadter and Michael Wallace, eds., *American Violence: A Documentary History* (New York: Alfred A. Knopf, Inc., 1971), p. 211.

6. James F. Richardson, *The New York Police: Colonial Times to 1901* (New York: Oxford University Press, 1970), p. 145.

draft . . . It takes more soldiers to enforce than we get by it."[7] A more recent critic, historian Samuel Eliot Morison, dismissed the Northern draft act as "a most imperfect law, a travesty of conscription."[8]

The South was not swept by the violent protest found in the North, but negative reactions by several governors were damaging to the cause. For example, Governor Joseph E. Brown of Georgia called the Southern draft law "a palpable assault upon the rights and the sovereignty of the State."[9] Brown wrote President Davis that "I cannot consent to commit the state to a policy which is in my judgment subversive of her sovereignty and at war with all the principles for the support of which Georgia entered into this revolution."[10] Although Brown eventually submitted, when the second conscription act was passed on September 27, 1862, he refused to allow it to go into operation until the state supreme court had passed on its validity. Even then, he continued as an obstructionist, listing some fifteen thousand persons as indispensable state officials not liable to the draft.

Nor was Governor Brown's opposition an isolated case. Governor Zebulon Vance of North Carolina charged that the draft was unconstitutional, and along with other governors he thwarted the operation of the draft by establishing many minor government jobs which carried exemption status. It is estimated that these actions deprived the Confederate Army of nearly ten thousand men.[11] Alexander Stephens, vice president of the Confederacy, was an outspoken opponent of conscription, as were many other government officials. The difficulty this created in the enforcement of the law is reflected in the statement of John S. Preston, Confederate superintendent of conscription: "From one end of the Confederacy to the other every constituted authority, every officer, every man and woman is engaged in opposing the enrolling officer in the execution of his duties."[12]

The inequities in each draft law were wholesale. The most odious clause of the Southern legislation became known as the "twenty-

7. Hill, *The Minute Man*, p. 71.
8. Samuel Eliot Morison, *The Oxford History of the American People* (New York: Oxford University Press, 1965), p. 666.
9. Lowell H. Harrison, "Conscription in the Confederacy," *Civil War Times Illustrated*, Vol. 9 (July, 1970), p. 16.
10. Charles P. Roland, *The Confederacy* (Chicago: University of Chicago Press, 1960), p. 60.
11. Harrison, "Conscription," p. 16.
12. Roland, *The Confederacy*, p. 144.

nigger law" because it exempted one owner or overseer on each plantation with twenty slaves that did not already have a draft-exempt male. Senator James Phelan of Mississippi expressed the feelings of a large number of Southerners about this exemption when he wrote President Jefferson Davis that "never did a law meet with more universal odium than the exemption of slave owners, its injustices denounced even by men whose position allows them to take advantage of its privilege. . . . It has aroused a spirit of rebellion . . . and bodies of men have banded together to desert."[13] Such pressure helped to reduce the exemption to fifteen slaves, and finally, in 1864, the exemption was eliminated, but it did untold damage to Confederate morale. Perhaps the best example of protest on the part of the draftee is expressed in the following comments to President Davis from a draftee about to desert:

> Your happy conscript would go to the faraway North whence the wind comes and leave you to reap the whirlwind with no one but your father the devil to reap and rake and bind after you. And he's going. It is with intense and multifariously proud satisfaction that he gazes for the last time upon our holy flag—that symbol . . . of an adored holy trinity, cotton, niggers, and chivalry. . . . Behind he leaves the legitimate chivalry of this unbounded nation centered in the illegitimate son of a Kentucky horsethief. . . . And now, bastard President of a political abortion, farewell. . . . Except it be in the army of the Union, you will not again see the conscript.[14]

The hiring of substitutes was permitted in the draft laws of both North and South. The finding of a replacement for service possessed a strong tradition from earlier times. In the South there was such an acute shortage of soldiers that by late 1863 Richmond newspapers were carrying advertisements offering as much as six thousand dollars for an acceptable substitute.[15] In the North, a commutation fee of three hundred dollars provided an additional means of escaping service until the next drawing. Although the commutation fee was often attacked as the most inequitable of the exemptions (by July, 1864, commutation fees could only be used by conscientious objectors), one study indicates that it proved fairer than substitution.[16] Since the price was set at three hundred

13. Randall and Donald, *Civil War and Reconstruction*, p. 265.
14. *Ibid.*
15. Harrison, "Conscription," p. 13.
16. Hugh G. Earlhuil, "Commutation: Democratic or Undemocratic?" *Civil War History*, Vol. 12 (June, 1966), pp. 132–44.

dollars, a laborer had a greater chance for escape by commutation than by prohibitively costly substitution.

Bounties were another holdover from earlier times. Active bidding for recruits erupted in the North among cities, counties, and states. This enabled a recruit to collect considerable sums of money over and above the federal bounty. One result of this "easy money" was the development of the "bounty jumper," who would enlist in one locality, collect an enlistment bounty, and, prior to induction, leave for another locale to enlist again and collect another bounty. One recruiting officer in Indiana reported that "out of three hundred and eighty-one enlistments . . . more than two hundred . . . deserted almost immediately on receiving their bounties."[17] Indiana ultimately resorted to actively arresting and prosecuting bounty jumpers. Several of the worst bounty jumpers were tried by court-martial, and three, one of whom admitted to having jumped bounty thirty times, were publicly shot in an attempt to discourage others from bounty jumping. Adjutant General W. H. H. Terrell of Indiana reported that "The severe measures adopted, ultimately suppressed the evil in this State by convincing those engaged in the business that the prospective gains were not commensurate with the inevitable risks."[18]

Fantastic sums were expended on bounties. For example, the counties of Illinois spent $13,711,389; those of New York spent over $86,000,000. The total for the states and localities for the second half of the war was over $286,000,000, and the national government's figure was over $300,000,000. The total expenditure for the Union's "bounty bill" is placed at $750,000,000.[19] These figures are even more astounding when one is aware that the bounties cost as much as the pay of its army and five times the cost of its ordnance.[20]

The Confederacy legalized conscription of Negro troops on March 13, 1865. Two days after passage of that law, General Robert E. Lee received a request from the 49th Georgia Infantry asking that much-needed recruits be filled by conscripted Negroes. The "Negro Draft" allowed the Confederate president to ask for the services of as many slaves as he needed for military service (both master and slave had to consent before a slave could serve).

17. James Barnett, "The Bounty Jumpers of Indiana," Civil War History, Vol. 4 (Dec., 1958), p. 431.
18. Ibid., p. 436.
19. Randall and Donald, Civil War and Reconstruction, p. 329.
20. Weigley, United States Army, p. 211.

If the requested number of slaves did not come forth, a call could be made for as many as 300,000 slaves.[21] Even after being drafted, a slave was not guaranteed freedom by the law.

In the North, after several inept attempts at recruiting freedmen and former slaves failed, an extended effort resulted in the recruitment of 186,017 blacks into regiments of United States Colored Volunteers. Although blacks had served in the American Revolution and in other earlier conflicts, they were barred from the regular army. In addition, the Militia Act of 1792 prevented blacks from joining state militias. Thus, the Civil War marked the first time in American history that blacks officially served in the Unites States Army.[22]

The draft during the Civil War was marked by inequities, lack of direct administration, and mass civil protest. It attempted, in both North and South, to subordinate the states by establishing a direct military obligation to the federal government. It failed as a direct means to produce manpower; however, it was responsible for prompting to action thousands of men who, when confronted with the unsavory stigma of being drafted, succumbed to the lucrative bounties for volunteering. Numerous loopholes existed due to practices of substitution and commutation—vestiges of earlier draft laws. The rich were still favored over the poor due to the belief of many legislators that certain sectors of society had to be protected. James G. Blaine, Republican congressman from Maine, stated that commutation would benefit "the great 'middle interest' of society— the class on which business and the prosperity of the country depend."[23] The disastrous effects of the draft riots in the North guaranteed that the more flagrant inequities would at last be removed from future draft legislation in the twentieth century.

All told, the Confederacy raised some 300,000 soldiers, or about one-third of its army, by the draft.[24] The Union's figure is less impressive—only approximately 46,000 draftees and 118,000 substitutes.[25] The Civil War marked the last conflict in which America would depend on both the organized militia and volunteers. Russell F. Weigley summarized the long-term implications of Civil War manpower policy as follows: "After reviewing the problems

21. Harrison, "Conscription," p. 18.
22. Weigley, *United States Army*, p. 212.
23. U.S., Selective Service System, *Backgrounds of Selective Service*, Vol. 1, p. 66.
24. Weigley, *United States Army*, p. 205.
25. *Ibid.*, p. 210.

and anomalies of the effort to maintain the volunteer armies of the
1860's, the United States would never again attempt to raise a mass
wartime army by that method. Federal conscription would be the
principal legacy of the Civil War experience to future American
armies."[26]

An overview of Civil War conscription emerged in a report by
General James Oakes, who supervised enrollment laws in Illinois.
Oakes recommended that it be the citizens' responsibility to register
in future drafts, and he suggested that substitution, commutation,
and bounties be rejected forever. Finally, the general strongly recommended that the central government take over full responsibility
for the draft rather than depend on the states for help. These suggestions, in the opinion of Oakes, would substantially reduce civil
opposition to the draft and provide a greatly improved and more
efficient system as well. This report played a significant role in
shaping the draft during the First World War.

The peace at Appomattox initiated a diminishing concern for
military matters in the United States. For the remainder of the
nineteenth century the regular army averaged about 26,000 men,
and the organized militia experienced a reduction in participation.
Few foreign threats and relative internal security encouraged an
increasing absorption with the industrialization which was trans-
forming American society.

The violent railroad strikes of the summer of 1877 helped bring
about a revived interest in the organized militia. The militia's in-
eptness in handling several strikes necessitated the use of the
regular army.[27] Men of property began to demand that the army
be increased, while Samuel Gompers complained that "standing
armies are always used to exercise tyranny over people, and are
one of the prime causes of a rupture in a country."[28] These conditions prompted the meeting in New York of delegates of organized
militia units from nineteen states. They proceeded to form the
National Guard Association in an effort to strengthen their role as
a military reserve. It should be noted that the National Guard of
the 1870's was frequently dominated by the wealthier classes of
society, who participated out of concern with the protection of private property and the preservation of law and order against the
wave of violent strikes that swept America. Thus, one can under-

26. *Ibid.*, p 216.
27. Walter Millis, *Arms and Men*, p. 143.
28. Weigley, *United States Army*, p. 282.

stand how the Seventh Regiment of New York was able to raise $500,000 from private donations for its own use.[29]

When the nation went to war again in 1898, the fighting was carried on by the regular army and volunteers—the bulk of whom came from National Guard units. The regular army, the National Guard, and other volunteers constituted a force of 225,000 men, two-thirds of whom never left the United States.[30]

The postwar period witnessed a return to the nation's traditional peacetime manpower posture—a small regular army and an organized militia now called the National Guard.[31]

13

As the numbers volunteering in support of the Confederate cause began to diminish in the early months of 1862, and as battlefield losses continued to mount, the Confederate armies began to face a manpower crisis, General Robert E. Lee recommended to President Davis that a conscription bill be enacted, and the Confederate Congress acted on this request on April 16, 1862, supporting the measure by a vote of more than two to one.

This law was, according to one historian, "a more Spartan measure than any other English-speaking land had ever enacted."[32] All white males between the ages of eighteen and thirty-five were liable to be inducted for a three-year period of service. Initially, a draftee was allowed to hire a substitute from among those not liable to service, but this policy was later rescinded. A thirty-day period was alloted between the call and the obligation to report so that the potential draftee could volunteer and thus escape the stigma of serving under compulsion. On September 27, 1862, the high age limit of eligibility for the draft was raised from thirty-five to forty-five, and on February 17, 1864, both high and low limits were extended to include ages seventeen to fifty.

29. Millis, *Arms and Men*, p. 144.
30. *Ibid.*, p. 170.
31. The National Guard had 112,507 men enrolled in 1893 as compared with 130,000 in 1860. This is significant in that the population for these two years was 72,000,000 and 32,000,000, respectively. This demonstrated a continuing decline in the participation of citizens in militia functions. See Hill, *The Minute Man*, p. 51, and Weigley, *United States Army*, p. 282.
32. Allan Nevins, *The War for the Union*, Vol. 2, *War Becomes Revolution, 1862–1863* (New York: Charles Scribner's Sons, 1971), p. 89.

Confederate Conscription Act, 1862

In view of the exigencies of the country and the absolute necessity of keeping in service our gallant army, and of placing in the field a large additional force to meet the advancing columns of the enemy now invading our soil: Therefore,

The Congress of the Confederate States of America do enact, That the President be, and he is hereby, authorized to call out and place in the military service of the Confederate states, for three years, unless the war shall have sooner ended, all white men who are residents of the Confederate States, between the ages of eighteen and thirty-five years of age at the time the call or calls may be made, who are not legally exempted from military service. All of the persons aforesaid who are now in the armies of the Confederacy, and whose term of service will expire before the end of the war, shall be continued in the service for three years from the date of the original enlistment, unless the war shall have been sooner ended. . . .

Sec. 9. *Be it further enacted,* That persons not liable for duty may be received as substitutes for those who are, under such regulations as may be prescribed by the Secretary of War. . . .

14

The first attempt of the federal government to use conscription was the Militia Act of 1862, which proved to be a "limping draft."[33] The act had moderate success, particularly in encouraging volunteering, but it proved inadequate to meet increasing demands for manpower. The next step, then, was a national conscription conducted entirely by the federal government, and this was accomplished by the Enrollment Act of March 3, 1863.

The draft act never achieved the degree of success that Provost Marshal General Fry had estimated; only 6 percent of the Union force was raised through the system.[34] Yet this was not the sole test of its effectiveness: "A failure it was; yet not entirely so. The Draft

Reprinted from *The Rebellion Record,* ed. by Frank Moore (New York, 1864), pp. 324–25.

33. Randall and Donald, *Civil War and Reconstruction,* p. 313.
34. Colonel Fry had projected an enrollment of 3,000,000 men, with approximately 425,000 of them called to service.

Act did something, as its authors had expected, to stimulate volunteering. A young man reaching twenty was obviously wiser to offer
his services, escape the stigma of conscription, get special state and
local benefits, and join the regiment he liked, than be taken by the
neck for service."[35] Viewed in that broader perspective, then, the
role of conscription in the Civil War is seen in its proper light.

Union Conscription Act, 1863

AN ACT FOR ENROLLING AND CALLING OUT THE NATIONAL FORCES, AND
FOR OTHER PURPOSES.

Whereas there now exists in the United States an insurrection and rebellion against the authority thereof, and it is, under the Constitution
of the United States, the duty of the government to suppress insurrection and rebellion, to guarantee to each State a republican form of government, and to preserve the public tranquility; and whereas, for these
high purposes, a military force is indispensable, to raise and support
which all persons ought willingly to contribute; and whereas no service
can be more praiseworthy and honorable than that which is rendered
for the maintenance of the Constitution and Union, and the consequent
preservation of free government:
Therefore—
*Be it enacted by the Senate and House of Representatives of the
United States of America in Congress assembled,* That all able-bodied
male citizens of the United States, and persons of foreign birth who
shall have declared on oath their intention to become citizens under
and in pursuance of the laws thereof, between the ages of twenty and
forty-five years, except as in hereinafter excepted, are hereby declared
to constitute the national forces, and shall be liable to perform military
duty in the service of the United States when called out by the President
for that purpose.

Sec. 2. *And be it further enacted,* That the following persons be, and
they are hereby, excepted and exempt from the provisions of this act,
and shall not be liable to military duty under the same, to wit: Such as
are rejected as physically or mentally unfit for the service; also, First
the Vice-President of the United States, the judges of the various courts
of the United States, the heads of the various executive departments of

Reprinted from *Statutes at Large,* Vol. 12, pp. 731–37.

35. Nevins, *War for the Union,* Vol. 2, p. 465.

the government, and the governors of the several States. Second, the only son liable to military duty of a widow dependent upon his labor for support. Third, the only son of aged or infirm parent or parents dependent upon his labor for support. Fourth, where there are two or more sons of aged or infirm parents subject to draft, the father, or, if he be dead, the mother, may elect which son may be exempt. Fifth, the only brother of children not twelve years old, having neither father nor mother dependent upon his labor for support. Sixth, the father of motherless children under twelve years of age dependent upon his labor for support. Seventh, where there are a father and sons in the same family and household, and two of them are in the military service of the United States as non-commissioned officers, musicians, or privates, the residue of such family and household, not exceeding two, shall be exempt. And no persons but such as are herein excepted shall be exempt: *Provided, however*, That no person who has been convicted of any felony shall be enrolled or permitted to serve in said forces.

Sec. 3. *And be it further enacted*, That the national forces of the United States not now in the military service, enrolled under this act, shall be divided into two classes: the first of which shall comprise all persons subject to do military duty between the ages of twenty and thirty-five years, and all unmarried persons subject to do military duty above the ages of thirty-five and under the age of forty-five; the second class shall comprise all other persons subject to do military duty, and they shall not, in any district, be called into the service of the United States until those of the first class shall have been called. . . .

Sec. 10. *And be it further enacted*, That the enrollment of each class shall be made separately, and shall only embrace those whose ages shall be on the first day of July thereafter between twenty and forty-five years.

Sec. 11. *And be it further enacted*, That all persons thus enrolled shall be subject, for two years after the first day of July succeeding the enrolment, to be called into the military service of the United States, and to continue in service during the present rebellion, not, however, exceeding the term of three years; and when called into service shall be placed on the same footing in all respects, as volunteers for three years, or during the war, including advance pay and bounty as now provided by law.

Sec. 12, *And be it further enacted*, That whenever it may be necessary to call out the national forces for military service, the President is hereby authorized to assign to each district the number of men to be furnished by said district; and thereupon the enrolling board shall, under the direction of the President, make a draft of the required number, and fifty per cent. in addition, and shall make an exact and complete roll of the names of the persons so drawn, and of the order in which they were drawn, so that the first drawn may stand first upon the said roll, and the second may stand second, and so on; and the persons so drawn shall be notified of the same within ten days thereafter, by a written or printed notice, to be served personally or by leaving a copy at the last place of residence, requiring them to appear at a designated rendezvous to report for duty. In assigning to the districts the number of men to be furnished therefrom, the President shall take into consideration the number of volunteers and militia furnished by and from the several states in which said districts are situated, and the period of their service since the commencement of the present rebellion, and shall so make said assignment as to equalize the numbers among the districts of the several states, considering and allowing for the numbers already furnished as aforesaid and the time of their service.

Sec. 13. *And be it further enacted,* That any person drafted and notified to appear as aforesaid, may, on or before the day fixed for his appearance, furnish an acceptable substitute to take his place in the draft; or he may pay to such person as the Secretary of War may authorize to receive it, such sum, not exceeding three hundred dollars, as the Secretary may determine, for the procuration of such substitute; which sum shall be fixed at a uniform rate by a general order made at the time of ordering a draft for any state or territory; and thereupon such person so furnishing the substitute, or paying the money, shall be discharged from further liability under that draft. And any person failing to report after due service of notice, as herein prescribed, without furnishing a substitute, or paying the required sum therefor, shall be deemed a deserter, and shall be arrested by the provost-marshal and sent to the nearest military post for trial by court-martial, unless, upon proper showing that he is not liable to do military duty, the board of enrolment shall relieve him from the draft.

Sec. 14. *And be it further enacted,* That all drafted persons shall, on arriving at the rendezvous, be carefully inspected by the surgeon of the board, who shall truly report to the board the physical condition of each one; and all persons drafted and claiming exemption from military duty on account of disability, or any other cause, shall present their claims to be exempted to the board, whose decision shall be final. . . .

Sec. 17. *And be it further enacted,* That any person enrolled and drafted according to the provisions of this act who shall furnish an acceptable substitute, shall thereupon receive from the board of enrolment a certificate of discharge from such draft, which shall exempt him from military duty during the time for which he was drafted; and such substitute shall be entitled to the same pay and allowances provided by law as if he had been originally drafted into the service of the United States.

Sec. 18. *And be it further enacted,* That such of the volunteers and militia now in the service of the United States as may reenlist to serve one year, unless sooner discharged, after the expiration of their present term of service, shall be entitled to a bounty of fifty dollars, one half of which to be paid upon such reenlistment, and the balance at the expiration of the term of reenlistment; and such as may reenlist to serve for two years, unless sooner discharged, after the expiration of their present term of enlistment, shall receive, upon such reenlistment, twenty five dollars of the one hundred dollars bounty for enlistment provided by the fifth section of the act approved twenty-second of July, eighteen hundred and sixty-one, entitled "An act to authorize the employment of volunteers to aid in enforcing the laws and protecting public property." . . .

Sec. 25. *And be it further enacted,* That if any person shall resist any draft for men enrolled under this act into the service of the United States, or shall counsel or aid any person to resist any such draft; or shall assault or obstruct any such officer in making such draft, or in the performance of any service in relation thereto; or shall counsel any drafted men not to appear at the place of rendezvous, or wilfully dissuade them from the performance of military duty as required by law, such person shall be subject to summary arrest by the provost-marshal, and shall be forthwith delivered to the civil authorities, and, upon conviction thereof, be punished by a fine not exceeding five hundred dollars, or by imprisonment not exceeding two years, or by both of said punishments.

15

The most serious opposition to the federal draft act occurred in New York City only two days after the law had been in operation when a draft office was attacked and left in smoldering ruins. This assault precipitated three days of widespread violence and looting. At the heart of much of the antagonism to the draft lay the realization that the commutation fee of $300, not to mention the possibility of hiring a substitute, was far beyond the means of most workingmen. This sense of inequity, combined with an awareness that the war was being fought to free the slaves, vented itself in a series of mob actions against Negroes which culminated in the burning of the Colored Orphan Asylum. The frenzy of the mob was eventually abated by the appearance of federal troops and an announcement that municipal funds would be made available for those too poor to provide their own commutation fee. Doctor John Torrey, one of the leading scientists of the day, provided a graphic eyewitness account of the disturbances in a letter to Doctor Asa Gray.

The New York Draft Riots

New York, July 13th, 1863

Dear Doctor—

We have had great riots in New York to-day and they are still in progress. They were reported to us at the Assay office about noon, but I thought they were exaggerated. Fresh accounts came in every half hour, and some of our Treasury officers (occupying the same building with us) were alarmed. I had made arrangements for visiting Eliza, at Snedens, this afternoon, but just as I was starting Mr. Mason came in and said that he saw a mob stop two 3rd. Avenue cars to take out some negroes and maltreat them. This decided me to return home, so as to protect my colored servants. I could go neither by the 3rd nor 6th Avenues, as the cars had stopped. Taking the 4th Av. I found the streets full of people, and when I reached the terminus (now 34th St.) I found the whole road way and sidewalks filled with rough fellows (and some equally rough women) who were tearing up rails, cutting down telegraph poles, and setting fire to buildings. I walked quietly along through the midst of them, without being molested. In 49 st. they were numerous, and made, as I was passing near the College, an attack upon one of a row of new houses in our street. The rioters were induced to go away by one or two Catholic priests, who made pacific speeches to them. I found Jane and Maggie a little alarmed, but not frightened. The mob had been in the College Grounds, and came to our house—wishing to know if a republican lived there, and what the College building was used for. They were going to burn Pres. King's house, as he was rich, and a decided republican. They barely desisted when addressed by the

Reprinted from "An Eyewitness Account of the New York Draft Riots, July, 1863," *Mississippi Valley Historical Review*, Vol. 47 (December, 1960), pp. 475–79, ed. by A. Hunter Dupree and Leslie H. Fishel, Jr., by permission of the Organization of American Historians. Original letter located in Harvard University.

Catholic priests. The furious bareheaded and coatless men assembled under our windows and shouted aloud for Jeff. Davis! We have some of the most valuable articles of small bulk, all packed and ready for removal at a moment's warning. All the family will remain the whole night with our clothes on, for there is no telling when they may return. Towards evening the mob, furious as demons, went yelling over to the Colored-Orphan Asylum in 5th Avenue a little below where we live—and rolling a barrel of kerosine in it, the whole structure was soon in a blaze, and is now a smoking ruin. What has become of the 300 poor innocent orphans I could not learn. They must have had some warning of what the rioters intended; and I trust the children were removed in time to escape a cruel death. Before this fire was extinguished, or rather burned out, for the wicked wretches who caused it would not permit the engines to be used, the northern sky was brilliantly illuminated, probably by the burning of the Aged Colored-woman's Home in 65th St.—or the Harlem R. Road Bridge—both of which places were threatened by the rioters. Just before dusk I took a walk a short distance down 5th Avenue, and seeing a group of rowdies in the grounds of Dr. Ward's large and superb mansion, I found they had gone there with the intention of setting fire to the building, which is filled with costly works of art! The family were all out, entreating the scamps to desist, as "they were all Brackenridge democrats and opposed to the *draft*." They finally went off, but may return before morning. I conversed with one of the ringleaders who told me they would burn the whole city before they got through. He said they were to take Wall St. in hand tomorrow! We will be ready for them at the Assay Office & Treasury. Strange to say the military were nowhere to be seen at my latest investigation. There may be bloody times tomorrow.

Wednesday, July 15. You doubtless learn from the newspapers that our city is still in the power of a brutal mob. We were not molested on Monday night, and I slept well, partly undressed. We are all quite calm and are chiefly concerned about our servants. Yesterday there were cars only on the lower part of the 4th Avenue.—all the others in the city, and the omnibuses were withdrawn. I was obliged to walk up from Wall St. in the heat of the day. On reaching home I found that we had been warned that all the College buildings were to be destroyed at night. Jane and Maggie had some of their most valuable articles packed, but we did not know where to send them. A friend took our basket of silver to her house. I look about to see what few articles I could put in a small travelling bag, but it was very difficult to make a selection. There were so many (to me) precious little souvenirs that it grieved me to think they would probably be destroyed. Then it *did* go hard with me to feel pretty well assured that the Herbarium and Botanical Books were to be given up! Yet we had a reprieve. Just as we were expecting the mob to come howling along, a person came in with a confidential message from a Catholic priest, that Gov. Seymour had taken the responsibility of stopping the draft, and the chief rioters were to be informed of this measure. So we made up our minds to take a good sleep. I was, however, mortified to find that the mob had, at least temporarily, triumphed. But we shall still have to finish the business with saltpetre.

This morning I was obliged to ride down to the office in a hired coach. A friend who rode with me had seen a poor negro hung an hour or two before. The man had, in a frenzy, shot an Irish fireman, and they immediately strung up the unhappy African. At our office there had been no disturbance in the night. Indeed the people there were "spoiling for a fight." They had a battery of about 25 rifle barrels, carrying 3 balls each, and mounted on a gun-carriage. It could be loaded and fired with rapidity. We had also 10-inch shells, to be lighted and thrown out of the windows. Likewise quantities of SO_3, with arrangements for projecting it on the mob. Walking home we found that a large number of soldiers—infantry, artillery and cavalry are moving about, and bodies of armed citizens. The worst mobs are on the 1st and 2nd and 7th Avenues. Many have been killed there. They are very hostile to the negroes, and scarcely one of them is to be seen. A person who called at our house this afternoon saw three of them hanging together. The Central Park has been a kind of refuge to them. Hundreds were there to-day, with no protection in a very severe shower. The Station Houses of the police are crowded with them.

Walking out on 5th Avenue near 48th st. a man who lives there told me that a few minutes before, in broad sunlight, three ruffians seized the horses of a gentleman's carriage and demanded money. By whipping up, they barely escaped. Immediately afterwards they stopped another carriage, turned the persons out of it, and then got in themselves, shouting and brandishing their clubs. So that concessions have not yet quieted the mob, and the soldiers cannot be every where. Reenforcements will doubtless arrive, and we shall have law and order. Thieves are going about in gangs, calling at houses, and demanding money—threatening the torch if denied. They have been across the street this afternoon, and I saw them myself. Perhaps they will give us a call: but we are all going to bed in a few minutes.

This evening there was a great light north of us—and I found, on looking with a spyglass, that it was from the burning a fine bridge over the Harlem valley—used by one of the railroads. There was some cannon-firing in the 1st Avenue, with what result I don't know.

The city looks very strangely. Nothing in Broadway but a few coaches. Most of the stores closed, but the side walks are full of people—and not a few ladies are out. It is half past 10 o'clock, and I must go to bed.

Thursday—U.S. Assay Office. The cars are running this morning, but the stores are closed in the greater part of the 3rd avenue. Herb. came up to breakfast. He had been up all night at the Assay Office, and had been drilling, under a U.S. officer, as an artillerist. They had 4 cannon and a rifle battery ready for the mob, at the office. I found a body of marines there this morning.—Just at this moment there was a false alarm, "every man at his post." The great doors were slammed too in a moment, and the arms were seized. I was amused to see an old *tar* quietly light his match rope, and swing it about to get it well on fire. He had the shells, to be thrown from the windows, in charge. Quiet was soon restored.—Passing down the Avenue, I saw the 7th Regt. at their armory, ready to go wherever they were needed. They will be as impartial as veterans. Thurber and young Etheredge have been at the Tribune Office all the week,—ready for service.

I shall try and do up some botany at the College to-day, as there is little to keep us at the Office. We feel that our chief danger is past. We are now afraid only of the small gangs of thieves.

Here I have given you a long account of what has been on our minds this week. I suppose you have been somewhat concerned about us. We were in the most dangerous part of the city, and have been kept more or less anxious on account of our colored servants, but I trust we shall not be driven from our home. A friend (Mr. Gibbons) who visits us almost every week, and is known to be an abolitionist, had his house smashed up yesterday.

Jane is going to spend a few days at Springfield, with Miss Day. She will probably leave home tomorrow. Eliza is still at her farm. Give my love your own good Jane.

Ever yours—
John Torrey

16

Governor Horatio Seymour of New York was a bitter opponent of the federal draft act, on the grounds of both its constitutionality and what he claimed were its unfair quotas for New York. On

August 3, 1863, he wrote President Lincoln an account of the draft riots in New York and requested a suspension of the August 19 draft call until the results of a recruiting drive were known. He also suggested a total suspension of the act until its constitutionality was determined by the Supreme Court. President Lincoln, in the following letter, rejected all of Seymour's recommendations.

Secretary of War Edwin Stanton was livid over this attempt to interfere with the functioning of the draft: "If the national Executive must negotiate with state executives in relation to the execution of an Act of Congress, then the problem which the rebellion desired to solve is already determined. . . . The governor of New York stands to-day on the platform of Slidell, Davis, and Benjamin; and if he is to be the judge whether the Conscription Act is constitutional and may be enforced or resisted as he or other state authorities may decide, then the rebellion is consummated and the national government abolished."[36]

President Lincoln to Governor Seymour

Executive Mansion,
Washington, August 7, 1863

His Excellency Horatio Seymour
Governor of New-York

Your communication of the 3rd Inst. has been received, and attentively considered.

I can not consent to suspend the draft in New-York, as you request, because among other reasons, *time* is too important. . . .

I do not object to abide a decision of the United States Supreme Court, or of the judges thereof, on the constitutionality of the draft law. In fact, I should be willing to facilitate the obtaining of it; but I can not consent to lose the *time* while it is being obtained. We are contending with an enemy who, as I understand, drives every able bodied man he can reach, into his ranks, very much as a butcher drives bullocks into a slaughter-pen. No time is wasted, no argument is used. This produces an army which will soon turn upon our now victorious soldiers already in the field, if they shall not be sustained by recruits, as they should be. It

Reprinted from *The Collected Works of Abraham Lincoln*, Vol. 6, ed. by Roy P. Basler (New Brunswick, N.J.: Rutgers University Press, 1953), pp. 369–70.

36. Edwin Stanton to James Brady, quoted in Benjamin P. Thomas and Harold M. Hyman, *Stanton: The Life and Times of Lincoln's Secretary of War* (New York: Alfred A. Knopf, 1962), p. 283.

produces an army with a rapidity not to be matched on our side, if we first waste time to re-experiment with the volunteer system, already deemed by congress, and palpably, in fact, so far exhausted, as to be inadequate; and then more time, to obtain a court decision, as to whether a law is constitutional, which requires a part of those not now in the service, to go to the aid of those who are already in it; and still more time, to determine with absolute certainty, that we get those, who are to go, in the precisely legal proportion, to those who are not to go.

My purpose is to be, in my action, just and constitutional; and yet practical, in performing the important duty, with which I am charged, of maintaining the unity, and the free principles of our common country.

Your Obt. Servt.
A. Lincoln

17

The following pamphlet, published anonymously in the wake of the uprising in New York City and similar disturbances in Ohio, Vermont, New Hampshire, and Massachusetts, questions what led so many people to this extremity. Are these outbreaks of violence —"outcroppings of one universal indignation"—to be the more greatly censured, or should the blame fall on the government for passing such a law? The pamphlet then goes on the analyze the impact of federal conscription on American society.

The Draft, or Conscription Reviewed by the People

The riotous demonstrations recently witnessed in New York and some other places, which have been occasioned by the *Draft*, are much to be deplored by all classes of citizens. No circumstances can justify such terrible proceedings, and their authors can offer no sufficient excuse for their conduct. But now, when the madness of the hour seems to have subsided, at least for the present, it may be wise for both people and rulers, to view the subject candidly and carefully. The public felt aggrieved by the proceedings under the conscription act; they felt that a great wrong had been done them; they murmured in secret and in public, and the disturbances which we have witnessed were only the out-

Reprinted from a pamphlet by an anonymous author, 1863.

cropings of one universal indignation. That the people were not right in resorting to violent means to redress a wrong, is everywhere acknowledged; but whether they or the government most deserve censure is a question. It seems to us that well informed, far seeing men might have anticipated such results from such legislation. If men are wanted for the army, the government should endeavor to raise them by constitutional and legitimate means. A very brief examination of the question should be sufficient to convince any unbiassed enquirer that Congress had no constitutional right to pass the obnoxious conscription act. The constitution of the United States confers no such authority upon Congress. And the uniform conduct of the government, both in war and peace, before the passing of this conscription act, clearly shows that no such power was delegated or intended to be delegated to Congress. . . . The general government confided in the intelligence and patriotism of the states. No insolent Marshals patroled the state, disturbing the quiet of its peaceful citizens. State authorities had an eye to the rights and interests of their own people, and state rights had not yet been swallowed up by the powers at Washington.

It must be recollected, that during the war of 1812, the governors of several of the New England states refused to allow their state conscripts to be marched out of their respective states, declaring that the general government had no authority to use the militia of any state, out of its own limits. To the principle thus laid down, the general government made no formal opposition, and there the matter seemed to rest as an established principle pertaining to state rights. Now if this was sound constitutional doctrine then, it must be so now, and Mr. Lincoln's administration has no more right to override the reserved rights of the states, than that of Mr. Madison had. . . .

But an attempt is made to justify the existing conscription act, on the ground that the war in which we are engaged at the present time, is not a foreign war, but only an insurrection, and therefore Congress has a right to use the militia to suppress it. In answer to this it may be said that this is no such insurrection or invasion as the constitution contemplates; 'tis no mob, nor riot, nor temporary insurrection to be suppressed by a hasty appeal to the militia. But it is open war of mammoth proportions, against an organized government, recognized by all Europe, and by our intercourse with its authorities, as a belligerent power, having in all respects the character of a foreign enemy, and however unwilling we may be to acknowledge the fact, we are compelled to treat this enemy, not as a band of insurgents, but precisely as we should an English or French army. . . . Much more might be said to show that this act and all proceedings under it are unauthorized by the Constitution of the United States, and in a legal sense absolutely void, but we have no time to pursue the investigation further. Whenever an appeal is made to the proper tribunal, it will undoubtedly be declared unconstitutional.

But if there was no constitutional impediment to the act, it must nevertheless be considered both unjust and unwise. By lot it inflicts a grievous wrong upon all who have the misfortune to fall under its ban. It is the most odious of all methods for raising troops, and belongs exclusively to despotic governments. It is said that Great Britain never during her long wars, ever resorted to this opprobrious method for recruiting her armies. During the fiery reign of Napoleon Bonaparte, when a military phrenzy had taken possession of all France, this odious method was resorted to, and much of the best blood of the nation was shed in obedience to its requirements. The system in its nature and history is exclusively despotic. In nations where the masses are profoundly ignorant, and accustomed to implicit obedience to superiors, this method obtains, and the conscript may go to the army with as little complaint as the ox to the slaughter. But our Congress, when they concocted and passed this law, greatly mistook the temper of the American people. Unlike the serfs of Russia or Austria, the great masses of our people are intelligent and high minded, and habituated to think and judge for themselves. They make and unmake their rulers, and approve or disapprove their acts as they think proper, and no administration can long continue to outrage their rights with impunity, as a day of reckoning is pretty sure to come sooner or later. Until the inauguration of the present scheme of conscription, the policy of our government has been to depend upon voluntary enlistments for the regular army, and to make use of the militia only for brief periods as occasion might require. The present is the first attempt in this country to create a regular army by arbitrary conscription, and it is such an audacious onslaught upon state rights and personal liberty as was never before witnessed in any free government. . . .

The present conscription measure is extremely unjust, because from the length of the service required it must work entire ruin to a considerable portion of those who are caught in its meshes. Many of them are young married men, farmers, merchants and mechanics, with small families and small means, just starting in business and beginning to live, with a hopeful prospect before them. Take the case of a young mechanic just engaged in a prosperous business, with all the fond endearments of home clustering round him—the die is cast, and he is drafted. The unrelenting decree puts a sudden stop to all his business arrangements, snatches him from the bosom of his family, and requires him to exchange the comforts of home for the hardships, privations and dangers of the camp and field of battle. He is doomed for three years, and whether he will live to return at the end of that time is a question that no one can answer; there is not more than an even chance in his favor. Perhaps he leaves a family without any adequate means for support. The town to which he belongs may mete out to his wife and children a stinted support during the time which he serves in the army, but if he falls in battle or by disease, the same blow that strikes him down, at the same instant cuts off the provision made for his family, and perhaps leaves them, forlorn and destitute, to the cold charities of an unfeeling world. But in whatever circumstances as to property such a family may be placed, it is left without its proper counsellor and guide, to struggle with the world as best it may. As to the conscript himself, if he survives, three years of camp life will work untold changes in him. If he returns at all, it will probably be with a constitution broken down, and with some lasting infirmity upon him; his mind brutalized and debased. Three years spent in indolence, amid all the corrupting influences of army life, demoralizes the once circumspect and industrious mechanic; his thoughts, habits and inclinations become changed, and he is unfitted for the quiet duties of civil life, in which the conscription found him. He may return, but not to the home he left—if he finds his family, they are strangers to him and he to them.

This conscription law is extremely unjust in its requirements. The service that should be shared by all as equally as possible, is arbitrarily demanded of a selected portion of the people, whilst nothing is required of others. There was no necessity for this. As before stated, the drafts in the revolutionary war, and also in the war of 1812, were for short periods, so that the able-bodied men took turns, and the service was shared very equally by all. The people of Rhode Island, always jealous of their equal rights and immunities, when they adopted their constitution, took care to insert in it a clause declaring that "the burdens of the state ought to be fairly distributed among its citizens." The conscription law violates this principle, and was evidently framed in utter disregard of all the rights, interests and wishes of the people. Its main features were borrowed from despotisms, and the whole act is little more than a transcript of the Russian system. If the service required had been for six, or even nine months, it would have been submitted to without any serious complaint, and all the riotous outbreaks and scenes of horror and bloodshed would have been prevented; a sufficient number of men would have been raised, and the nation would have been saved from the

mortification of its failure. The act was certainly very unwise, and
does little credit to the heads or the hearts of its authors. The disturbance and universal opposition which it everywhere meets with, is doing more to strengthen and encourage the rebels than any victory of
theirs ever has done. Again, the act is unjust, because the price of exemption is the same for the poor and the rich. From the rich it exacts an inconsiderable trifle, whilst it often takes from the poor man all he has.
Some sell their little homes, others mortgage them to raise the money;
many give their last dollar, and others borrow of their friends. The poor
man must go or part with all he has. The curse has fallen upon him—he
is broken up and ruined if he goes, and made a beggar if he stays; whilst
the rich man, whose interest at stake is a thousand fold more than that
of the poor man, is in no way incommoded. If the call had been per-
emptory: included the rich as well as the poor, and allowed neither
substitutes nor a money commutation, the poor man would readily have
marched to the scenes of conflict, shoulder to shoulder with his wealthy
neighbor, and cheerfully have shared with him every danger and hardship. Such a course would make the condition of a soldier respectable,
promote a spirit of genuine patriotism, and give character and efficiency
to the army. Such men would feel that they had something at stake besides their own persons. One such man would be worth more than a
score of simple hirelings. The rebels have had much the advantage of
us in this respect; their men of substance have fought in the ranks, and
their presence has inspired others with courage and devotion to their
cause.

If there is any one clause in that act that is more reprehensible than
another, it is that which provides that if the conscript fails to appear at
the time and place designated, he shall be considered a deserter and
dealt with accordingly. Without having committed any crime, or being
guilty of the least offence, the absentee is by the law condemned as a deserter, and the penalty is death. The annals of tyranny may be searched
in vain for a parallel to this. We would not rashly censure the conduct
of our national legislature, or willingly impugn the motives of its members, but we are bound to regard the act under consideration as a sad
mistake, which must inevitably seriously injure our cause, and dishonor
us at home and abroad. The sovereign people have already pronounced
their disapprobation of it; and it is much to be hoped that the government will somehow modify or repeal it, and quiet the popular murmurs.
Yet we are aware that governments are too prone to turn a deaf ear to
the complaints and admonitions of the common people, until the surges
of popular indignation sweep over them.

But after all that may be said of the palpable injustice of the act in question, and the obvious disquietude which attend the proceedings under it, let it everywhere be distinctly understood that the proper remedy is not to be found in open and violent resistance. Such demonstrations are painful evidences of public sentiment, but cannot directly correct the wrong. Therefore we earnestly entreat everyone wholly to abstain from all unlawful proceedings, to be patient and bide his time, until the wrong can be corrected in a constitutional manner; and if the constituted authorities fail to set the matter right, the sovereign people will most assuredly do it in their own good time.

18

The federal draft act failed to make any provision for conscientious objection. It was only through the labors of congressional leaders such as Charles Sumner and Thaddeus Stevens that certain accommodations were made to provide for conscientious objectors. On December 15, 1863, the War Department decided that conscientious objectors who were unwilling to use the existing avenues of staying out of the army—namely, paying the commutation fee or hiring a substitute—"shall ... be put on parole ... to report when called for."[37] On February 24, 1864, in an amendment to the draft act, it was provided that religious objectors were to be considered noncombatants when called to service and were to be assigned to duty in hospitals or caring for freedmen or were, instead, to pay a $300 commutation fee, these funds to be used on behalf of wounded soldiers.

The two following selections from Edward N. Wright's *Conscientious Objectors in the Civil War* illustrate the differing response on the part of members of the administration to the problem.

Conscientious Objectors in the Civil War

. . . Lincoln's sympathetic attitude towards those who actually suffered for conscience's sake is well illustrated by the case of Henry D.

Reprinted from Edward N. Wright, *Conscientious Objectors in the Civil War* (Philadelphia: University of Pennsylvania Press, 1931), pp. 124–25, 130–31 [original citations].

37. Randall and Donald, *Civil War and Reconstruction*, p. 319.

Swift, a member of the Society of Friends, and a resident of South Dedham, Massachusetts.[38] Swift was drafted in 1863, and when he went to Concord, where the conscripts were being mobilized, he was ordered to take part in the military drills.

> This he resolutely refused to do, it being contrary to the dictates of his conscience. For this he was put into the guard-house, but he adhered to his determination and refrained from all military activity at Concord, as well as later on, when sent to Long Island, and to Boston Harbor. From here troops were being constantly sent south to replenish armies in the field. While at Long Island he gladly helped in hospital services, but refused all remuneration for his services. He was "bucked down" and finally told by the officers that he would be shot for refusal to obey orders. He was then taken from the guard-house and made to witness an execution, and was told that that would be his fate if he persisted in his insubordination; but he still remained firm. He was tried by court-martial and sentenced to be shot.

During his stay at Long Island, he was visited by Stephen A. Chase, of Lynn, and Charles R. Tucker, of New Bedford, both prominent members of the Society of Friends. They went to Washington and stated the facts of Henry D. Swift's case to President Lincoln and Secretary Stanton. When the matter was considered by the President he directed that an honorable parole be made out. This was done and delivered to Henry Swift shortly before the time he had been informed his execution was to take place. This was in the fall of 1863. . . .

The attitude of the other members of Lincoln's Cabinet is not clearly known, but one incident, which has been preserved, would tend to show that Secretary Seward had far less patience with objectors than did Stanton. A Quaker, by the name of Ethan Foster, while visiting Washington on behalf of several New England young Friends who had been conscripted, said:

> Soon after we entered the War Office, the Secretary of State (William H. Seward) came in and took a seat. He remained silent until our conference with Secretary Stanton was concluded; when Charles Perry (who had an impression that Seward, when Governor of New York, had recommended the passage of a law to exempt from military service those who were consciously opposed to war)

38. The account of Henry D. Swift's experiences was first published in the Worcester, Mass., *Gazette*, Mar. 1, 1916, and afterwards reprinted in condensed form in the *Bulletin of Friends' Historical Society*, Vol. 7 (1916), pp. 37–38.

turned to him expecting a word of sympathy and encouragement, and remarked that he would perceive why we were there; upon which he suddenly and with much vehemence of manner asked, "Why don't the Quakers fight?" Charles replied, "Because they believe it wrong, and cannot do it with a clear conscience." He reprimanded us severely because we refused to fight. After a little pause I said, "Well, if this world were all, perhaps we might take thy advice"; to which he responded, "The way to get along in the next world is to do your duty in this." I replied, 'That is what we are trying to do; and now I want to ask thee one question, and I want thee to answer it; whose prerogative is it to decide what my duty is, thine or mine?" He did not answer the question, became more angry and excited; asked, "Why, then, don't you pay the commutation?" We told him we could see no difference between the responsibility of doing an act ourselves and that of hiring another to do it for us. On this he sprang from his seat and strided around in a circle of some eight or ten feet across, exclaiming, *"Then I'll pay it for you,"* and thrusting his hand into his coat pocket, added, *"I'll give you my check!"*

Immediately after this exhibition, we took our leave in much sadness, at the treatment so opposite to that we had expected from Secretary Seward.[39]

19

Although the Supreme Court never had cause to decide on the constitutionality of the federal draft law during the Civil War, there is evidence available which reveals how Chief Justice Roger Taney might have decided if the circumstance were to have arisen. Among the Taney papers is a lengthy document, entitled "Thoughts on the Conscription Law of the U. States," which contains Taney's assessment of the constitutionality of the draft. Taney found the law to be unconstitutional, involving federal interference in an area of state sovereignty.

There is no certainty that these thoughts would have emerged as Taney's opinion in an actual case, nor can the degree of support they would have won from his colleagues on the court be sur-

39. Ethan Foster, *The Conscript Quakers* (Cambridge, Mass.: Riverside Press, 1883), pp. 14–16.

mised. Nonetheless, Taney's resolute argumentation indicates that the Lincoln administration was fortunate in having avoided a test of its conscription law before the Supreme Court.

Taney on the Constitutionality of the Draft

By the Act of Congress entitled an Act for enrolling and calling out the national forces and for other purposes (generally called the conscription law) all able bodied male citizens of the United States between the ages of twenty and forty-five years except as thereinafter excepted are declared to constitute the national forces and liable to perform military duty in the service of the United States when called out by the President for that purpose.

The 2nd Section excepts and exempts from operation of the Law, the Vice President of the United States, the Judges of the various Courts of the United States, the head of the various executive departments of the government, and the governors of the several States, sundry other descriptions of persons are also exempted from family considerations, or want of health, whose exemption is not material to the matter now before the Court.

The 18th Section provides that the persons called out shall be liable to serve for a period not exceeding three years.

The question to be decided is,—Does Congress under the Constitution of the United States possess the power it has in this instance exercised?

In determining this question it is necessary that we should fix clearly in our minds the relative powers of the general and State governments, and the attitude in which they stand to each other when exercising their respective powers.

The confederation which existed prior to the adoption of the present constitution was a mere league of independent States. Each State retained the entire sovereignty within its own territorial limits, and the confederate power could not exercise forcibly any authority civil or military by its own officers within the territories of a State without its consent nor did it possess any power within these limits in any case paramount and superior to that of a State.

It was under these circumstances and in this state of things that the present Constitution was formed.

Reprinted from Roger Taney, "Thoughts on the Conscription Law of the U. States," *Tyler's Quarterly Historical and Genealogical Magazine,* Vol. 18 (1936), pp. 74–87, ed. by Philip G. Auchampaugh [original citations].

By adopting this Constitution, the people of the several States created the government of the United States and delegated to it certain specified powers of sovereignty within their respective territories;[40] but in express terms retained all the powers not thereby conferred on the U. States, in their own hands. Two separate governments are thus to exercise powers of sovereignty over the same territory and the same people at the same time. The line of division between them is marked out. Each of them is altogether independent of the other in the sphere of action assigned to it. The power of the Federal government is paramount to that of the State within the limits of its delegated powers. The authority of the several States is equally paramount within the limits retained by the States—neither owes allegiance to, or is inferior to the other.,[41] being both sovereignties they stand on equal ground—and the Citizen owes allegiance to the General government to the extent of the powers conferred on it and no further—and he owes equal allegiance to the State to the extent of the sovereign powers[42] they reserved,—The rule as to allegiance and the reason of the rule are clearly stated in I Blackstone's Commentaries, 366, in the following words: "Allegiance is the tie or ligament which binds the subject to the King in return for that protection which the King affords to the subject."— And as neither the Federal government, nor that of a State, could lawfully afford protection to the Citizen beyond the limits of their respective powers, no allegiance can be claimed or is due from the Citizen to either government beyond those limits. It is a divided allegiance but

40. Judge Taney at this point claims that the people delegated powers to the federal government. In Ableman vs. Booth he says "it was necessary that many of the rights of sovereignty which the states then possessed should be ceded to the general government" (21 Howard 517). In neither case does he say a new nation was created. In the Booth case he also pointed out that the courts were a substitute for an appeal to arms. Perhaps we might draw the conclusion that even a bad decision might be more desirable than a bad war.

41. It would seem to follow that to refuse to obey an unconstitutional act or order of either government would be no treason. Thus the ancient Calvinistic doctrine and the spirit of Magna Charta seems to put on new life from this reading of the Constitution. There seems to be suggested a constitutional right of resistance to ungranted powers.

42. The word sovereignty, as Daniel Webster so ably pointed out in the case of the Bank of Augusta vs. Earle, does not occur in the Constitution. Persons who remember Webster only for his nationalistic arguments in his Reply to Hayne might be both interested and surprised at his demarcation of state and federal sovereignty so well stated in this later case. It would seem that Taney's essay suggests more points in harmony with those views than either George Ticknor Curtis or Alexander H. Stephens reveals in his debate on the subject after the War Between the States (see Alexander H. Stephens, *Reviewers Reviewed*, New York, 1872, pp. 61–123). When Webster chose to argue for the reserved sovereignty of the states he could state it with all his accustomed ability.

not inconsistent—the boundaries of each sovereignty being defined and established, and not interfering with one another, and each independent of the other in its own sphere of action.

These principles were decided by this Court unanimously and upon much consideration in the case of Ablemore vs. Booth,[43] 21 How. 366. But the great importance of the case now before the Court makes it proper that I should again refer to the clauses in the Constitution which bear upon the subject. Clause 16, S. 8, Article I. authorizes Congress "to make all laws which shall be necessary and proper for carrying into execution the foregoing powers and all other powers vested by this Constitution in the government of the United States, or in any Department or officer thereof. And again the second clause of the 6 article declares that this constitution and the laws of the United States which shall be made in pursuance thereof, and all treaties made or which shall be made under the authority of the United States shall be the supreme law of the land, and the Judges in every State shall be bound thereby, anything in the Constitution or laws of any State to the contrary notwithstanding.

And Article 11 of the amendments to the Constitution declares "that the powers not delegated to the United States by the Constitution nor prohibited by it to the States are reserved to the States respectively or to the people.

These clauses show that the sovereignty of the general government is not a general & pervading one—but is confined to the powers delegated by the Constitution. And all the rights and powers of sovereignty not delegated are reserved to the States. The sovereignty of the State therefore to the extent of this reservation is wholly independent of the general government.[44]

The last mentioned clause it will be observed was an amendment to the original Constitution after it had been fully discussed before the people and in the conventions of the different States, and was manifestly adopted to show more clearly than the original instrument was sup-

43. It has seemed to me that this paper of Judge Taney is even clearer on the rights and extent of state sovereignty than the able exposition of the subject given in the Booth case. But even at that time when Taney was upholding the powers of the federal government against the defiance of a state Taney was careful to call attention to the "voluntary" entrance of the states into the compact of the federal union. The meaning of the word contract has been virtually converted into the word organic by writers of the federalist and nationalist schools of thought.

44. This relationship still exists. Should the New Deal and even the federal government perish in some frightful political cataclysm the states would, legally at least, remain with their rights of sovereignty and allegiance unimpaired.

posed to do, that no general supremacy over the States was intended to be conferred on the Federal government, and to show by the plainest and most positive words that the States were still sovereignties in their character.

Indeed the sovereignty of the States is expressly recognized in the 2d clause of the 2d Sect. of the 4th Article which provides that "a person charged in any State with treason, felony or other crime who shall flee from justice and be found in another State shall on demand of the Executive authority of the State from which he fled, be delivered up to be removed to the State having jurisdiction of the crime." The State must be sovereign,[45] and the party accused must owe it allegiance in return for the protection it affords him, or the crime of high treason could not be committed against it, nor its Courts have jurisdiction of the offence.

It follows from what is above stated, that the Federal government has no inherent, and original powers of sovereignty. It has only what the States delegated—and any exercise of sovereign power beyond these limits would be a usurpation[46] of State sovereignty—and consequently illegal.[47]

This brings me to inquire whether the power exercised in passing the Conscription Act above mentioned has been delegated to the Federal government.

In pursuing this inquiry we must not confine our attention to a single clause and construe it as if it stood by itself apart from all other provisions. The whole instrument must be taken together—general words in one clause may be restrained in the meaning by other provisions in the instrument and no construction can by any just rule of construction, be given to any one clause, that would make it repugnant to the plain

45. This enunciation is a great victory for states' rights and state sovereignty, for it locates a residual sovereignty powerful to defend itself within the language of the constitution itself. It is an argument which could be used either by the Calhoun followers or by those of Taney. Taney was no worshipper or follower of Calhoun. Indeed he seems to have either distrusted or disliked him. See Carl Brent Swisher's *Roger B. Taney*, New York, 1935, p. 451.

46. See note 41.

47. This paragraph reminds us of a part of President Buchanan's Message of December 1860. One of the instances of this doctrine of limitation will be found in Taney's opinion in Commonwealth of Kentucky vs. Dennison, Governor of Ohio, (241 Howard 107). In this case, it will be remembered, Taney overruled the fugitive slave law in favor of non-coercion of the Governor. President Buchanan's message in 1860 in favor of the non-coercion of a state found some critics but some of his friends and certain of his foes held that the Supreme Court had in this case sustained his argument, e.g. Charles Warren, *The Supreme Court*, Boston, 1932, Vol. II, p. 367.

words of another and make the Constitution so carefully and deliberately prepared inconsistent with itself.

Guided by this well established and familiar rule of construction–I proceed to examine the clauses in the Constitution which bear directly on the question.

The Constitution establishes and recognizes two kinds of military force entirely different from each other in their character, obligations and duties.–The 12th clause of the 8th Section of the 1st Article gives to Congress the power to raise and support armies. The power is general,–the number is not limited and it embraces times of peace as well as times of war, when raised it is exclusively subject to the control of the United States authorities.–It is a body of men separated from the general mass of citizen–subject to a different code of laws liable to be tried by Military Courts instead of the Civil Tribunals.–and may be employed at all times in or out of the United States, at the pleasure of Congress–and willing or not willing forced to obey the orders of their superior officers. And in the 3rd clause of the 10th Section of the 1st Article it is provided that "no State shall without the consent of Congress keep troops or ships of war in time of peace."–The powers given to the general government to raise and support armies, necessarily carries with it the power to appoint their officers, and the power to make rules and regulations for its government is given by the 14th clause of the Section and Article last above referred to. These rules and regulations so far as they concern the individuals who compose the army are altogether independent of State authority,–and the control of the whole body is exclusively and absolutely in the general government.–They compose the national forces,–or what is called in the Constitution the land forces of the United States.

The other description of military force is the militia over which by the express provisions of the Constitution the general government can exercise no power in time of peace, and but a limited and specified power in time of war.–It will be observed that as relates to the Army the power is given to raise and support it, a power which Congress in its discretion may or may not exercise. But the militia is spoken of, as a known military force, always existing and needing no law to bring it into existence and merely requiring organization, discipline and training to make it efficient.

Thus the clause 16–in the Section and Article aforesaid declares that Congress shall have power "to provide for organizing, arming and disciplining the militia and governing such part of them as may be employed in the service of the United States reserving to the States respectively the appointment of the officers and the authority of training the militia according to the discipline prescribed by Congress."

The clause immediately preceding (15) gives Congress the power to provide for calling forth the militia to execute the laws of the Union, suppress insurrection, and repel invasion. But what description of persons composes the militia who are thus to be officered and trained by the State,—and may be called to aid the general government in the emergencies above mentioned? The answer will be found in the 2d amendment to the Constitution which declares that "A well regulated militia being necessary to the security of a free State, this right of the people to keep and bear arms shall not be infringed." The militia is therefore to be composed of Citizens of the States, who retain all their rights and privileges as citizens who when called into service by the United States are not to be fused[48] into one body—nor confounded with the Army of the United States, but are to be called out as the militia of the several States to which they belong and consequently commanded by the officers appointed by the State. It is only in that form or organization that they are recognized in the Constitution as a military force.[49]

The United States can exercise no authority over them except only in the contingencies specified in the Constitution.

This . . . is plainly and distinctly expressed in the 1st clause of the 2nd Section of the Second Article which declares that—

"The President shall be commander in chief of the Army and Navy of the United States and of the *militia of the several States* when called into the actual service of the United States."

The distinction between the Army of the United States and the Militia of the several States and the power which the President may exercise over them respectively is here clearly stated. He has no power over the Militia unless when called into the actual service of the United States. They are then called out in the language of the Constitution, as the militia of the several States. The General government has no militia, it has only the Army and Navy—The militia force duly organized and

48. A second oath is still used to federalize the militia.
49. Marshall, before he went on the bench, seemed to hold that the states had the right to resist federal usurpations by force of arms if necessary. Madison once spoke in the same strain. See P. C. Centz (alias for Sage), *The Republic of Republics*, Boston, 1881, pp. 389, 392; Elliot's Debates, Vol. III, 414, 420. Governor John Floyd of Virginia defined Andrew Jackson's intention to coerce South Carolina as treason. He was not only prepared to resist it but if necessary to die in the struggle. Charles H. Ambler, Ed., *The Life and Diary of John Floyd*, Richmond, 1918, pp. 204, 206. As a result of Floyd's defiant attitude federal troops were sent by sea instead of through the Old Dominion. No actual engagement was fought at the time and the question rested until 1861.

ready to be called out belongs to the several States and may be called on in the emergencies mentioned to aid the land and naval forces of the United States.

But if the act of Congress of which I am speaking can be maintained all of the clauses in the Constitution above referred to are abrogated. There is no longer any militia—it is absorbed in the Army.—Every able bodied Citizen, not exempted by that law, belongs to the national forces —that is to the Army of the United States. They are not to be called out as the Militia of a State—but as a part of its land forces—and subject as soon as called on to all the obligations of a private soldier, in the ranks of the regular army.

The Generals, Colonels and other Officers appointed by the State according to the provisions of the Constitution are reduced to the ranks, and compelled march as private soldiers and obey the orders of such persons as the President may select to command them, and they and every other able bodied citizen except those whom it has been the pleasure of Congress to exempt, are compelled against their will to subject themselves to military law, to be tried by military Courts instead of the civil tribunals—and to be treated as deserters if they refuse to surrender their civil rights.

It appears to me impossible to believe that a Constitution and form of government framed by such men can contain provisions so repugnant to each other. For if the conscription law be authorized by the Constitution, then all of the clauses so elaborately prepared in relation to the militia, coupled as they are with the declaration "that a well regulated militia is necessary for the security of a free state", are of no practical value and may be set aside and annulled whenever Congress may deem it expedient.

The power to do this is, I understand, claimed under the clause which gives Congress the power to raise and support armies.

It is true that the power is delegated without specifying the manner in which the armies are to be raised.[50] But no inference can be drawn from these general words that would render null and inoperative the plain and specific provisions in regard to the militia, to which I have above referred. No just rule of construction can give any weight to inferences drawn from general words, when these inferences are opposed to special and express provisions, in the same instrument.

50. Lincoln saw this difficulty but nevertheless claimed the power for the federal government. Professor Andrew C. MacLaughlin in his able but very federalistic volume, *Constitutional History of the United States* (New York, 1935, pp. 628, 629, quoting Lincoln's works, Vol. II, p. 381), extols Lincoln's policy.

But apart from this consideration the words themselves, even if they stood alone, will not, according to their known and established use and meaning in the English language, justify this construction.

During the period when the United States were English Colonies, the Army of England,—the standing army,—was always raised by voluntary enlistments,[51]—and the right to coerce all the able bodied subjects of the Crown into the ranks of the Army and subject them to military law, was not claimed or exercised by the English government—and when the power to raise and support armies was delegated to Congress, the words of the grant necessarily implied that they were to be raised in the usual manner.[52]—And the general government has always heretofore so understood them and has uniformly by its own officers recruited the ranks of its "land forces" by voluntary enlistments for a specified period.

The general words "to provide and maintain a navy" could with much more apparent plausibility be construed to authorize coercion when a sufficient number of volunteer seamen could not be obtained. For at the time the Constitution was adopted and long before it had been the practice of the British government to compel by force seamen to serve on board its ships of war whenever there was a deficiency of volunteers—and it might be said with some appearance of reason, that the power to provide and maintain a navy, implied that it was to be provided and maintained in the same manner that it had been provided and maintained by the government under which we had before lived.— I do not think the Whalers and Fishermen, and Seamen of the Northern States would assent to such a construction or admit it to be correct.—It certainly would not be correct—for such a power over landsmen or

51. Chief Justice White, himself a Confederate Veteran, took a different view of the subject in the draft cases in 1918, (245 U.S. 366). Although he stressed the changes wrought by the 14th Amendment in that case, he seemed unwilling to admit that Elliot's Debates would have denied him a similar conclusion. Taney had knowledge of these debates and came to a different conclusion. According to Doctor Steiner, Taney thought what had sufficed for Washington ought to be sufficient for Lincoln. We managed to survive the Revolution without a draft by the central authority and ought to have been able to do as well under the stronger union of 1789. He held that the same method was ample in either event. After all it is a sad commentary on democracy when the so-called sovereign people have to be forced by their alleged agents to continue a slaughter. Both governments in the War of '61 had to resort to conscription, and both found much opposition in their paths. Taney hoped that both sides would call a convention and settle their differences. See Smith's *Roger B. Taney,* p. 190, Durham, N.C., 1935.

52. For the unpopularity of the draft during the War of 1812, see McMaster, *A History of the People of the United States,* Vol. IV, pp. 241, 242. This action was against a foreign enemy.

seamen would have been repugnant to the principles of the government which was then framed and adopted.

It is true also that the act recites in the preamble that an insurrection and rebellion exists against the authority of the United States, and that it is its duty to suppress it.—But this is the very crisis which the framers of the Constitution foresaw might happen and has given to the general government the powers they deemed adequate to meet it, or safe to grant.

It is the state of things in which Congress is authorized to provide for calling out the militia of the several States and if that course was pursued, the forces called out would be commanded by officers appointed by the State,—and it can hardly be maintained that where a specific power is given to Congress in a certain contingency, Congress may when the contingency happens repudiate the means prescribed in the Constitution and adopt others which it may deem more effectual, —such a construction would make the Constitution of no higher authority than an act of Congress,—and every provision in it liable to be repealed and altered or disregarded whenever in the judgment of a majority of the Legislature the public interest would be promoted by the exercise of powers not conferred.[53]

Much has been said in Courts of Justice as well as elsewhere of the war powers of the general government, and it seems to be assumed that the Constitution was made for a time of peace only and that there is no provision for a time of war. I can see no ground whatever for this argument. The war power of the Federal government is as clearly defined in the Constitution as its powers in time of peace.—Congress may raise and support armies,—it may provide and establish a Navy,—it may lay an embargo,—it may provide for calling out the militia of the several States—it may grant letters of marque and reprisal,—it may suspend the habeas corpus,—it may quarter soldiers in a house without the consent of the owner, in a manner to be regulated by law, which it cannot do in time of peace. These are all war powers—powers to be exercised in time of war—or in preparation for war,—And when we find these powers and none others enumerated and conferred for war purposes, it is conclusive proof that they are all that were deemed necessary, and that it was not deemed safe or prudent to trust more in the hands of the new government. This conclusion seems inevitable when we find that all powers not delegated to the general government or forbidden to the

53. Evidently Taney would not have held that the governors, who refused to call out the militia in answer to Lincoln's orders, were guilty of misconduct. Such governors who refused were either silent or questioned the constitutionality of the call.

States were reserved to the States and the people. The same considerations apply with equal force to the case of an insurrection or rebellion against the authority of the United States. The Habeas Corpus may be suspended and the militia called out to suppress it,—The Constitution has armed the general government with these powers to meet the emergency mentioned in the preamble to this law. But it seems to be supposed that these measures are not adequate to meet the crisis,—and that the Federal government may for the time disregard the limitations of power contained in the Constitution and adopt any measures it may deem necessary to put down the rebellion. This view of the subject, in its effect, puts aside the government created by the Constitution and establishes a temporary or provisional government in its place.—But the Judiciary who derive all the power they possess from the Constitutional government—and have all sworn to support it, would hardly be justified in violating any of its provisions—or in sanctioning their violation by any other Department of the government.—They can never be called on to execute or enforce unconstitutional laws or recognize as justifiable assumptions of power which the Constitution has not conferred.

But there is a more serious objection to this act of Congress—than those above stated.—It enables the general government to disorganize at its pleasure the government of the States,—by taking forcibly from them the public officers necessary to the execution of its laws.

I have already spoken of the sovereignty reserved to the States, as altogether independent of the sovereignty of the United States and in no respect subordinate to it. It had high duties to perform in the protection of the persons and property of the citizen in preserving the peace and promoting the prosperity of the Citizens of the State. And as the militia when called into the service of the United States were to be taken from the people of the State it is essential to the existence of State Sovereignty that its governors, judges and civil officers necessary for the purpose of carrying on the government should not be taken away, and the government thereby disorganized and rendered incapable of fulfilling the duties for which it was created, what officers are required for that purpose, the State sovereignty alone can judge, accordingly we find in the clause of the Constitution herein before referred to, that no power is granted to the Federal government to determine what description of persons shall compose the military force called the militia; the power to provide for organizing, arming and disciplining the militia, was necessarily delegated to Congress to make that arm of the military force efficient by conforming that organization and discipline to that of the army, so that when called into the service of the United States they might conveniently act together.

But the power prescribed who shall be liable to be called on and who exempted, is not given, not any power from which it can be inferred, on the contrary the right to appoint the officers and train the men is reserved to the State—The State must therefore determine who are to be trained, and they are to be selected from the people or the State.—It would necessarily happen that many from age or infirmity were unfit for military duty—and many would hold official stations essential to the existence and exercise of the State government; of this the people of the State have the sole right to judge. And such persons would not be enrolled and trained by the State because their duties required them to be elsewhere. And if the services of the militia were called for by the United States those only who were enrolled and trained under the State officers would be required by the State to respond to the call, and the State government would go on fulfilling its functions without interruption or inconvenience.

But the Act of Congress assumes the right of the General government to enroll in the national forces of the United States, and is in the army or "land forces" as they are called in the Constitution, every able bodied male citizen of the State without regarding the position he may hold in the State government—neither the judges nor executive officers, except the governor, are exempted and are made liable to trial by military court, and to punishment as deserters, if they refuse to march when ordered by the President.—What is to become of the people of a State if their executive officers and judges are taken away, and their Courts of Justice shut up? It will hardly be said in defence of the law that the Governor may appoint others to fill their places; for I believe it will be found that the people of no one of the States anticipated the possibility of such a state of things and have not therefore made provisions in their respective Constitutions to meet it. And indeed if every able bodied citizen is liable to the Conscription unless exempted by Congress, the Governors of the States, if they had not been specially exempted, might be forced into the army, and find themselves standing by the side of their generals and Judges as privates in the ranks and commanded and disciplined by officers appointed by a different sovereignty.

Neither does the privilege of hiring substitutes or paying $300. lessen the constitutional objections to the law. For the State Officers could not be required to furnish substitutes or pay $300. unless the power exists to compel them to serve in person.

There can be no actual government without proper officers to exercise its powers and execute its laws. The act in question shows that Congress was fully sensible of this,—and has exempted all of the executives and judicial officers of the United States, whose services are required to carry on the government.—That government is preserved in the full, free and uninterrupted exercise of all its powers. But it exempts none of the Officers of the State governments, but the Governor—and it leaves him without any other officer, executive or judicial. How is the peace of the State to be preserved, and the laws efficiently executed, if the whole or even a part of the officers of the State to whom these duties have been assigned are taken away and forced into the Army of the United States? No one I think can believe that the men who framed the Constitution could have intended to give to the new sovereignty they then created the power to paralyze or cripple the old ones, so as to disable them from executing the power expressly reserved to them,[54]—powers essential to the safety of the people of the State and which the State government alone could exercise under the provisions of the Constitution.

I speak of the Constitutional and lawful power, not of the physical power which the Constitution has placed in the hands of the Federal government.[55]

For in a contest of mere force, a State would meet the United States upon very unequal terms—prepared as the latter always is with a disciplined army and navy at its command.—But so far from intending to give the general government the power to disorganize the government of a State they have carefully and jealously excluded it from any right to interfere in the domestic controversies and difficulties of a State, even where its aid might be supposed to be useful. For in the case of rebellion or insurrection against the State government, the United States is not allowed to interfere in it, to support the State authority,

54. This same type of reasoning appears in Kentucky vs. Dennison. When the conscription act of the Confederacy was challenged the opponents of the act used this same line of attack. Their reasoning is as clear as Taney's statement. Moreover the Confederate Constitution like the Articles of Confederation left no doubt as to its position in the matter of state sovereignty. Yet the Virginia Court before which the case was tried, rejected this point of view and sustained the Confederate draft. (John Randolph Tucker, The Constitution of the United States, Chicago, 1897, Vol. 11, pp. 579, 580). It was the same line of reasoning which Chief Justice White accepted in the draft cases in 1918. Thus a broad construction view of a Confederate Court became part of the law of the land during the World War. Had Taney decided the matter in the 60's his opinion in Kentucky vs. Dennison seems to indicate that he would not have sustained a Federal Conscription Act. His essay leaves no doubt concerning his personal views on the subject.

55. These excellent distinctions between right and might deserve a wider circulation.

unless its assistance is applied for by the Legislature of the State or by the Executive where the Legislature cannot be convened (Art.–4, S. 4.) scarcely any provision could more strongly show how anxiously and jealously the sovereignty of the States was guarded from any interposition by the United States.–It is not permitted even to defend it, unless their assistance is asked for by the State authorities.

The circumstance that the Federal government pervades the whole union, and that its power within the sphere of action assigned to it, is supreme over that of the States, is perhaps calculated to create an impression upon the minds of those whose pursuits have not led them to examine particularly the provisions of the Constitution,–that its supremacy over the State extends to all cases where the general government may choose to exercise it.–The character of the powers assigned to it, and in which its power is supreme, is also calculated to attract the public attention far more than the quiet exercise of State powers, in any single State.–But it must be remembered that State Sovereignty also pervades every part of the Union and in that respect is coextensive with that of the United States,–In every part of the Union (except the territories) there is a State government, exercising independently of the general government, all the powers not delegated to the United States. These powers although not so striking as those exercised by the general Government are not less important to the happiness of the people.–For while the powers conferred on the general government contain mainly our foreign relations and the intercourse between the different States, it is the State Sovereignty which preserves tranquillity in the State, and guards the life, liberty and property of the individual Citizen, and protects him in his home and in his ordinary business pursuits.

It cannot be that the men who framed the Constitution, or the people who adopted it could have regarded these interests as of less value than those committed to the care of the Federal government,–and could have intended on that account to give the latter the power, whenever it deemed it expedient to paralyze the action of the State governments, –and leave the people to choose between anarchy on the one side, or a purely unlimited military despotism on the other, to be coerced by the U. States.

For the reasons[56] above stated, I am of opinion that this Act of Congress is unconstitutional and void,–and confers no lawful authority on the persons appointed to execute it.

---

56. Despite the defeat of the states rights section in the "War of Conquest" these remarks and truths are to a great extent still with us. We are not yet in all things a consolidated republic.

20

At the end of the Civil War, Brevet Brigadier General James Oakes, assistant provost marshal general and administrator of the draft laws in Illinois, furnished a report of his operations to his superior, General James Fry. His long and precisely detailed analysis of the system pointed out its deficiencies and recommended improvements for any future contingency. One of the real handicaps, according to Oakes, was the policy of having enrolling officers seek out the eligible men rather than placing the obligation upon the men to register. He also attacked, in scathing terms, that widespread phenomenon of the Civil War years, the substitute broker —"the vampires who fatten upon the profits." The payment of bounties, with town, county, state, and federal governments in competition for recruits, also met with Oakes's disapproval. This report lay, for a long time, virtually unnoticed in War Department files until, when the nation was preparing itself once again for the draft in World War I, it was discovered and its recommendations were put into effect.

Report on the Draft in Illinois

Office Acting Assistant Provost Marshal General, Illinois

Springfield, August 9, 1865

General: In compliance with the request contained in your communication of April 27, 1865, I have the honor to submit the following Historical Report of the operations of this office since it commenced business, with such remarks and suggestions as my experience and observation may seem to warrant. . . .

2. ENROLMENT

The starting point and basis of the whole system of replenishing the national army through the agency of the Bureau of the Provost Marshal General, is the enrolment of the arms-bearing population of the country. Upon its completeness and correctness depends the equity of credits allowed and quotas imposed. If the enrolment is right, all is right; if

Reprinted from *Backgrounds of Selective Service*, Special Monograph No. 1, Vol. 1 (Washington, D.C.: U.S. Selective Service System, 1949), pp. 154–91.

wrong, all is wrong. To no other subject have I given more attention and thought. It cannot be denied that the enrolments made under existing laws were far from being perfect; and it is equally undeniable, I think, that the errors contained in said enrolments were not due so much to remissness on the part of enrolling officers (some of whom, doubtless, were incompetent and unfaithful), as to grave defects in the laws themselves under which they acted. In fact, it is believed that most of the imperfections can never be avoided under the present system.

It is not intimated that the several enrolment acts were not as carefully matured and as wisely adapted to the end in view as was possible at the time; much less is it intended to challenge the wisdom and necessity of the policy of military conscription, or the administrative ability of the Provost Marshal General.

The organization of the bureau was, in my estimation, an absolute necessity of the government, and contributed to an incalculable extent toward the final overthrow and destruction of the rebellion. Its aid was essential and invaluable not only on account of the vast accessions to the army secured through its direct agency, but also, indirectly, through the significant revelation which it afforded to our enemies, at home and abroad, of the ability of the government to summon to the national defence the whole military strength of the country, and that, too, by the stern ordeal of the draft. And the conduct of the bureau has, in my judgment, been characterized by great ability, energy and prudence. The defects of the present laws are, for the most part, such as no forecast could anticipate, and which could only be developed by experience and time.

I am, therefore, clearly convinced that a radically different policy should be adopted, in case the agency of your bureau should again be called into requisition. Instead of endeavoring to search out and hunt up every person liable to military service, through the agency of a vast multitude of petty enrolling officers, upon whose capacity and fidelity it is not possible in all cases to rely, I think the government should impose its supreme demands *directly upon the people themselves,* and require them, under the sternest penalties, *to report themselves* for enrolment. If the government has a right to the military service of its citizens in times of public peril, rebellion, and war, it has a right to secure such services in the simplest, cheapest and most direct manner.

The policy advocated is not new; it is as old as the principles and method of federal, State, and local taxation. It is the duty of taxpayers to call at the office of the collector and discharge their indebtedness, or, in default, to suffer their property to be sold by public auction. The collector does not go to the taxpayer, but the tax-payer comes to the collector; and so, I think, it should be with a military enrolment.

As soon as the emergency requiring a conscription can be foreseen, let the acting assistant provost marshals general of States be required, through their respective district provost marshals and otherwise, to give general and emphatic public notice through the newspapers, circulars and hand-bills, etc., that a draft is impending, and that all persons between the prescribed ages must appear before the board of enrolment of their district, and be duly enrolled or exempted for cause, as the case may be, or suffer the consequences. Let the several boards be required to hold meetings for that purpose in a sufficient number of places in each county, for the proper and speedy accommodation of all liable to enrolment, and let a sufficient time be allowed for the purpose at each point. Immediately upon the termination of the period assigned for reporting, let public notice be likewise given that the lists will be finally closed with a certain time—say ten days—after which all voluntarily failing to report shall be subject to the penalties and liabilities provided by law. Let it be enacted that any person liable to enrolment, and finally failing or refusing to report to the proper officers for that purpose, shall be heavily fined, or imprisoned, or both, as Congress shall prescribe, and that all such persons failing to report, but whose names may be communicated through other sources to the board of enrolment, shall, if drafted and accepted, be compelled to *serve personally*. Let the foregoing rule apply to aliens, to persons having conscientious scruples against bearing arms, and to all classes and descriptions of persons, without distinction, whose ages are within the prescribed limits. . . .

It will be seen that under the operation of such an enrolment act as is here proposed, not only is the original enrolment made with incomparably less difficulty, time, and expense, but it becomes thereafter throughout the whole continuance of the war, and without any additional expense whatever, *self-revising*, so that each State will thereafter be always ready for any new assignment of quotas, and any additional drafts. It is also morally certain that an enrolment made under the provisions of such a law would be far more complete and reliable than by the present or any other system; for, beyond all question, just as but a very small percentage of the tax-payers of a community incur the hazard of losing their estates by neglecting to pay their taxes, so, a like unimportant portion of the arms-bearing population of any subdistrict would voluntarily incur the stern penalties of imprisonment and fine, by seeking to evade the requirements of such a military enactment; and not only would the number of delinquents be very small, from the nature of the case, but it would be constantly and rapidly reduced by the hearty resistance rendered by all who had themselves complied with the law, every one of whom would be urged by the strongest incentives of personal interest to bring forward such delinquents, or report them for punishment. . . .

4. SUBSTITUTE BROKERS

In my judgement, the strong hand of the government should be laid upon the whole heartless crew of substitute brokers, whether as principals or subordinates, and all others who would make merchandise of the necessities and calamities of the country. The whole business is founded upon a supreme and sordid selfishness, and prosecuted with a degree of unprincipled recklessness and profligacy unparalleled in the annals of corruption and fraud. The traffic is too odious to be engaged in by respectable men, or, if such persons do embark in it with honest intentions at first, they soon become so corrupted by the nefarious practices to which competition compels them to resort, as to lose all claim to the character of honorable men. The whole thing is demoralizing to those engaged in it, whether as agents or subjects, and a disgrace to the people who connive at it, and the government that tolerates it. It presses into the service, by devices which no vigilance can wholly prevent, great numbers of men wholly unfit for military duty. It disgraces the honest soldier and the service, by conferring the dignity of the federal uniform upon branded felons; upon blotched and bloated libertines and pimps; upon thieves, burglars, and vagabonds; upon the riff-raff of corruption and scoundrelism of every shade and degree of infamy which can be swept into the insatiable clutches of the vampires who fatten upon the profits of the execrable business. It is the parent and support also of the herd of bounty-jumpers who have prowled the country during the last twelve months, scandalously selling themselves again and again to the highest bidder, regardless of their plighted faith and the solemnities of their oaths to the government.

The enormous gains of the business clothe its agents with a power of bribery, against which there is reason to fear that not a few of the commissioned officers of the government have proved unable to stand. Many well-known facts render this more than a mere surmise. Members of boards of enrolment, who were penniless when they received their commissions, have retired from the service with a display of means utterly incompatible with the assumption of their honesty, and yet so adroitly has the business been conducted that no clue can be obtained whereby to prove their guilt.

A business that thus interferes with the military operations of the government, demoralizing and corrupting both people and soldiery, and bringing the force of a tremendous temptation to bear upon the very officers of the government to swerve them from rectitude; a business that makes bounty-jumpers by hundreds a set of dastards who to the crime of desertion add the meanness of constructive theft and robbery; a business that ends to stain the proud name of the soldier of the republic, and entail, by vilest fraud, an expense of untold thousands— such a business not only cannot be right, but must be considered as falling within the sphere of the national authority in time of war.

I therefore suggest and recommend that substitute brokerage be suppressed by proper authority, as a military offence, and that all persons found guilty of engaging therein be liable to summary trial and punishment by court-martial or military commission. . . .

6. BOUNTIES

It has seemed to me that if the government deems it expedient to offer large bounties as an inducement to volunteer, it would be more prudent not to pay any part or instalment of such bounties in *advance*. The large amount received from the government by the soldier before he leaves the general rendezvous, added to the local bounty which is often still larger, constitutes a very strong temptation to desert—too strong, in many instances, for resistance. I would therefore recommend, should the policy of large bounties be hereafter continued, that no part be paid until after the soldier has served a certain time.

But I am of the opinion that a still better policy would be, in future wars, to dispense with government bounties altogether as a means of promoting volunteering, and, instead, to increase the regular pay of the soldier to such an extent as would enable him, with prudence and economy, to support his family or dependents while in the army; relying upon the spirit of the people and such local bounties as particular communities might offer to secure volunteers, and when these resources failed, call in the aid of the draft.

The drain upon the national treasury to pay such large bounties to such vast numbers of men is prodigious, and if continued would be absolutely ruinous. The amount of bounty necessary to secure a given result, at successive stages of a war, is, moreover, necessarily greater and greater. A sum that secures volunteers enough to fill one call will prove inadequate for the next call; and so the amount must be increased as the war goes on, until the resources of the federal treasury become unequal to the demand. Nor is this the only evil. Those who respond to the first call of their country, and enter the service without any stimulus but patriotism, regard with disfavor those who could only be induced to take up arms by the pressure of pecuniary motives, while those who subsequently receive a still larger bounty are disliked, in turn, by their predecessors to whom a less amount was paid; and so the effect is not only to engender bitter and jealous feelings among the soldiers, but also to induce those not yet enlisted to wait for still greater offers, and thus defeat the very end in view.

The bad effects above mentioned have been realized in this State to a large extent. The ill-nature produced by the disparity of benefits received by different portions of the regiment has, in many instances, been injurious to the *morale* of the whole command, while taunts and retorts, criminations and recriminations, have impaired the efficiency of the men by diverting attention from duty to angry disputations. I am convinced that, upon the whole, the evils of large government bounties are greater than the benefits, and do not doubt that a different policy should obtain in case great armies are again to be called into service. . . .

8. Resistance

At the time I was ordered to take post in this city, as acting assistant provost marshal general of Illinois, no signal success had crowned the national arms, and the public mind was much depressed and in a state of feverish apprehension. Advantage was taken of this discouraging aspect of affairs by the enemies of the government, and threats of resistance and defiance to the provisions of the enrolment act, then just passed, were freely made in various parts of the State, eliciting much uneasiness on the part of good men. Though not sharing in the fears that were entertained respecting the imminence of an actual outbreak, I deemed it prudent to enjoin upon my subordinates the exercise of great circumspection and forbearance, and the careful avoidance of all unnecessary irritation while in the discharge of their duties. The measure about to be inaugurated by the government was not only now and hitherto untried in this country, but one against which the people had conceived a most violent prejudice; and common sagacity dictated the pursuance of such a course as would allay the excitement and fears of the people and lead them gradually to a more rational view of the nature and necessity of conscription, while the inflexible purpose of the government to enforce the law regardless of all opposition and menace was at the same time firmly exhibited.

Under instructions in harmony with the foregoing policy, the work began and progressed rapidly and satisfactorily in almost every district. The disloyal elements of the State, which were not lacking in numbers or virulence, were awed by the calm strength and quiet determination exhibited by the government, and shrank from open collision; while the friends of a stern prosecution of the war rapidly discarded their fears and prejudices and ranged themselves firmly on the side of the government and its officers.

At a very early period after the work commenced, an enrolling officer was assaulted and almost killed in the streets of Chicago; but the summary arrest and condign punishment of the miscreant settled the question at once in that city and district, and exerted a wholesome influence upon the disaffected in other portions of the State.

At a later period more serious resistance was made in the 9th, 10th, 11th and 13th districts, in each of which the aid of the military was, at different times, called to the assistance of the provost marshals. One county of the 13th district (Williamson) was obliged to be enrolled in the presence and by the aid of a company of cavalry, and a bitter and dangerous spirit was for a time manifested; but the certainty of invoking upon themselves the prompt and irresistable strength of the military arm dissuaded the insurgents from the hazards of actual collision, and the excitement gradually died away. . . .

The difficulties above mentioned nearly all occurred in connexion with the enrolment. The only serious opposition after the draft was connected with the service of notices upon drafted men, and occurred chiefly in Fulton, Clarke, and Fayette counties. But the presence of troops held the leaders in check, and the notices were finally served in every instance.

Although but few actual collisions have occurred in the State, a bitter and dangerous temper has frequently been manifested and formidable combinations have existed in various localities, with the avowed purpose of armed resistance to the enforcement of the laws; and I am entirely satisfied that the presence in the State of the requisite military force was all that prevented the bloody culmination of their threats in many localities, if not a general and formidable insurrection, especially toward the close of the year 1864. . . .

It is not needful to look for the *causes* of nearly all the opposition which I have encountered in this State. It is due mainly to the (as I think) mistaken clemency of the government in dealing with deserters, upon which I have elsewhere remarked, and the machinations of a few disloyal political leaders, aided by the treasonable utterances of corrupt and profligate newspapers. The swarm of deserters whom assured impunity brought to the State, exerted a most baleful and contaminating influence both in preventing enlistments, and also in giving head and venom to the lawless gangs that attempted to resist and defy the authorities.

But the grand cause—the only really guilty and formidable source of dangers through which Illinois has passed—is to be found in the steady streams of political poison and arrant treason which have been permitted to flow from the wicked, reckless and debauched newspaper press of the State. But for this, the enrolment and draft would have passed off with scarcely a ripple of disturbance. The terrible effect of such daily teachings upon the ignorant and deluded masses can well be imagined. The government, with all its officers, aims and purposes, has been maligned, calumniated, aspersed and defied, with a persistent fiendishness and a truculent hatred that would have seemed incredible and impossible. And chief among these instigators of insurrection and treason, the foul and damnable reservoir which supplied the lesser sewers with political filth, falsehood and treason, has been the Chicago Times—a newspaper which would not have needed to change its course an atom, if its place of publication had been Richmond or Charleston, instead of Chicago—a sheet that has been bought by tens of thousands by southern emissaries, with southern gold, for gratuitous southern distribution, to keep alive the delusion and spirits of the southern people, and protract the war—a paper that rebel leaders have ever regarded as their best northern ally in Illinois, and whose editorials have been read with delight by Davis and his fellow-traitors since the war began. The pestilent influence of that paper in this State has been simply incalculable. I have not the slightest doubt that it is responsible for the shedding of more drops of the patriot blood in Illinois soldiers than there are types in all of its four pages of political slime and scandal. The conspiracy that came so near wrapping Chicago in flames and drenching her streets with blood was fomented and encouraged by the teachings of the Chicago Times; without that paper there would have been no conspiracy. In my opinion, without desiring in the least to abridge the regulated liberty of the press, it is as much the duty of the government to suppress such newspapers in time of public danger and war, as it is to storm the fortresses, sink the navies, and destroy the armies of the common enemy;

and should war break out I would urge the prompt adoption of that policy. . . .

CONCLUSION

It is to be hoped that the great lessons of this war will not be lost upon the country. Aside from its glorious termination, the rich experiences and teachings which it has left as a legacy to us and our children are not few or small. It has accustomed our people to the disabilities and hardships incident to a state of war. It has demonstrated to the world the invincible power of citizen soldiery in a just cause, and how soon they may acquire the discipline and steadiness of veterans. It has especially taught us how to raise, arm, equip, muster, organize, drill, and employ great armies. And if these lessons are wisely improved, the nation would embark in another war, whether foreign or domestic, with incomparably greater advantages for its successful prosecution than were possessed at the commencement of the late rebellion. . . .

I am, general, very respectfully, your obedient servant,

James Oakes
Bvt. Brig. Gen. U.S.A.,
Act. Assist.
Provost Marshal General, Ill.

Brigadier General James B. Fry
Provost Marshal General, Washington, D.C.

1900-1940:
Conscription
Comes of Age

☆

THE "SPLENDID LITTLE WAR" of 1898, while not testing the nation's military capacity, did reveal the army's structural and administrative inadequacies. The new secretary of war appointed in 1899, Elihu Root, set out to remedy these deficiencies. A lawyer by profession, Root determined to master the relevant military literature in order to formulate a more efficient army organization.

Drawing upon the theories of German, British, and French military thinkers, as well as the analysis of Civil War General Emory Upton, Root concluded that a number of fundamental changes were necessary. American preparations for war in the past, the secretary of war determined, had depended upon the assumption that the national character and spirit would prove "superior to system, or rather absence of system."[1] Future wars would not allow for any such fond hopes, and procedures would have to be developed to prepare for any contingency.

The "Root reforms" that emerged from this planning included the establishment of a general staff headed by a chief of staff, the creation of a number of service schools to provide advanced training for officers, an enlarged regular army with a minimum force of sixty thousand, and a redefinition of the army's relationship with

1. T. Harry Williams, *Americans at War*, p. 112.

the militia.[2] The last of these achievements was embodied in the Militia Act of January 21, 1903, more commonly known as the Dick Act.

The Dick Act served to remove the confusion which surrounded the term *militia*, which had been interchangeably used to designate the organized military companies of the states, now known as the National Guard, and the entire unorganized military manpower potential of the nation.[3] The law reaffirmed the traditional universal military obligation but directed its primary attention to the affiliation between the regular army and the National Guard. This "organized militia" would receive an annual congressional appropriation for arms and equipment. It would drill regularly, maintain a state of preparedness, and be reviewed periodically by regular army officers. The Dick Act provided then, according to Russell Weigley, "a foundation for cooperation of a continually improving kind between the Regular Army and the only reserve force that in 1903 was feasible."[4]

The modernization introduced by Root placed the army on the soundest footing in its peacetime history. The question that arose, however, when Europe plunged into war in the summer of 1914, was whether the army, in its form at that time, was capable of guaranteeing the national defense.

President Woodrow Wilson addressed that issue in his State-of-the-Union message to Congress on December 8, 1914. Wilson assured that body that as long as "we retain our present principles and ideals" we shall never have a large standing army. We should be prepared to defend the nation, but this did not require turning America into a "military camp" or asking "young men to spend the best years of their lives making soldiers of themselves." Volunteering and the strengthening of the National Guard were adequate enough measures. Congress stood cheering as Wilson finished his address.[5] That enthusiasm, however, would soon dissipate in the face of increasing American involvement in the war and the mounting campaign waged by the advocates of preparedness.

The preparedness movement enlisted a growing number of adherents during the early months of 1915, with former President Theodore Roosevelt and former Chief of Staff General Leonard

2. *Ibid.*, p. 115.
3. Russell F. Weigley, *History of the United States Army*, p. 321.
4. *Ibid.*, pp. 321–22.
5. Arthur Link, *Wilson: The Struggle for Neutrality, 1914–1915* (Princeton: Princeton University Press, 1960), p. 140.

Wood as its ablest recruiting sergeants. Wood, as "military publicist,"[6] argued the case for compulsory military training as a corollary of universal manhood suffrage and insisted that many social benefits would accrue from such a program.[7] He became the guiding spirit of the Plattsburg movement, a voluntary military training program whose organizers included Theodore Roosevelt, Jr., and Elihu Root, Jr. These camps, attended by prominent business and professional men, would not only serve to provide basic military training for the participants but, more importantly from Wood's perspective, would serve to sell the public on the advantages of universal military training.

Wilson proved somewhat responsive to the demands for an improved national defense posture. In December, 1915, he recommended that Congress increase the regular army to 142,000 men and expand the reserves to 400,000. The National Defense Act of June 3, 1916, went beyond Wilson's proposed figures, providing for a regular army of 175,000 men, with further increments over the next five years, and a reserve force of 450,000. These additional forces were to be raised by volunteering, and Wilson, when questioned as to whether a sufficient number would come forward, replied, "Why, if they did not, it is not the America that you and I know. . . . I am sorry for the skeptics who believe that the response would not be tremendous."[8]

The skeptics, as it turned out, had made the more realistic judgment. When America entered the war ten months later, the army's strength stood at slightly less than 380,000. The soaring national spirit served to induce only 36,000 young men to volunteer in the following two weeks.[9] William Jennings Bryan's earlier boast that a million men would spring to arms overnight had proved to be embarrassingly hollow.

The administration submitted a proposal for a draft to Congress on April 6, 1917. The opposition, although not numerically strong, was vitriolic in its attack upon the proposed legislation. Speaker of the House Champ Clark (D., Mo.) avowed that he saw "precious

6. Samuel Huntington, *The Soldier and the State*, p. 273.

7. Wood, a rather ineffectual public speaker, nonetheless accepted every invitation that would provide a forum for his views. He kept a meticulous account of these engagements, listing 156 talks between November, 1915, and June, 1916, with a total audience of 137,000. Hermann Hagedorn, *Leonard Wood*, 2 vols. (New York, 1939), Vol. 2, p. 173.

8. Warren S. Tryon, "The Draft in World War I," *Current History*, Vol. 55 (June, 1968), p. 340.

9. *Ibid.*

little difference between a conscript and a convict,"[10] while his fellow Missourian, Senator James Reed, predicted that blood would flow in the streets if a draft were enacted. The flamboyance of Clark's and Reed's rhetoric appeared to have little effect on their colleagues. The measure passed by overwhelming majorities in both houses on April 28.

The Senate and House versions of the draft bill differed in several respects, and this difference delayed the enactment of the legislation. The question of the age range for draftees was finally settled at ages twenty-one through thirty (later extended to eighteen through thirty-five). The issue of allowing the continuance of volunteering while conscription was in operation, a politically charged topic, since Theodore Roosevelt wished to command a volunteer division, finally came to a compromise resolution: the president could, if he wished, continue to accept volunteers. Wilson signed the bill into law on May 18, 1917, and set June 5 as the date for registration.

Secretary of War Newton Baker, anxious that the new law win public acceptance, advised Wilson to have "the registration and selection by draft . . . conducted under such circumstances as to excite a strong patriotic feeling and silence as far as possible the prejudice which remains . . . in the popular mind against a draft by reason of Civil War memories."[11] The president, in his registration message, exhorted the enrollees to step forward "in one solid rank in defense of the ideals to which this nation is consecrated. It is important to those ideals no less than to the pride of this generation in manifesting its devotion to them, that there be no gaps in the ranks." There were, as it turned out, large "gaps in the ranks," with over 300,000 men resisting or evading the draft.[12]

Despite the opposition, the operation of the draft in World War I marked a major improvement over its Civil War antecedent. The lessons of that sorry enterprise had been well learned, and its pitfalls had not been repeated. The payment of bounties and the hiring of substitutes were disallowed, and the carrying out of the functions of conscription now lay not in the hands of the military but with

10. U.S., Congress, House, *Congressional Record*, 65th Cong., 1st sess., April 25, 1917, p. 1102.

11. Tryon, "The Draft," p. 344.

12. *Ibid.*, p. 368. For more detailed accounts of antagonism toward the draft, see Robert W. Dubay, "The Opposition to Selective Service, 1916–1918," *The Southern Quarterly*, Vol. 7 (Apr., 1969), pp. 301–22; and Horace C. Peterson and Gilbert C. Fite, *Opponents of War, 1917–1918.*

local civilian boards. Close to three million men, approximately
two-thirds of the armed forces, were drafted under the act, a sizable
leap over the 6 percent produced by the Civil War draft.

Under the provisions of the act, only members of the "historic
peace churches" were entitled to noncombatant status, and 20,873
men were inducted on that basis.[13] There was no provision in the
law for those men who were conscientiously opposed to war but
were not affiliated with the peace churches. However, President
Wilson, in an Executive Order issued on March 20, 1918, allowed
those who objected to the war because of "conscientious scruples"
to also serve in a noncombatant capacity.[14] Some 4,000 men claimed
conscientious objection under this arrangement. A commission consisting of Major Walter Kellogg of the judge advocate's office, Judge
Julian W. Mack, and Dean Harlan F. Stone of Columbia University
Law School was established by the secretary of war to visit army
camps and investigate many of these claims, some 2,300 in all. Of
the 4,000 objectors, 1,300 were eventually assigned to serve in the
military in a noncombatant status, some 1,200 accepted farm and
industrial furloughs, where they had that portion of their pay over
thirty dollars a month donated to the Red Cross, and 504 men refused any accommodation whatsoever on their part to the authority
of the military. Of this latter group, 450 were convicted in courts-
martial, with 142 of them receiving life sentences, and 17 were
sentenced to death, although all of the death sentences were eventually commuted.

The World War I draft act terminated with the armistice, but
proponents of universal military training sought to carry conscription over into peacetime. They developed several proposals,
the most significant being a provision in the Army Reorganization
Bill, introduced in July, 1919, that all nineteen-year-old males be
required to undergo three months of military training. The Senate
Military Affairs Committee reported the bill out in January, 1920,
with the period of training lengthened to four months, still a far
cry from the War Department's preference for eleven months. The
Democratic caucus, which met while the House Military Affairs
Committee had the bill under consideration, voted 106–7 against
the universal military training section. The committee passed the
bill with that section intact, but agreed, four days later, to delete it.

13. U.S., Selective Service System, *Conscientious Objection*, Vol. 1, p. 53.
14. *Ibid.*, p. 57.

The Senate bill eventually suffered a similar fate when an amendment was adopted providing for *voluntary* universal military training at summer camps.

Popular interest in adopting universal military training had clearly peaked in the period immediately prior to America's entrance into the war. The martial spirit did not long survive the armistice. With no enemy visible on the horizon, it proved increasingly difficult to argue the military necessity for so costly a program. Even so fervent an advocate as General Leonard Wood, when he sought the Republican presidential nomination in 1920, had to play down his commitment in the face of increasing public resistance.[15] Universal military training was relegated to a political limbo for the next two decades.[16]

Although general interest in compulsory training waned, the army and the navy provided for continued study on a more specialized level. The National Defense Act of 1920 had assigned to the general staff the responsibility of planning for the mobilization of manpower. During the early twenties, G-1, the army's personnel section, produced many analyses, memoranda, and bills. On January 22, 1926, the secretary of war recommended to the secretary of the navy that the Joint Army-Navy Selective Service Committee be established to draw up the necessary regulations and procedures for the organization of a selective service system. The secretary of the navy agreed, and the committee came into being. For the next ten years, the committee involved itself with research and analysis, critical evaluations of prospective legislation, and plans for setting up national and state headquarters for the system. From 1936 onward, the group extended its activities, convening training conferences and programs designed to prepare the personnel to implement the system if it came into existence.

The activities of the Joint Army-Navy Selective Service Committee, however, were of limited interest in a nation still immersed in the throes of economic depression. Only when war erupted once again in Europe, and the sense of threat grew ominously large in this country, would the nation once again engage the issue of compulsory military training.

15. Huntington, *The Soldier*, p. 282.
16. Chase C. Mooney and Martha E. Layman, "Some Phases of the Compulsory Military Training Camp Movement, 1914–1920," *Mississippi Valley Historical Review*, Vol. 28 (Mar., 1952), pp. 633–56.

21

The principal theorist of American military policy in the post–Civil War years was Emory Upton. Upton, an 1861 West Point graduate, served with distinction throughout the Civil War, emerging a brevet major general. In 1875 he was appointed by General William Tecumseh Sherman to head a three-man military commission to study the organization of military forces around the world. Upton then began a history of American military policy designed to illustrate his principal thesis—America had, time and again, been unprepared for war because of a mistaken reliance on the militia and on the ability of a citizen soldiery to immediately spring to arms. What was needed instead was continuous preparedness to be achieved by a regular professional army which could readily be expanded, in time of war, into a mass army.

Upton's study had only progressed partially through the Civil War when, in 1881, suffering severe pain because of a brain tumor, he took his own life. The study was widely circulated in manuscript form, and finally, in 1904, it was published by the government under the auspices of Secretary of War Elihu Root. Its argument was taken up by other writers on military policy, and an Uptonian school eventually emerged.

Emory Upton on Preparedness

. . . But bad as is our system it would be unpatriotic to attack it if at the same time no remedy could be suggested. In order that this work may not be misjudged we will first indicate to the reader the chief causes of weakness of our present system, and next will outline the system which ought to replace it.

The causes of the weakness are as follows:

First. The employment of militia and undisciplined troops commanded by generals and officers utterly ignorant of the military art.

Second. Short enlistments from three months to three years, instead of for or during the war.

Third. Reliance upon voluntary enlistments, instead of voluntary enlistments coupled with conscription.

Reprinted from Emory Upton, *The Military Policy of the United States* (Washington, D.C.: Government Printing Office, 1912), pp. xiii–xv.

Fourth. The intrusion of the States in military affairs and the consequent waging of all our wars on the theory that we are a confederacy instead of a nation.

Fifth. Confusing volunteers with militia and surrendering to the States the right to commission officers of volunteers the same as officers of militia.

Sixth. The bounty—a national consequence of voluntary enlistments.

Seventh. The failure to appreciate military education, and to distribute trained officers as battalion, regimental, and higher commanders in our volunteer armies.

Eighth. The want of territorial recruitment and regimental depots.

Ninth. The want of post-graduate schools to educate our officers in strategy and the higher principles of the art of war.

Tenth. The assumption of command by the Secretary of War.

The main features of the proposed system are as follows:

First. In time of peace and war the military forces of the country to consist of—

The Regular Army.

The National Volunteers, and

The Militia.

The Regular Army in time of peace to be organized on the expansive principle and in proportion to the population, not to exceed one thousand in one million.

The National Volunteers to be officered and supported by the Government, to be organized on the expansive principle and to consist in time of peace of one battalion of two hundred men to each Congressional district.

The Militia to be supported exclusively by the States and as a last resort to be used only as intended by the Constitution, namely, to execute the laws, suppress insurrections, and repel invasions.

The author is well aware that in suggesting this system he will be accused of favoring centralization and strong government. This is a charge which he would neither covet nor deny. No soldier in battle ever witnessed the flight of an undisciplined army without wishing for a strong government, but a government no stronger than was designed by the fathers of the Republic.

Founded in the affections of the people, the Constitution in time of danger gives Congress absolute power to raise and support armies and to lay its hands upon every man and every dollar within the territory of the nation.

Recognizing, moreover, that the individual life is to be sacrificed to the life of a state, the same Constitution permits the suspension of the writ of habeas corpus, giving to Congress and to the President power not only over life and property, but over the liberty of every citizen of the Republic. It is a popular delusion that armies make wars; the fact is wars inevitably make armies. No matter what the form of government, war, at the discretion of the rulers, means absolute despotism, the danger from which increases as the war is prolonged. Armies in time of peace have seldom if ever overthrown their governments, but in time of anarchy and war the people have often sought to dictate, and purchase peace at the expense of their liberty. If we would escape this danger we should make war with a strong arm. No foreign invader should be allowed a foothold on our soil. Recognizing, too, that under popular institutions the majority of the people create the government and that the majority will never revolt, it should be our policy to suppress every riot and stamp out every insurrection before it swells to rebellion. This means a strong government, but shall we find greater safety in one that is weaker?

Military resources are one thing and military strength another. For military resistance, the strength of a government is the power it can wield on the field of battle. In the War of 1812 the strength of the Government at the battle of Bladensburg was measured by 6,000 militia; at Bull Run it was measured by 35,000 of the same kind of troops. In one case the capital fell into the hands of the enemy, while in the other our existence as a nation possibly depended upon the irresolution and supineness of a band of insurgents. At Gettysburg the wave of rebellion was resisted by 80,000 veteran troops; had we trusted to the same number of militia the capital would have been captured and the Government hopelessly destroyed. Unable to suppress in two years an insurrection which culminated in a great rebellion, the representatives of the people were forced to adopt conscription and to concentrate in the hands of the President all the war powers granted by the Constitution, whereupon weakness gave place to strength, but at the expense of a needless sacrifice of life and property.

If in time of rebellion our own Government grew more despotic as it grew stronger, it is not to be inferred that there is any necessary connection between despotism and military strength.

Twenty thousand regular troops at Bull Run would have routed the insurgents, settled the question of military resistance, and relieved us from the pain and suspense of four years of war.

China, the most despotic of Governments, has no military strength; numbering 400,000,000 people, she has been twice conquered by a few despised Tartars, and only a few years ago 20,000 English and French dictated peace at the walls of the capital. In Persia the Shah can lop off the heads of his subjects or wall them up alive at his pleasure, and yet it has been said that a single foreign battalion could overthrow his throne, while a brigade would starve in his dominions.

In seeking to avoid the dangers of weakness and despotism the author would not have it imagined that his work will produce immediate effect, or that his system will be adopted in five, ten or even twenty years. Such a revolution in our military policy must be preceded by a change in popular sentiment.

Foreign governments for more than a hundred years have recognized us as a nation, but strange to say, a fact patent to all the world, is as yet recognized by scarcely a majority of our people.

Our forefathers hated Great Britain because she repeatedly subverted the government of the colonies. A large portion of their descendants, confusing states rights with state sovereignty, look upon the General Government as equally hostile to the States. When this feeling is abandoned; when it is understood that the life of the State is bound up in the life of the nation; when it is appreciated that republicanism, State and national, guaranteed by the Constitution, is the natural bulwark against the two forms of despotism—absolute monarchy on the one side and absolute democracy on the other—then, and not til then, will the views of the author be accepted. Should his work be received unkindly he will at least have the satisfaction that he has sought to be true to the Republic, and that in view of its increasing grandeur he has endeavored to present a military system which, recognizing the opposition to large standing armies, will still be compatible with the safety, honor, and the liberty of our people.

22

William James, troubled by the inadequacies and deficiencies he felt implicit in much of the pacifist program, addressed himself to this problem in an essay entitled "The Moral Equivalent of War." James discussed the need to keep the martial virtues viable, not by perpetual warfare but rather by using them in a more positive context, by placing them at the service of society. Published in 1910 by the Association for International Conciliation, the pamphlet met an immediate response. James's biographer, Ralph Barton Perry, re-

ferred to the volume of affirmative mail he received in response to
the essay "not only from confirmed pacifists, but from many, including army officers, who were attracted by James's candid recognition of the psychological and moral claims of war." [17] Programs
quite similar to James's have been widely advocated in recent
years, [18] and, indeed, they have been partially realized in organizations such as the Peace Corps, Vista, and others.

William James's "The Moral Equivalent of War," 1910

. . . At the present day, civilized opinion is a curious mental mixture.
The military instincts and ideals are as strong as ever, but are confronted
by reflective criticisms which sorely curb their ancient freedom. Innu-
merable writers are showing up the bestial side of military service. Pure
loot and mastery seem no longer morally avowable motives, and pretexts
must be found for attributing them solely to the enemy. England and
we, our army and navy authorities repeat without ceasing, arm solely
for "peace," Germany and Japan it is who are bent on loot and glory.
"Peace" in military mouths to-day is a synonym for "war expected." The
word has become a pure provocative, and no government wishing peace
sincerely should allow it ever to be printed in a newspaper. Every up-
to-date dictionary should say that "peace" and "war" mean the same
thing, now *in posse*, now *in actu*. It may even reasonably be said that the
intensely sharp competitive *preparation* for war by the nations *is the
real war*, permanent, unceasing; and that the battles are only a sort of
public verification of the mastery gained during the "peace" interval.

It is plain that on this subject civilized man has developed a sort of
double personality. If we take European nations, no legitimate interest
of any one of them would seem to justify the tremendous destructions
which a war to compass it would necessarily entail. It would seem as
though common sense and reason ought to find a way to reach agreement
in every conflict of honest interests. I myself think it our bounden duty
to believe in such international rationality as possible. But, as things
stand, I see how desperately hard it is to bring the peace-party and the

Reprinted from *The Writings of William James*, ed. by John J. McDermott (New
York: Random House, Inc., 1967), pp. 662–69.

17. Ralph Barton Perry, *The Thought and Character of William James: A Briefer
Version* (Cambridge, Mass.: Harvard University Press, 1948), p. 229.
18. Robert S. McNamara, speech delivered to the American Society of Newspaper
Editors, May 18, 1967; and Margaret Mead, "A National Service System as a Solution to a Variety of National Problems," in Sol Tax, ed., *The Draft*, pp. 99–109.

war-party together, and I believe that the difficulty is due to certain
deficiencies in the program of pacificism which set the militarist imagi-
nation strongly, and to a certain extent justifiably, against it. In the
whole discussion both sides are on imaginative and sentimental ground.
It is but one utopia against another, and everything one says must be
abstract and hypothetical. Subject to this criticism and caution, I will
try to characterize in abstract strokes the opposite imaginative forces,
and point out what to my own very fallible mind seems the best utopian
hypothesis, the most promising line of conciliation. . . .

All these beliefs of mine put me squarely into the anti-militarist party.
But I do not believe that peace either ought to be or will be permanent
on this globe, unless the states pacifically organized preserve some of
the old elements of army-discipline. A permanently successful peace-
economy cannot be a simple pleasure-economy. In the more or less so-
cialistic future towards which mankind seems drifting we must still
subject ourselves collectively to those severities which answer to our
real position upon this only partly hospitable globe. We must make new
energies and hardihoods continue the manliness to which the military
mind so faithfully clings. Martial virtues must be the enduring cement;
intrepidity, contempt of softness, surrender of private interest, obedience to command, must still remain the rock upon which states are built
—unless, indeed, we wish for dangerous reactions against common-
wealths fit only for contempt, and liable to invite attack whenever a
centre of crystallization for military-minded enterprise gets formed
anywhere in their neighborhood.

The war-party is assuredly right in affirming and reaffirming that the
martial virtues, although originally gained by the race through war,
are absolute and permanent human goods. Patriotic pride and ambition
in their military form are, after all, only specifications of a more general
competitive passion. They are its first form, but that is no reason for
supposing them to be its last form. Men now are proud of belonging to a
conquering nation, and without a murmur they lay down their persons
and their wealth, if by so doing they may fend off subjection. But who
can be sure that *other aspects of one's country* may not, with time and
education and suggestion enough, come to be regarded with similarly
effective feelings of pride and shame? Why should men not some day
feel that it is worth a blood-tax to belong to a collectivity superior in *any*
ideal respect? Why should they not blush with indignant shame if the
community that owns them is vile in any way whatsoever? Individuals,
daily more numerous, now feel this civic passion. It is only a question of
blowing on the spark till the whole population gets incandescent, and

on the ruins of the old morals of military honor, a stable system of morals of civic honor builds itself up. What the whole community comes to believe in grasps the individual as in a vise. The war-function has grasped us so far; but constructive interests may someday seem no less imperative, and impose on the individual a hardly lighter burden.

Let me illustrate my idea more concretely. There is nothing to make one indignant in the mere fact that life is hard, that men should toil and suffer pain. The planetary conditions once for all are such, and we can stand it. But that so many men, by mere accidents of birth and opportunity, should have a life of *nothing else* but toil and pain and hardness and inferiority imposed upon them, should have *no* vacation, while others natively no more deserving never get any taste of this campaigning life at all,—*this* is capable of arousing indignation in reflective minds. It may end by seeming shameful to all of us that some of us have nothing but campaigning, and others nothing but unmanly ease. If now—and this is my idea—there were, instead of military conscription a conscription of the whole youthful population to form for a certain number of years a part of the army enlisted against *Nature,* the injustice would tend to be evened out, and numerous other goods to the commonwealth would follow. The military ideals of the hardihood and discipline would be wrought into the growing fibre of the people; no one would remain blind as the luxurious classes now are blind, to man's relations to the globe he lives on, and to the permanently sour and hard foundations of his higher life. To coal and iron mines, to freight trains, to fishing fleets in December, to dish-washing, clothes-washing, and window-washing, to road-building and tunnel-making, to foundries and stoke-holes, and to the frames of skyscrapers, would our gilded youths be drafted off, according to their choice, to get the childishness knocked out of them, and to come back into society with healthier sympathies and soberer ideas. They would have paid their blood-tax, done their own part in the immemorial human warfare against nature; they would tread the earth more proudly, the women would value them more highly, they would be greater fathers and teachers of the following generation.

Such a conscription, with the state of public opinion that would have required it, and the many moral fruits it would bear, would preserve in the midst of a pacific civilization the manly virtues which the military party is so afraid of seeing disappear in peace. We should get toughness without callousness, authority with as little criminal cruelty as possible, and painful work done cheerily because the duty is temporary, and threatens not, as now, to degrade the whole remainder of one's life. I spoke of the "moral equivalent" of war. So far, war has been the only force that can discipline a whole community, and until an equivalent discipline is organized, I believe that war must have its way. But I have no serious doubt that the ordinary prides and shames of social man, once developed to a certain intensity, are capable of organizing such a moral equivalent as I have sketched, or some other just as effective for preserving manliness of type. It is but a question of time, of skilful propagandism, and of opinion-making men seizing historic opportunities. . . .

23

President Woodrow Wilson in his 1914 State-of-the-Union message addressed himself to the question of national defense. Despite the events in Europe of the previous summer, there was, Wilson felt, no need for America to depart from its military tradition. This nation had never permitted the growth of a large standing army, nor should it move in that direction by instituting a peacetime draft. Its military needs could and should be satisfied by volunteers. To go beyond this tradition "carries with it a reversal of the whole history and character of our polity. More than this, proposed at this time, permit me to say, would mean merely that we had lost our self-possession, that we had been thrown off our balance by a war with which we have nothing to do, whose causes can not touch us. . . ." This notion of American insularity raised by Wilson was, even at that time, in a process of deterioration which would bring it to dissolution in slightly more than two years.

Wilson's State-of-the-Union Message, 1914

. . . The other topic I shall take leave to mention goes deeper into the principles of our national life and policy. It is the subject of national defense.

It can not be discussed without first answering some very searching questions. It is said in some quarters that we are not prepared for war. What is meant by being prepared? Is it meant that we are not ready upon brief notice to put a nation in the field, a nation of men trained to arms? Of course we are not ready to do that; and we shall never be in time of

Reprinted from *The State of the Union Messages of the Presidents, 1790–1966*, Vol. 3, ed. by Fred L. Israel (New York: R. R. Bowker Co., 1966), pp. 2557–59.

peace so long as we retain our present political principles and institutions. And what is it that it is suggested we should be prepared to do?
To defend ourselves against attack? We have always found means to do
that, and shall find them whenever it is necessary without calling our
people away from their necessary tasks to render compulsory military
service in times of peace. . . .

From the first we have had a clear and settled policy with regard to
military establishments. We never have had, and while we retain our
present principles and ideals we never shall have, a large standing army.
If asked, Are you ready to defend yourself? we reply, Most assuredly, to
the utmost; and yet we shall not turn America into a military camp. We
will not ask our young men to spend the best years of their lives making
soldiers of themselves. There is another sort of energy in us. It will know
how to declare itself and make itself effective should occasion arise. And
especially when half the world is on fire we shall be careful to make our
moral insurance against the spread of the conflagration very definite and
certain and adequate indeed.

Let us remind ourselves, therefore, of the only thing we can do or will
do. We must depend in every time of national peril, in the future as in
the past, not upon a standing army, nor yet upon a reserve army, but
upon a citizenry trained and accustomed to arms. It will be right enough,
right American policy, based upon our accustomed principles and practices, to provide a system by which every citizen who will volunteer for
the training may be made familiar with the use of modern arms, the
rudiments of drill and maneuver, and the maintenance and sanitation of
camps. We should encourage such training and make it a means of discipline which our young men will learn to value. It is right that we
should provide it not only, but that we should make it as attractive as
possible, and so induce our young men to undergo it at such times as
they can command a little freedom and can seek the physical development they need, for mere health's sake, if for nothing more. Every means
by which such things can be stimulated is legitimate, and such a method
smacks of true American ideas. It is right, too, that the National Guard
of the States should be developed and strengthened by every means
which is not inconsistent with our obligations to our own people or with
the established policy of our Government. And this, also, not because
the time or occasion specially calls for such measures, but because it
should be our constant policy to make these provisions for our national
peace and safety.

More than this carries with it a reversal of the whole history and
character of our polity. More than this, proposed at this time, permit me

to say, would mean merely that we had lost our self-possession, that we had been thrown off our balance by a war with which we have nothing to do, whose causes can not touch us, whose very existence affords us opportunities of friendship and disinterested service which should make us ashamed of any thought of hostility or fearful preparation for trouble. This is assuredly the opportunity for which a people and a government like ours were raised up, the opportunity not only to speak but actually to embody and exemplify the counsels of peace and amity and the lasting concord which is based on justice, and fair and generous dealing. . . .

24

General Leonard Wood, chief of staff from 1910 to 1914, was a leading advocate of universal military training. On leaving his duties as chief of staff, General Wood assumed command of the First Military District, and this position furnished him sufficient time to write and speak extensively on the preparedness movement. In the following excerpt, General Wood argues the case for a general obligation for military service, which "is the basic principle upon which truly representative government, or free democracy, rests and must rest if it is successfully to withstand the shock of modern war."

Leonard Wood on Military Obligation, 1916

Our past military policy, so far as it concerns the land forces, has been thoroughly unsound and in violation of basic military principles. We have succeeded not because of it, but in spite of it. It has been unnecessarily and brutally costly in human life and recklessly extravagant in the expenditure of treasure. It has tended greatly to prolong our wars and consequently has delayed national development.

Because we have succeeded in spite of an unsound system, those who do not look beneath the surface fail to recognize the numerous shortcomings of that system, or appreciate how dangerous is our further dependence upon it.

The time has come to put our house in order through the establishment of a sound and dependable system, and to make such wise and

Reprinted from Leonard Wood, *Our Military History, Its Facts and Fallacies* (Chicago: The Reilly and Britton Co., 1916), pp. 193–206.

prudent preparation as will enable us to defend successfully our country and our rights.

No such system can be established which does not rest upon equality of service for all who are physically fit and of proper age. Manhood suffrage means manhood obligation for service in peace or war. This is the basic principle upon which truly representative government, or free democracy, rests and must rest if it is successfully to withstand the shock of modern war.

The acceptance of this fundamental principle will require to a certain extent the moral organization of the people, the building up of that sense of individual obligation for service to the nation which is the basis of true patriotism, the teaching of our people to think in terms of the nation rather than in those of a locality or of personal interest.

This organization must also be accompanied by the organization, classification and training of our men and the detailed and careful organization of the material resources of the country with the view to making them promptly available in case of need and to remedying any defects.

In the organization of our land forces we must no longer place reliance upon plans based upon the development of volunteers or the use of the militia. The volunteer system is not dependable because of the uncertainty as to returns, and in any case because of lack of time for training and organization.

Modern wars are often initiated without a formal declaration of war or by a declaration which is coincident with the first act of war.

Dependence upon militia under state control or partially under state control, spells certain disaster, not because of the quality of the men or officers, but because of the system under which they work. . . .

The main reliance in a war with a first-class power will ultimately be the great force of citizen soldiers forming a purely federal force, thoroughly organized and equipped with reserves of men and material. This force must be trained under some system which will permit the instruction to be given in part during the school period or age, thereby greatly reducing the time required for the final intensive period of training, which should be under regular officers and in conjunction with regular troops. In brief, the system must be one which utilizes as far as possible the means and opportunities now available, and interferes as little as possible with the educational or industrial careers of those affected. . . .

Each year about one million men reach the military age of 18; of this number not more than fifty per cent are fit for military service, this being about the average in other countries. Far less than fifty per cent come up to the standards required for the regular army, but the minor defects rejecting them for the regular army would not reject them for general military service. Assuming that some system on the general lines of the Australian or Swiss must be eventually adopted in this country, it would seem that about 500,000 men would be available each year for military training. If the boys were prepared by the state authorities, through training in schools and colleges, and in state training areas—when the boys were not in school—to the extent that they are in Switzerland or Australia, it would be possible, when they come up for federal training, to finish their military training—so far as preparing them for the duties of enlisted men is concerned—within a period of approximately three months. We should be able to limit the period of first line obligation to the period from eighteen to twenty-five, inclusive, or seven years, or we could make the period of obligatory service begin two years later and extend it to twenty-seven. This procedure would give in the first line approximately three and one-half millions of men at the age of best physical condition and of minimum dependent and business responsibility. From men of certain years (classes) of this period, organizations of federal forces should be built up to the extent of at least twenty-five divisions. They would be organized and equipped exactly like the regular army and would be held ready for immediate service as our present militia would be were it under federal control.

Men of these organizations would not live in uniform but would go about their regular occupations as do the members of the militia to-day, but they would be equipped, organized and ready for immediate service. If emergency required it, additional organizations could be promptly raised from the men who were within the obligatory period.

There should be no pay in peace time except when the men were on duty and then it should be merely nominal. The duty should be recognized as a part of the man's citizenship obligation to the nation. The organizations to be made up of men within the period of obligatory service, could be filled either by the men who indicated their desire for such training or by drawing them by lot. This is a matter of detail. The regular army as organized would be made up as to-day; it would be a professional army. The men who came into it would be men who had received in youth this citizenship training. They would come into the regular army because they wanted to be professional soldiers. The regular army would be to a certain extent the training nucleus for the citizen soldier organizations and would be the force garrisoning our over-sea possessions. It would be much easier to maintain our regular army in a highly efficient condition, as general military training would have produced a respect for the uniform and an appreciation of the importance of a soldier's duty.

The reserve corps of officers would be composed of men who had had longer and more advanced training, and could be recruited and maintained as indicated below, through further training of men from the military schools and colleges and those from the officers' training corps units of the nonmilitary universities and colleges. There would also be those from the military training camps and other sources, such as men who have served in the army and have the proper qualifications. This would give a military establishment in which every man would be physically fit to play his part and would have finished his obligation in what was practically his early manhood, with little probability of being called upon again unless the demands of war were so great as to require more men than those of the total first line, eighteen to twenty-five years, inclusive. Then they would be called by years as the occasion required, and would be available for service up to their forty-fifth year. It would give us a condition of real national preparedness, a much higher type of citizenship, a lower criminal rate and an enormously improved economic efficiency. Pending the establishment of such a system, every effort should be made to transfer the state militia to federal control. By this is meant its complete removal from state control and its establishment as a purely federal force, having no more relation to the states than the regular army has at present. This force under federal control will make a very valuable nucleus for the building up of a federal force of citizen soldiers. . . .

25

General Hugh Scott, in his annual report for 1916 as chief of staff, argued that the volunteer system was an outmoded and inadequate method of developing a modern army. In its place Scott recommended universal military training, and in December, 1916, he ordered the War College division of the general staff to develop such a plan. Although it was intended for use on a permanent basis, much of it proved to be of immediate advantage the following spring when America entered World War I.

Hugh Scott on Universal Military Training, 1916

. . . In my judgment, the country will never be prepared for defense until we do as other great nations do that have large interests to guard, like Germany, Japan, and France, where everybody is ready and does perform military service in time of peace as he would pay every other tax and is willing to make sacrifices for the protection he gets and the country gets in return. The volunteer system in this country, in view of the highly organized, trained, and disciplined armies that our possible opponents possess, should be relegated to the past. There is no reason why one woman's son should go out and defend or be trained to defend another woman and her son who refuses to take training or give service. The only democratic method is for every man in his youth to become trained in order that he may render efficient service if called upon in war. . . .

Universal military training has been the corner stone upon which has been built every republic in the history of the world, and its abandonment the signal for decline and obliteration. This fact was fully recognized by the makers of our Constitution and evidenced in our early laws. A regular army was regarded as inconsistent with the principles of free government, dangerous to free institutions, and apart from the necessities of the times. All were imbued with a patriotism which would make them stand shoulder to shoulder in upholding the laws, and in the defense of the common country, sharing equally the blessings of peace and the hardship of war. The law required every able-bodied male between 18 and 45 years to keep himself provided with rifle and ammunition and to attend muster, and was in effect compulsory military service. They were called together for training at muster time only, for the outdoor life of the early settlers was considered sufficient training for any military duty they were then liable to be called upon to perform. Unfortunately the doctrine of States rights crept in to prevent the enforcement of Federal law, and each State was left to build up its militia. The Regular Army existed as a small force to protect the western march of civilization from Indian foray, and notwithstanding its brilliant record, the attitude of a great mass of our people continued hostile to the soldier, so much so that several States and Congress have in recent times had to pass laws to insure respect to the uniform and its wearers in public places. Some of our States, while extending the right to vote to aliens of a few months' residence who have declared their intention to become

Reprinted from *War Department Reports, 1916,* Vol. 1 (Washington, D.C.: U.S. Department of War, 1917), pp. 159–62.

citizens, deny it absolutely to persons in the military and naval service of the United States, putting them in a class with the criminal and the insane.

It is vital that our ideas with reference to military service be regenerated. For our small army we go into the labor market for recruits. When the demand for labor is lax, the stipend of the soldier attracts; when the daily wage goes up, recruiting is at its lowest ebb. There is no appeal to patriotism, no appeal for the individual to obtain military training as the highest duty of his citizenship. . . .

During the months of May and June hundreds of thousands marched in so-called preparedness parades to the plaudits of onlookers. But when the militia was called out in June to protect our border, it was with the utmost difficulty that its units were recruited to the small number required, and some were never filled. The spirit was rife to let somebody else do it. Not only is there evidence of the volunteer spirit being moribund, but the States have for years been unable to make an efficient showing with the militia, even with the generous assistance of the General Government in qualified instructors and supplies. It would seem that the self-reliance of the individual, like that of the States, had given way to dependence upon others. The fine volunteer spirit of the States militia was injured in the demand for Federal pay in time of peace. It sounded the knell of patriotic military training for individuals and commercialized the highest duty that a State can demand from its people. We have fallen away from the teaching of the Fathers, for there is no longer instilled into our people the fundamental doctrine that every man owes a military as well as a civil obligation to his Government. . . .

26

With the American entrance into the war on April 6, 1917, there was an immediate need for adequate forces. Supporters of voluntarism were shaken by the small number of men who offered their services in the first two weeks. The administration saw a draft as the only logical means of developing a large army, not only because of the regular increments of manpower it allowed for but also because it enabled the government to achieve a proper balance between the industrial work force and the fighting force.

Debate on the draft was heated in both houses of Congress, but the bills eventually passed with only eight senators and twenty-four members of the House voting in opposition. A conference committee was set up to reconcile the differences in the bills, and the bill which emerged, signed into law on May 18, reflected the hard-earned experience of the Civil War draft. For one thing, at Secretary of War Newton Baker's suggestion, the enforcement apparatus was to be manned not by the army but by civilians. Substitution was not permitted, nor was the paying of commutation fees. With these adaptations, the law operated far more efficiently than its Civil War predecessor.

World War I Draft Act, 1917

AN ACT TO AUTHORIZE THE PRESIDENT TO INCREASE TEMPORARILY THE MILITARY ESTABLISHMENT OF THE UNITED STATES

Be it enacted by the Senate and House of Representatives of the United States of America in Congress assembled, That in view of the existing emergency, which demands the raising of troops in addition to those now available, the President be, and he is hereby, authorized—

First. Immediately to raise, organize, officer and equip all or such number of increments of the Regular Army provided by the national defense Act approved June third, nineteen hundred and sixteen, or such parts thereof as he may deem necessary; to raise all organizations of the Regular Army, including those added by such increments, to the maximum enlisted strength authorized by law. Vacancies in the Regular Army created or caused by the addition of increments as herein authorized which can not be filled by promotion may be filled by temporary appointment for the period of the emergency or until replaced by permanent appointments or by provisional appointments made under the provisions of section twenty-three of the national defense Act, approved June third, nineteen hundred and sixteen, and hereafter provisional appointments under said section may be terminated whenever it is determined, in the manner prescribed by the President, that the officer has not the suitability and fitness requisite for permanent appointment. . . .

Sec. 2. That the enlisted men required to raise and maintain the organizations of the Regular Army and to complete and maintain the organizations embodying the members of the National Guard drafted into the service of the United States, at the maximum legal strength as by this Act provided, shall be raised by voluntary enlistment, or if and

Reprinted from *Statutes at Large*, Vol. 40, pp. 76–80.

whenever the President decides that they cannot effectually be so raised
or maintained, then by selective draft; and all other forces hereby authorized, except as provided in the seventh paragraph of section one,
shall be raised and maintained by selective draft exclusively; but this
provision shall not prevent the transfer to any force of training cadres
from other forces. Such draft as herein provided shall be based upon
liability to military service of all male citizens, or male persons not alien
enemies who have declared their intention to become citizens, between
the ages of twenty-one and thirty years, both inclusive, and shall take
place and be maintained under such regulations as the President may
prescribe not inconsistent with the terms of this Act. Quotas for the
several States, Territories and District of Columbia, or subdivisions
thereof, shall be determined in proportion to the population thereof, and
credit shall be given to any State, Territory, District, or subdivision
thereof, for the number of men who were in the military service of the
United States as members of the National Guard on April first, nineteen
hundred and seventeen, or who have since said date entered the military
service of the United States from any such State, Territory, District or
subdivision, either as members of the Regular Army or the National
Guard. . . .

Sec. 3. No bounty shall be paid to induce any person to enlist in the
military service of the United States; and no person liable to military
service shall hereafter be permitted or allowed to furnish a substitute
for such service; nor shall any substitute be received, enlisted, or enrolled in the military service of the United States; and no such person
shall be permitted to escape such service or to be discharged therefrom
prior to the expiration of his term of service by the payment of money or
any other valuable thing whatsoever as consideration for his release
from military service or liability thereto.

Sec. 4. That the Vice President of the United States, the officers, legislative, executive, and judicial of the United States and of the several
States, Territories, and the District of Columbia, regular or duly ordained ministers of religion, students who at the time of the approval of
this act are preparing for the ministry in recognized theological or
divinity schools, and all persons in the military or naval service of the
United States shall be exempt from the selective draft herein prescribed;
and nothing in this Act contained shall be construed to require or compel any person to serve in any of the forces herein provided for who is
found to be a member of any well-recognized religious sect or organization at present organized or existing and whose existing creed or principles forbid its members to participate in war in any form and whose

religious convictions are against war or participation therein in accordance with the creed or principles of said religious organizations, but no person so exempted shall be exempted from service in any capacity that the President shall declare to be noncombatant; and the President is hereby authorized to exclude or discharge from said selective draft and from the draft under the second paragraph of section one hereof, or to draft for partial military service only from those liable to draft as in this Act provided, persons of the following classes: County and municipal officials; customhouse clerks; persons employed by the United States in the transmission of the mails; artificers and workmen employed in the armories, arsenals, and navy yards of the United States, and such other persons employed in the service of the United States as the President may designate; pilots; mariners actually employed in the sea service of any citizen or merchant within the United States; persons engaged in industries, including agriculture, found to be necessary to the maintenance of the Military Establishment or the effective operation of the military forces or the maintenance of national interest during the emergency; those in a status with respect to persons dependent on them for support which renders their exclusion or discharge advisable; and those found to be physically or morally deficient. No exemption or exclusion shall continue when a cause therefor no longer exists: *Provided,* That notwithstanding the exemptions enumerated herein, each State, Territory, and the District of Columbia shall be required to supply its quota in the proportion that its population bears to the total population of the United States.

The President is hereby authorized, in his discretion, to create and establish throughout the several States and subdivisions thereof and in the Territories and the District of Columbia local boards, and where, in his discretion, practicable and desirable, there shall be created and established one such local board in each county or similar subdivision in each State, and one for approximately each thirty thousand of population in each city of thirty thousand population or over, according to the last census taken or estimates furnished by the Bureau of Census of the Department of Commerce. Such Boards shall be appointed by the President, and shall consist of three or more members, none of whom shall be connected with the Military Establishment, to be chosen from among the local authorities of such subdivisions or from other citizens residing in the subdivision or area in which the respective boards will have jurisdiction under the rules and regulations prescribed by the President. Such boards shall have power within their respective jurisdictions to hear and determine, subject to review as hereinafter provided, all questions of exemption under this Act, and all questions of or claims for including or discharging individuals or classes of individuals from the selective draft, which shall be made under rules and regulations prescribed by the President, except any and every question or claim for including or excluding or discharging persons or classes of persons from the selective draft under the provisions of this Act authorizing the President to exclude or discharge from the selective draft "Persons engaged in industries, including agriculture, found to be necessary to the maintenance of the Military Establishment, or the effective operation of the military forces, or the maintenance of national interest during the emergency."

The President is hereby authorized to establish additional boards, one in each Federal judicial district of the United States, consisting of such number of citizens, not connected with the Military Establishment, as the President may determine, who shall be appointed by the President. The President is hereby authorized, in his discretion, to establish more than one such board in any Federal judicial district of the United States, or to establish one such board having jurisdiction of an area extending into more than one Federal judicial district.

Such district boards shall review on appeal and affirm, modify, or reverse any decision of any local board having jurisdiction in the area in which any such district board has jurisdiction under the rules and regulations prescribed by the President. Such district boards shall have exclusive original jurisdiction within their respective areas to hear and determine all questions or claims for including or excluding or discharging persons or classes of persons from the selective draft, under the provisions of this Act, not included within the original jurisdiction of such local boards.

The decisions of such district boards shall be final except that, in accordance with such rules and regulations as the President may prescribe, he may affirm, modify or reverse any such decision.

Any vacancy in any such local board or district board shall be filled by the President, and any member of any such local board or district board may be removed and another appointed in his place by the President, whenever he considers that the interest of the nation demands it.

The President shall make rules and regulations governing the organization and procedure of such local boards and district boards, and providing for and governing appeals from such local boards to such district boards, and reviews of the decisions of any local board by the district board having jurisdiction, and determining and prescribing the several areas in which the respective local boards and district boards shall have jurisdiction, and all other rules and regulations necessary to carry out the terms and provisions of this section, and shall provide for the issuance of certificates of exemption, or partial or limited exemptions, and for a system to exclude and discharge individuals from selective draft.

Sec. 5. That all male persons between the ages of twenty-one and thirty, both inclusive, shall be subject to registration in accordance with regulations to be prescribed by the President; and upon proclamation by the President or other public notice given by him or by his direction stating the time and place of such registration it shall be the duty of all persons of the designated ages, except officers and enlisted men of the Regular Army, the Navy, and the National Guard and Naval Militia while in the service of the United States, to present themselves for and submit to registration under the provisions of this Act; and every such person shall be deemed to have notice of the requirements of this Act upon the publication of said proclamation or other notice as aforesaid given by the President or by his direction; and any person who shall willfully fail or refuse to present himself for registration or to submit thereto as herein provided, shall be guilty of a misdemeanor and shall upon conviction in the district court of the United States having jurisdiction thereof, be punished by imprisonment for not more than one year, and shall thereupon by duly registered: *Provided,* That in the call of the docket, precedence shall be given, in courts trying the same, to the trial of criminal proceedings under this Act: *Provided further,* That persons shall be subject to registration as herein provided who shall have attained their twenty-first birthday and who shall not have attained their thirty-first birthday on or before the day set for the registration, and all persons so registered shall be and remain subject to draft into the forces hereby authorized, unless exempted or excused therefrom as in this Act provided: *Provided further,* That in the case of temporary absence from actual place of legal residence of any person liable to registration as provided herein such registration may be made by mail under regulations to be prescribed by the President. . . .

27

Registration day under the draft act was set for June 5, 1917, and provided a vivid contrast with the Civil War picture of enrolling officers hunting down potential enrollees. At local draft boards across the nation over 9,500,000 men came forward on that day to sign up. It was felt that the most equitable way to choose the 687,000 men immediately needed would be by lottery, and so, on July 20, the first number was selected from a large glass bowl by the blindfolded secretary of war.

President Wilson composed the following statement, to be published along with the notification of the obligation to register, in which he tried to minimize the note of coerciveness in the drafting process. Despite the Wilsonian rhetoric, over one-third of a million men were eventually to be classed as draft evaders.

Wilson's "Registration for the Draft," 1917

. . . The power against which we are arrayed has sought to impose its will upon the world by force. To this end it has increased armament until it has changed the face of war. In the sense in which we have been wont to think of armies there are no armies in this struggle. There are entire nations armed. Thus, the men who remain to till the soil and man the factories are no less a part of the army that is France than the men beneath the battle flags. It must be so with us. It is not an army that we must shape and train for war; it is a nation. To this end our people must draw close in one compact front against a common foe. But this cannot be if each man pursues a private purpose. All must pursue one purpose. The nation needs all men; but it needs each man, not in the field that will most pleasure him, but in the endeavor that will best serve the common good. Thus, though a sharpshooter pleases to operate a trip-hammer for the forging of great guns, and an expert machinist desires to march with the flag, the Nation is being served only when the sharpshooter marches and the machinist remains at his levers. The whole nation must be a team in which each man shall play the part for which he is best fitted. To this end, Congress has provided that the nation shall be organized for war by selection and that each man shall be classified for service in the place to which it shall best serve the general good to call him.

The significance of this cannot be overstated. It is a new thing in our history and a landmark in our progress. It is a new manner of accepting and vitalizing our duty to give ourselves with thoughtful devotion to the common purpose of us all. It is in no sense a conscription of the unwilling; it is, rather, selection from a nation which has volunteered in mass. It is no more a choosing of those who shall march with the colors

Reprinted from *Statutes at Large*, Vol. 40, part 2, p. 1666.

than it is a selection of those who shall serve an equally necessary and devoted purpose in the industries that lie behind the battle line.

The day here named is the time upon which all shall present themselves for assignment to their tasks. It is for that reason destined to be remembered as one of the most conspicuous moments in our history. It is nothing less than the day upon which the manhood of the country shall step forward in one solid rank in defense of the ideals to which this nation is consecrated. It is important to those ideals no less than to the pride of this generation in manifesting its devotion to them, that there be no gaps in the ranks.

It is essential that the day be approached in thoughtful apprehension of its significance and that we accord to it the honor and the meaning that it deserves. Our industrial need prescribes that it not be made a technical holiday, but the stern sacrifice that is before us, urges that it be carried in all our hearts as a great day of patriotic devotion and obligation when the duty shall fall upon every man, whether he is himself to be registered or not, to see to it that the name of every male person of the designated ages is written on these lists of honor.

28

President Wilson's statement on registration met with an immediate rebuttal from one of the most vociferous of the antiwar critics, Max Eastman, editor of *The Masses*. In one of the last issues of *The Masses* before its suppression by the government, Eastman attacked the casuistry of Wilson's semantics in regard to the draft. Eastman was eventually indicted under the Sedition Act and brought to trial twice, both instances resulting in a hung jury, and the indictment was eventually dropped.

Max Eastman's Attack on Wilson and the Draft, 1917

President Wilson has to breathe an atmosphere of optimistic emotion. He always automatically idealizes a bad business, and he generally does this with skill and plausibility. But in declaring that his selective draft is "in no sense a conscription of the unwilling; it is, rather, selec-

Reprinted from *The Masses*, Vol. 9 (July, 1917), p. 18.

tion from a nation which has volunteered in mass," he builds himself up
to a height of casuistic complaisance from which the fall may be tragic
and terrible.

If anything is true, it is true that this nation has not volunteered
either in mass or any other way. The people here, happy in their geo-
graphic security and divided in their reminiscent patriotisms, have
long and deeply abhorred the idea of carrying war into Europe. So
universal is this abhorrence that every tradition and prediction of political history was overthrown last fall, and Woodrow Wilson elected
to the White House as a peace President, in the face of stalwart Republicanism, Rooseveltism, and Wall Street united in a solemn compact
of blood to beat him.

During the time of this event and after, this peace President, under
influences perhaps too subtle for political analysis, appears to have
changed into a man of the Army and Navy. He has declared a European
war, in face of the people's manifest will that he refrain—in face even
of the will of a majority of the House of Representatives, if that house
had possessed the courage to make its will known. Acknowledging that
to this war, undesired by the people, he could not raise a volunteer
army of 500,000 free citizens, he has forced upon Congress the principle
of conscriptive draft—a principle which even when adopted for military
purposes within the boundaries of the United States, and for the very
defense of the Union, and at the hands of Abraham Lincoln, met
riotous resistance from the devotees of individual liberty. . . .

For what specific purposes are you shipping our bodies, and the
bodies of our sons, to Europe?

For my part I do not recognize the right of a government to draft me
to a war whose purposes I do not believe in. But to draft me to a war
whose purposes it will not so much as communicate to my ear, seems
an act of tyranny, discordant with the memory even of the decent
kings. . . .

29

With the entrance of the United States into the First World War,
organizational rifts developed in the American Union against Militarism. The A.U.M. had led the fight against the preparedness
movement from 1914 onward, but with America's participation in
the war many of its members felt that the organization should avoid

any policies which might bring it into conflict with the government. A dissenting group, led by Roger Baldwin, established the National Civil Liberties Bureau, the forerunner of the American Civil Liberties Union, to defend and protect the rights of those persons who took objection to the government's wartime legislation. Baldwin himself was a conscientious objector and refused to report for his physical examination prior to induction. The following speech, in which he explains the basis of his opposition, was delivered to the court prior to sentencing.

Roger Baldwin's Speech on the Draft, 1918

Your Honor, I presume that myself, and not the National Civil Liberties Bureau, is on trial before this court this morning. I do not object to the reading into this record of the letters which the Government's attorney has read. Some of them I did not write. They represent one side of a work which I have been conducting as the Executive Officer of that organization during the past year. Our work is backed up and supported both by those who call themselves Pro-War Liberals, who are supporters of the war, and by those who are so-called Pacifists.

I have not engaged in personal propaganda. I have not made public addresses, except upon the subject matter of this Bureau. I have not written articles, except upon the subject matter of the Bureau, and I have felt throughout that it was a work which could be supported genuinely and honestly by those who opposed the war in principle, and by those who were supporting the war. I believe that the examination of the records of the Bureau now being made by the Department of Justice will conclusively demonstrate that the work has been undertaken with that sole purpose in view, and that it has been in the interest of the solution of certain democratic problems that this country has to face during war time.

I will say, in that connection for instance, that although the Post Office censorship throughout the war has been intolerant, narrow, and stupid, but one little pamphlet which we have issued—and we have issued a great many of them—has been excluded from the mails, and that in this Court within the last two weeks an injunction was issued, requiring the Post-Master of New York to accept for mailing all the pamphlets of this Bureau. I think that demonstrates pretty clearly that

Reprinted from *The Agitator in American Society*, ed. by Charles W. Lomas (Englewood Cliffs, N.J.: Prentice-Hall, Inc., 1968), pp. 114–19.

where the law is narrowly interpreted, rigidly interpreted, arbitrarily interpreted, as it is in the Post-Office Department of Washington, no exception has been taken to the general matter which has been sent out by this organization.

I know that the Government's Attorney is merely attempting to put before this Court my state of mind in taking the position I have about this act—in coming here as its deliberate violator.

I want to read to the Court, if I may, for purposes of record, and for purposes of brevity too, a statement which I have prepared, and which I hope will get across a point of view which the United States Attorney does not consider logical, but which I trust, at least, with the premises I hold, is consistent.

I am before you as a deliberate violator of the draft act. On October 9, when ordered to take a physical examination, I notified my local board that I declined to do so, and instead presented myself to the United States Attorney for prosecution. I submit herewith for the record the letter of explanation which I addressed to him at the time.

I refused to take bail, believing that I was not morally justified in procuring it, and being further opposed to the institution of bail on principle. I have therefore been lodged in the Tombs Prison since my arraignment on October 10. During that period I have been engaged daily at the Department of Justice offices in systematizing the files of the National Civil Liberties Bureau, of which I have been the director. These files had been voluntarily turned over to the Department for examination, and had, through much handling, become seriously disarranged. That work being completed, I am before you for sentence.

And, by the way, may I take this occasion, your honor—this is quite aside from the proceedings—to express my thanks for the courtesy of every officer of this court, and of the Department of Justice, through these trying weeks. It has been exceptional.

The compelling motive for refusing to comply with the draft act is my uncompromising opposition to the principle of conscription of life by the State for any purpose whatever, in time of war or peace. I not only refused to obey the present conscription law, but I would in the future refuse to obey any similar statute which attempts to direct my choice of service and ideals. I regard the principle of conscription of life as a flat contradiction of all our cherished ideals of individual freedom, democratic liberty, and Christian teaching.

I am the more opposed to the present act, because it is for the purpose of conducting war. I am opposed to this and all other wars. I do not believe in the use of physical force as a method of achieving any end, however good.

The District Attorney calls your attention, your Honor, to the inconsistency in my statement to him that I would, under extreme emergencies, as a matter of protecting the life of any person, use physical force. I don't think that is an argument that can be used in support of the wholesale organization of men to achieve political purposes in nationalistic or domestic wars. I see no relationship at all between the two.

My opposition is not only to direct military service but to any service whatever designed to help prosecute the war. I could accept no service, therefore, under the present act, regardless of its character.

Holding such profound convictions, I determined, while the new act was pending, that it would be more honest to make my stand clear at the start and therefore concluded not even to register, but to present myself for prosecution. I therefore resigned my position as director of the National Civil Liberties Bureau so as to be free to follow that personal course of action. But on the day my resignation took effect (August 31) agents of the Department of Justice began an examination of the affairs of that organization, and I was constrained to withdraw my resignation and to register in order to stand by the work at a critical moment. With that obligation discharged, I resigned, and took the next occasion, the physical examination, to make my stand clear.

I realize that to some this refusal may seem a piece of wilful defiance. It might well be argued that any man holding my views might have avoided the issue by obeying the law, either on the chance of being rejected on physical grounds, or on the chance of the war stopping before a call to service. I answer that I am not seeking to evade the draft; that I scorn evasion, compromise, and gambling with moral issues. It may further be argued that the War Department's liberal provisions for agricultural service on furlough for conscientious objectors would be open to me if I obey the law and go to camp, and that there can be no moral objection to farming, even in time of war. I answer first, that I am opposed to any service under conscription, regardless of whether that service is in itself morally objectionable and second, that, even if that were not the case, and I were opposed only to war, I can make no moral distinction between the various services which assist in prosecuting the war—whether rendered in the trenches, in the purchase of bonds or thrift stamps at home, or in raising farm products under the lash of the draft act. All serve the same end—war. Of course all of us render involuntary assistance to the war in the processes of our daily living. I refer only to those direct services undertaken by choice.

I am fully aware that my position is extreme, that it is shared by comparatively few, and that in the present temper it is regarded either as unwarranted egotism or as a species of feeble-mindedness. I cannot, therefore, let this occasion pass without attempting to explain the foundations on which so extreme a view rests.

I have had an essentially American upbringing and background. Born in a suburban town of Boston, Massachusetts, of the stock of the first settlers, I was reared in the public schools and at Harvard College. Early my mind was caught by the age-old struggle for freedom; America meant to me a vital new experiment in free political institutions; personal freedom to choose one's way of life and service seemed the essence of the liberties brought by those who fled the mediaeval and modern tyrannies of the old world. But I rebelled at our whole autocratic industrial system—with its wreckage of poverty, disease, and crime, and childhood robbed of its right to free growth. So I took up social work upon leaving college, going to St. Louis as director of a settlement and instructor in sociology at Washington University. For ten years I have been professionally engaged in social work and political reform, local and national. That program of studied, directed social progress, step by step, by public agitation and legislation, seemed to me the practical way of effective service to gradually freeing the mass of folks from industrial and political bondage. At the same time I was attracted to the solutions of our social problems put forth by the radicals. I studied the programs of socialism, the I.W.W., European syndicalism and anarchism. I attended their meetings, knew their leaders. Some of them became my close personal friends. Sympathizing with their general ideals of a free society, with much of their program, I yet could see no effective way of practical daily service. Some six years ago, however, I was so discouraged with social work and reform, so challenged by the sacrifices and idealism of some of my I.W.W. friends, that I was on the point of getting out altogether, throwing respectability overboard and joining the I.W.W. as a manual worker.

I thought better of it. My traditions were against it. It was more an emotional reaction than a practical form of service. But ever since, I have felt myself heart and soul with the worldwide radical movements for industrial and political freedom—wherever and however expressed —and more and more impatient with reform.

Personally, I share the extreme radical philosophy of the future society. I look forward to a social order without any external restraints upon the individual, save through public opinion and the opinion of friends and neighbors. I am not a member of any radical organization, nor do I wear any tag by which my views may be classified. I believe that all parts of the radical movement serve the common end—freedom of the individual from arbitrary external controls.

When the war came to America, it was an immediate challenge to me to help protect those ideals of liberty which seemed to me not only the basis of the radical economic view, but of the radical political view of the founders of this Republic, and of the whole mediaeval struggle for religious freedom. Before the war was declared I severed all my connections in St. Louis, and offered my services to the American Union Against Militarism to help fight conscription. Later, that work developed into the National Civil Liberties Bureau, organized to help maintain the rights of free speech and free press, and the Anglo-Saxon tradition of liberty of conscience, through liberal provisions for conscientious objectors. This work has been backed both by pro-war liberals and so-called pacifists. It is not anti-war in any sense. It seemed to me the one avenue of service open to me, consistent with my views, with the country's best interest, and with the preservation of the radical minority for the struggle after the war. Even if I were not a believer in radical theories and movements, I would justify the work I have done on the ground of American ideals and traditions alone—as do many of those who have been associated with me. They have stood for those enduring principles which the revolutionary demands of war have temporarily set aside. We have stood against hysteria, mob-violence, unwarranted prosecution, the sinister use of patriotism to cover attacks on radical and labor movements, and for the unabridged right of a fair trial under war statutes. We have tried to keep open those channels of expression which stand for the kind of world order for which the President is battling today against the tories and militarists.

Now comes the Government to take me from that service and to demand of me a service I cannot in conscience undertake. I refuse it simply for my own peace of mind and spirit, for the satisfaction of that inner demand more compelling than any consideration of punishment or the sacrifice of friendships and reputation. I seek no martyrdom, no publicity. I merely meet as squarely as I can the moral issue before me, regardless of consequences.

I realize that your Honor may virtually commit me at once to the military authorities, and that I may have merely taken a quicker and more inconvenient method of arriving at a military camp. I am prepared for that—for the inevitable pressure to take an easy way out by non-combatant service—with guard-house confinement—perhaps brutalities, which hundreds of other objectors have already suffered and are suffering today in camps. I am prepared for court martial and sentence to military prison, to follow the 200–300 objectors already sentenced to terms of 10–30 years for their loyalty to their ideals. I know that the way is easy for those who accept what to me is compromise, hard for those who refuse, as I must, any service whatever. And I know further, in military prison I shall refuse to conform to the rules for military salutes and the like, and will suffer solitary confinement on bread and water, shackled to the bars of a cell eight hours a day—as are men of like convictions at this moment.

I am not complaining for myself or others. I am merely advising the court that I understand full well the penalty of my heresy, and am prepared to pay it. The conflict with conscription is irreconcilable. Even the liberalism of the President and Secretary of War in dealing with objectors leads those of us who are "absolutists" to a punishment longer and severer than that of desperate criminals.

But I believe most of us are prepared even to die for our faith, just as our brothers in France are dying for theirs. To them we are comrades in spirit—we understand one another's motives, though our methods are wide apart. We both share deeply the common experience of living up to the truth as we see it, whatever the price.

Though at the moment I am of a tiny minority, I feel myself just one protest in a great revolt surging up from among the people—the struggle of the masses against the rule of the world by the few—profoundly intensified by the war. It is a struggle against the political state itself, against exploitation, militarism, imperialism, authority in all forms. It is a struggle to break in full force only after the war. Russia already stands in the vanguard, beset by her enemies in the camps of both belligerents —the Central Empires break asunder from within—the labor movement gathers revolutionary force in Britain—and in our own country, the Nonpartisan League, radical labor, and the Socialist Party hold the germs of a new social order. Their protest is my protest. Mine is a personal protest at a particular law, but it is backed by all the aspirations and ideals of the struggle for a world freed of our manifold slaveries and tyrannies.

I ask the Court for no favor. I could do no other than what I have done, whatever the court's decree. I have no bitterness or hate in my heart for any man. Whatever the penalty, I shall endure it, firm in the faith, that whatever befalls me, the principles in which I believe will bring forth out of this misery and chaos, a world of brotherhood, harmony, and freedom for each to live the truth as he sees it.

I hope your Honor will not think that I have taken this occasion to make a speech for the sake of making a speech. I have read you what I have written in order that the future record for myself and for my friends may be perfectly clear, and in order to clear up some of the matters to which the District Attorney called your attention. I know that it is pretty nigh hopeless in times of war and hysteria to get across to any substantial body of people, the view of an out and out heretic like myself. I know that as far as my principles are concerned, they seem to be utterly impractical—mere moon-shine. They are not the views that work in the world today. I fully realize that. But I fully believe that they are the views which are going to guide in the future.

Having arrived at the state of mind in which those views mean the dearest things in life to me, I cannot consistently, with self-respect, do other than I have, namely, to deliberately violate an act which seems to me to be a denial of everything which ideally and in practice I hold sacred.

30

The treatment of many World War I conscientious objectors in prison was barbarous; as Roger Baldwin noted in his speech, refusal to work under military command often resulted in the offender's being manacled to the bars of a cell for eight hours. A strike of objectors at Leavenworth in January, 1919, publicized these inhumane conditions and brought about some reform, but it was not until two years after the armistice that the last of the objectors was released from prison and not until 1933, when President Franklin Roosevelt issued a Christmas amnesty, that they had their civil rights restored.

In the following selection, Norman Thomas examines the experience of these men and attempts to place that experience in a larger perspective.

Norman Thomas on Conscientious Objectors

This insignificant fraction of the youth of America challenged the power of the state when it was mightiest and the philosophy of war when it was most pervasive. They said, "You may kill us but you cannot make us fight against our will." They said it not as men who court martyrdom but as men who serve principle; not as those who despised the state but as those who refused to make it God. If enough of them had said that thing in every land there would have been no war. If enough had said it in any one land it might not have been left to Gandhi in India to organize passive resistance to a foreign conqueror. (Colonel Sedgwick Rice, once Commandant at Fort Leavenworth could, one suspects, bear testimony that there was in the objectors a capacity for non-cooperation which a German war lord would have found it difficult to break.) The fact that the government was forced to treat with these men at all, that it dared not kill them and could not force them to kill is a significant precedent. In this war the objectors were few. But the memory of their defiance may some day help to break the spell which holds the patient masses like dumb, driven cattle in obedience to the financiers and diplomats for whose intrigues they pay with their lives under the grip of "the homicidal mania men call patriotism."

It is not likely that wars will be ended by the refusal of men to fight. Those who have resolved that there must be no more war should not forget that unless the causes of war are removed, well-founded fears and hatreds may submerge the popular desire for peace. But it is significant that in many countries today former soldiers and others are pledging themselves against participation in new international wars— some of the pledges extend to all war—and that labor organizations are disposed to indorse that idea. A small minority of determined objectors to conscription for the next war will give a definiteness and driving force to the amorphous peace movement which the old peace societies quite lacked. That minority, thanks to conscientious objectors in this war, ought to have a more definite understanding of the meaning of their struggle than those opponents of conscription who yielded to the herd instinct.

The example of the conscientious objectors in war time ought also to strengthen a wholesome iconoclasm in peace time directed against that extraordinary idol, the political state, which in Lord Acton's words, "suffers neither limit nor equality, and is bound by no duty to nations

Reprinted from Norman Thomas, *The Conscientious Objector in America* (New York: B. W. Huebsch, Inc., 1923), pp. 284–92.

or to men, that thrives on destruction, and sanctifies whatever things contribute to increase of power." . . .

The duty of civil disobedience which Thoreau preached and the objectors practiced is not a thing to be undertaken lightly; it is not a cloak for a cynical contempt of law; rather it is a social principle which in extremity is the last recourse of brave and sincere souls. It is unlikely that a sense of comradeship rather than the pressure of coercion can ever become the bond of social union until state worship has submitted to the test of such rigorous criticism as was involved in conscientious objection.

Yet the history of conscientious objection in the last war will not make the American state slow to impose conscription in another war. On the contrary, a wise government looking back on the experience of Mr. Baker and Mr. Keppel will find in it instructive lessons on how to bargain with men possessed of scruples against fighting. There will probably always be works of mercy; the raising of food, and other tasks of importance, which men who cannot be dragooned by threats into combatant service may perform under direction of the state to its own advantage. Mennonite farmers are more useful in war time raising wheat than are the same young men dead or in prison. . . .

All objectors to some degree challenged the religion of the state at the moment when war had raised it to its greatest exaltation. Only the absolutists challenged it utterly. And only absolutists will make the issue sharp and clear if and when the next war comes.

Therefore no sympathetic historian of conscientious objection can speak of the past or of the future without emphasizing the significance of precisely that group of objectors which was most despised, derided, and persecuted. Their names will not be remembered; their deeds may be forgotten; yet if the day finally dawns when human society will be a fellowship of freemen not the least of the prophets and pioneers of that dawning will be the absolutists of 1918 who, manacled to the bars of their dark cells like wild beasts, endured the interminable procession of the hours in solitary confinement.

31

A number of cases concerning the constitutionality of the 1917 draft act were contested in the federal court system and eventually progressed to the Supreme Court. The cases, assigned the collective title of "Selective Draft Law Cases," were decided in January, 1918, and the Court, without division, upheld the constitutionality of the act. Chief Justice Edward D. White, speaking for the Court, declared the draft to be a legitimate exercise of Congress's war-making powers. The argument that compulsory service was in violation of the Thirteenth Amendment's prohibition of involuntary servitude was rejected, as was the claim that the granting of exemptions on religious grounds constituted an establishment of religion in violation of the First Amendment.

This decision has become, in the words of a historian of the Court, "the basic statement of the Court on the power of the federal government to conscript military manpower."[19]

Selective Draft Law Cases

We are here concerned with some of the provisions of the Act of May 18, 1917, entitled, "An Act to authorize the President to increase temporarily the Military Establishment of the United States." The law, as its opening sentence declares, was intended to supply temporarily the increased military force which was required by the existing emergency, the war then and now flagrant. The clause we must pass upon and those which will throw light on their significance are briefly summarized:

The act proposed to raise a national army, first, by increasing the regular force to its maximum strength and there maintaining it; second, by incorporating into such army the members of the National Guard and National Guard Reserve already in the service of the United States (Act of Congress of June 3, 1916), and maintaining their organizations to their full strength; third, by giving the President power in his discretion to organize by volunteer enlistment four divisions of infantry; fourth, by subjecting all male citizens between the ages of twenty-one and thirty to duty in the national army for the period of the existing emergency after the proclamation of the President announcing the necessity for their service; and fifth, by providing for selecting from the body so called, on the further proclamation of the President, 500,000 enlisted men, and a second body of the same number should the President in his discretion deem it necessary. To carry out its purposes the

Reprinted from The Selective Draft Law Cases, 245 U.S. 375–390 [citations deleted].

19. Carl B. Swisher, "The Supreme Court and Conscription," Current History, Vol. 55 (June, 1968), p. 353.

act made it the duty of those liable to the call to present themselves for registration on the proclamation of the President so as to subject themselves to the terms of the act and provided full federal means for carrying out the selective draft. It gave the President in his discretion power to create local boards to consider claims for exemption for physical disability or otherwise made by those called. The act exempted from subjection to the draft designated United States and state officials as well as those already in the military or naval service of the United States, regular or duly ordained ministers of religion and theological students under the conditions provided for, and, while relieving from military service in the strict sense the members of religious sects as enumerated whose tenets excluded the moral right to engage in war, nevertheless subjected such persons to the performance of service of a non-combatant character to be defined by the President.

The proclamation of the President calling the persons designated within the ages described in the statute was made, and the plaintiffs in error, who were in the class and under the statute were obliged to present themselves for registration and subject themselves to the law, failed to do so and were prosecuted under the statute for the penalties for which it provided. They all defended by denying that there had been conferred by the Constitution upon Congress the power to compel military service by a selective draft, and asserted that even if such power had been given by the Constitution to Congress, the terms of the particular act for various reasons caused it to be beyond the power and repugnant to the Constitution. The cases are here for review because of the constitutional questions thus raised, convictions having resulted from instructions of the courts that the legal defenses were without merit and that the statute was constitutional.

The possession of authority to enact the statute must be found in the clauses of the Constitution giving Congress power "to declare war . . . to raise and support armies, but no appropriation of money to that use shall be for a longer term than two years . . . to make rules for the government and regulation of the land and naval forces." Article I, Sec. 8. And of course the powers conferred by these provisions like all other powers given carry with them as provided by the Constitution the authority "to make all laws which shall be necessary and proper for carrying into execution the foregoing powers." Article I, Sec. 8.

As the mind cannot conceive an army without the men to compose it, on the face of the Constitution the objection that it does not give power to provide for such men would seem to be too frivolous for futher notice. It is said, however, that since under the Constitution as originally framed state citizenship was primary and United States citizenship but derivative and dependent thereon, therefore the power conferred upon Congress to raise armies was only coterminous with United States citizenship and could not be exerted so as to cause that citizenship to lose its dependent character and dominate state citizenship. But the proposition simply denies to Congress the power to raise armies which the Constitution gives. That power by the very terms of the Constitution, being delegated, is supreme. Article VI. In truth the contention simply assails the wisdom of the framers of the Constitution in conferring authority on Congress and in not retaining it as it was under the Confederation in the several States. Further it is said, the right to provide is not denied by calling for volunteer enlistments, but it does not and cannot include the power to exact enforced military duty by the citizen. This however but challenges the existence of all power, for a governmental power which has no sanction to it and which therefore can only be exercised provided the citizen consents to its exertion is in no substantial sense a power. It is argued, however, that although this is abstractly true, it is not concretely so because as compelled military service is repugnant to a free government and in conflict with all the great guarantees of the Constitution as to individual liberty, it must be assumed that the authority to raise armies was intended to be limited to the right to call an army into existence counting alone upon the willingness of the citizen to do his duty in time of public need, that is, in time of war. But the premise of this proposition is so devoid of foundation that it leaves not even a shadow of ground upon which to base the conclusion. Let us see if this is not at once demonstrable. It may not be doubted that the very conception of a just government and its duty to the citizen includes the reciprocal obligation of the citizen to render military service in case of need and the right to compel it. To do more than state the proposition is absolutely unnecessary in view of the practical illustration afforded by the almost universal legislation to that effect now in force. In England it is certain that before the Norman Conquest the duty of the great militant body of the citizens was recognized and enforcible. It is unnecessary to follow the long controversy between Crown and Parliament as to the branch of the government in which the power resided, since there never was any doubt that it somewhere resided. So also it is wholly unnecessary to explore the situation for the purpose of fixing the sources whence in England it came to be understood that the citizen or the force organized from the militia as such could not without their consent be compelled to render service in a foreign country, since there is no room to contend that such principle ever rested upon any challenge of the right of Parliament to impose compulsory duty wherever the public exigency exacted, whether at home or abroad. This is exemplified by the present English Service Act.

In the Colonies before the separation from England there cannot be the slightest doubt that the right to enforce military service was unquestioned and that practical effect was given to the power in many cases. Indeed the brief of the Government contains a list of Colonial acts manifesting the power and its enforcement in more than two hundred cases. And this exact situation existed also after the separation. Under the Articles of Confederation it is true Congress had no such power, as its authority was absolutely limited to making calls upon the States for the military forces needed to create and maintain the army, each State being bound for its quota as called. But it is indisputable that the States in response to the calls made upon them met the situation when they deemed it necessary by directing enforced military service on the part of the citizens. In fact the duty of the citizen to render military service and the power to compel him against his consent to do so was expressly sanctioned by the constitutions of at least nine of the States, an illustration being afforded by the following provision of the Pennsylvania constitution of 1776. "That every member of society hath a right to be protected in the enjoyment of life, liberty, and property, and therefore is bound to contribute his proportion towards the expense of that protection, and yield his personal service when necessary, or an equivalent thereto." While it is true that the States were sometimes slow in exerting the power in order to fill their quotas—a condition shown by resolutions of Congress calling upon them to comply by exerting their compulsory power to draft and by earnest requests by Washington to Congress that a demand be made upon the States to resort to drafts to fill their quotas —that fact serves to demonstrate instead of to challenge the existence of the authority. A default in exercising a duty may not be resorted to as a reason for denying its existence.

When the Constitution came to be formed it may not be disputed that one of the recognized necessities for its adoption was the want of power in Congress to raise an army and the dependence upon the States for their quotas. In supplying the power it was manifestly intended to give it all and leave none to the States, since besides the delegation to Congress of authority to raise armies the Constitution prohibited the States, without the consent of Congress, from keeping troops in time of peace or engaging in war. Article I, Sec. 10.

To argue that as the state authority over the militia prior to the Constitution embraced every citizen, the right of Congress to raise an army should not be considered as granting authority to compel the citizen's service in the army, is but to express in a different form the denial of the right to call any citizen to the army. Nor is this met by saying that it does not exclude the right of Congress to organize an army by voluntary enlistments, that is, by the consent of the citizens, for if the proposition be true, the right of the citizen to give consent would be controlled by the same prohibition which would deprive Congress of the right to compel unless it can be said that although Congress had not the right to call because of state authority, the citizen had a right to obey the call and set aside state authority if he pleased to do so. And a like conclusion demonstrates the want of foundation for the contention that, although it be within the power to call the citizen into the army without his consent, the army into which he enters after the call is to be limited in some respects to services for which the militia it is assumed may only be used, since this admits the appropriateness of the call to military service in the army and the power to make it and yet destroys the purpose for which the call is authorized—the raising of armies to be under the control of the United States.

The fallacy of the argument results from confounding the constitutional provisions concerning the milita with that conferring upon Congress the power to raise armies. It treats them as one while they are different. . . .

The line which separates it from the army power is not only inherently plainly marked by the text of the two clauses, but will stand out in bolder relief by considering the condition before the Constitution was adopted and the remedy which it provided for the military situation with which it dealt. The right on the one hand of Congress under the Confederation to call on the States for forces and the duty on the other of the States to furnish when called, embraced the complete power of government over the subject. When the two were combined and were delegated to Congress all governmental power on that subject was conferred, a result manifested not only by the grant made by the limitation expressly put upon the States on the subject. The army sphere therefore embraces such complete authority. But the duty of exerting the power thus conferred in all its plenitude was not made at once obligatory but was wisely left to depend upon the discretion of Congress as to the arising of the exigencies which would call it in part or in whole into play. There was left therefore under the sway of the States undelegated the control of the militia to the extent that such control was not taken away by the exercise by Congress of its power to raise armies. This did not diminish the military power or curb the full potentiality of the right to exert it but left an area of authority requiring to be provided for (the militia area) unless and until by the exertion of the military power of Congress that area had been circumscribed or totally disappeared. This, therefore, is what was dealt with by the militia provision. It diminished the occasion for the exertion by Congress of its military power beyond the strict necessities for its exercise by giving the power to Congress to direct the organization and training of the militia (evidently to prepare such militia in the event of the exercise of the army power) although leaving the carrying out of such command to the States. It further conduced to the same result by delegating to Congress the right to call on occasions which were specified for the militia force, thus again obviating the necessity for exercising the army power to the extent of being ready for every conceivable contingency. This purpose is made manifest by the provision preserving the organization of the militia so far as formed when called for such special purposes although subjecting the militia when so called to the paramount authority of the United States. But because under the express regulations the power was given to call for specified purposes without exerting the army power, it cannot follow that the latter power when exerted was not complete to the extent of its exertion and dominant. Because the power of Congress to raise armies was not required to be exerted to its full limit but only as in the discretion of Congress it was deemed the public interest required, furnishes no ground for supposing that the complete power was lost by its partial exertion. Because, moreover, the power granted to Congress to raise armies in its potentiality was susceptible of narrowing the area over which the militia clause operated, affords no ground for confounding the two areas which were distinct and separate to the end of confusing both the powers and the weakening or destroying both.

And upon this understanding of the two powers the legislative and executive authority has been exerted from the beginning. From the act of the first session of Congress carrying over the army of the Government under the Confederation to the United States under the Constitution down to 1812 the authority to raise armies was regularly exerted as a distinct and substantive power, the force being raised and recruited by enlistment. Except for one act formulating a plan by which the entire body of citizens (the militia) subject to military duty was to be organized in every State which was never carried into effect, Congress confined itself to providing for the organization of a specified number distributed among the States according to their quota to be trained as directed by Congress and to be called by the President as need might require. When the War of 1812 came the result of these two forces composed the army to be relied upon by Congress to carry on the war. Either because it proved to be weak in numbers or because of insubordination developed among the forces called and manifested by their refusal to cross the border, the Government determined that the exercise of the power to organize an army by compulsory draft was necessary and Mr. Monroe, the Secretary of War, (Mr. Madison being President) in a letter to Congress recommended several plans of legislation on that subject. It suffices to say that by each of them it was proposed that the United States deal directly with the body of citizens subject to military duty and call a designated number out of the population between the ages of eighteen and forty-five for service in the army. The power which it was recommended be exerted was clearly an unmixed federal power dealing with the subject from the sphere of the authority given to Congress to raise armies and not from the sphere of the right to deal with the militia as such, whether organized or unorganized. A bill was introduced giving effect to the plan. Opposition developed, but we need not stop to consider it because it substantially rested upon the incompatibility of compulsory military service with free government, a subject which from what we have said has been disposed of. Peace came before the bill was enacted.

Down to the Mexican War the legislation exactly portrayed the same condition of mind which we have previously stated. In that war, however, no draft was suggested, because the army created by the United States immediately resulting from the exercise by Congress of its power to raise armies, that organized under its direction from the militia and the volunteer commands which were furnished, proved adequate to carry the war to a successful conclusion.

So the course of legislation from that date to 1861 affords no ground for any other than the same conception of legislative power which we have already stated. In that year when the mutterings of the dread conflict which was to come began to be heard and the Proclamation of the President calling a force into existence was issued it was addressed to the body organized out of the militia and trained by the States in accordance with the previous acts of Congress. That force being inadequate to meet the situation, an act was passed authorizing the acceptance of 500,000 volunteers by the President to be by him organized into a national army. This was soon followed by another act increasing the force of the militia to be organized by the States for the purpose of being drawn upon when trained under the direction of Congress, the two acts when considered together presenting in the clearest possible form the distinction between the power of Congress to raise armies and its authority under the militia clause. But it soon became manifest that more men were required. As a result the Act of March 3, 1863, was adopted entitled, "An Act for enrolling and calling out the National Forces and for other purposes." By that act which was clearly intended to directly exert upon all the citizens of the United States the national power which it had been proposed to exert in 1814 on the recommendation of the then Secretary of War, Mr. Monroe, every male citizen of the United States between the ages of twenty and forty-five was made subject by the direct action of Congress to be called by compulsory draft to service in a national army at such a time and in such numbers as the President in his discretion might find necessary. In this act, as in the one of 1814, and in this one, the means by which the act was to be enforced were directly federal and the force to be raised as a result of the draft was therefore typically national as distinct from the call into active service of the militia as such. And under the power thus exerted four separate calls for draft were made by the President and enforced, that of July 1863, of February and March 1864, of July and December, 1864, producing a force of about a quarter of a million men. It is undoubted that the men thus raised by draft were treated as subject to direct national authority and were used either in filling the gaps occasioned by the vicissitudes of war in the ranks of the existing national forces or for the purpose of organizing such new units as were deemed to be required. It would be childish to deny the value of the added strength which was thus afforded. Indeed in the official report of the Provost Marshal General reviewing the subject it was stated that it was the efficient aid resulting from the forces created by the draft at a very critical moment of the civil strife which obviated a disaster which seemed impending and carried that struggle to a complete and successful conclusion.

Brevity prevents doing more than to call attention to the fact that the organized body of militia within the States as trained by the States under the direction of Congress became known as the National Guard. And to make further preparation from among the great body of the citizens, an additional number to be determined by the President was directed to be organized and trained by the States as the National Guard Reserve.

Thus sanctioned as is the act before us by the text of the Constitution, and by its significance as read in the light of the fundamental principles with which the subject is concerned, by the power recognized and carried into effect in many civilized countries, by the authority and practice of the colonies before the Revolution, of the States under the Confederation and of the Government since the formation of the Constitution, the want of merit in the contentions that the act in the particulars which we have been previously called upon to consider was beyond the constitutional power of Congress, is manifest. Cogency, however, if possible, is added to the demonstration by pointing out that in the only case to which we have been referred where the constitutionality of the Act of 1863 was contemporaneously challenged on grounds akin to, if not absolutely identical with, those here urged, the validity of the act was maintained for reasons not different from those which control our judgment. And as further evidence that the conclusion we reach is but the inevitable consequence of the provisions of the Constitution as effect follows cause, we briefly recur to events in another environment. The seceding States wrote into the constitution which was adopted to regulate the government which they sought to establish, in identical words the provisions of the Constitution of the United States which we here have under consideration. And when the right to enforce under that instrument a selective draft law which was enacted, not differing in principle from the one here in question, was challenged, its validity was upheld, evidently after great consideration, by the courts of Virginia, of Georgia, of Texas, of Alabama, of Mississippi, and of North Carolina, the opinions in some of the cases copiously and critically reviewing the whole grounds which we have stated.

In reviewing the subject, we have hitherto considered it as it has been argued, from the point of view of the Constitution as it stood prior to the adoption of the Fourteenth Amendment. But to avoid all misapprehension we briefly direct attention to that Amendment for the purpose of pointing out, as has been frequently done in the past, how completely it broadened the national scope of the Government under the Constitution by causing citizenship of the United States to be paramount and dominant instead of being subordinate and derivative, and therefore, operating as it does upon all the powers conferred by the Constitution, leaves no possible support for the contentions made, if their want of merit was otherwise not so clearly made manifest.

It remains only to consider contentions which, while not disrupting power, challenge the act because of the repugnancy to the Constitution supposed to result from some of its provisions. First, we are of opinion that the contention that the act is void as a delegation of federal power to state officials because of some of its administrative features, is too wanting in merit to require further notice. Second, we think that the contention that the statute is void because vesting administrative officers with legislative discretion has been so completely adversely settled as to require reference only to some of the decided cases. A like conclusion also adversely disposes of a similar claim concerning the conferring of judicial power. And we pass without anything but statement the proposition that an establishment of a religion or an interference with the free exercise thereof repugnant to the First Amendment resulted from the exemption clauses of the act to which we at the outset referred, because we think its unsoundness is too apparent to require us to do more.

Finally, as we are unable to conceive upon what theory the exaction by government from the citizen of the performance of his supreme and noble duty of contributing to the defense of the rights and honor of the nation, as the result of a war declared by the great representative body of the people, can be said to be the imposition of involuntary servitude in violation of the prohibitions of the Thirteenth Amendment, we are constrained to the conclusion that the contention to that effect is refuted by its mere statement.

Affirmed

32

The following Supreme Court case arose out of an attempt to obstruct the operations of the draft act during World War I. The defendant, Charles T. Schenck, argued that the First Amendment guarantees of freedom of speech and of the press protected his antiwar utterances and publications. The Supreme Court, in a unanimous verdict, upheld Schenck's conviction by a lower court. The case has taken on a larger significance, however, because it is here that Justice Oliver Wendell Holmes offered the first statement of the "clear and present danger" test in regard to public utterances.

Schenck v. United States, 1919

Holmes, J. This is an indictment in three counts. The first charges a conspiracy to violate the Espionage Act of June 15, 1917 . . . by causing and attempting to cause insubordination, etc., in the military and naval forces of the United States, and to obstruct the recruiting and enlistment

Reprinted from *Schenck v. United States*, 249 U.S. 47, pp. 48–53 [citations deleted].

service of the United States, when the United States was at war with
the German Empire, to wit, that the defendants wilfully conspired to
have printed and circulated to men who had been called and accepted
for military service under the Act of May 18, 1917, a document set forth
and alleged to be calculated to cause such insubordination and obstruction. The count alleges overt acts in pursuance of the conspiracy, ending
in the distribution of the document set forth. . . . They set up the First
Amendment to the Constitution forbidding Congress to make any law
abridging the freedom of speech, or of the press, and bringing the case
here on that ground have argued some other points also of which we
must dispose.

It is argued that the evidence, if admissible, was not sufficient to
prove that the defendant Schenck was concerned in sending the documents. According to the testimony Schenck said he was the general
secretary of the Socialist party and had charge of the Socialist headquarters from which the documents were sent. He identifies a book
found there as the minutes of the Executive Committee of the party.
The book showed a resolution of August 13, 1917, that 15,000 leaflets
should be printed on the other side of one of them in use, to be mailed
to men who had passed exemption boards, and for distribution. Schenck
personally attended to the printing. On August 20 the general secretary's
report said, "Obtained new leaflets from printer and started work ad-
dressing envelopes" etc.; and there was a resolve that Comrade Schenck
be allowed $125 for sending leaflets through the mail. He said that he
had about fifteen or sixteen thousand printed. There were files of the
circular in question in the inner office which he said were printed on the
other side of the one sided circular and were there for distribution. Other
copies were proved to have been sent through the mails to drafted men.
Without going into confirmatory details that were proved, no reasonable
man could doubt that the defendant Schenck was largely instrumental
in sending the circulars about. . . .

The document in question upon its first printed side recited the first
section of the Thirteenth Amendment, said that the idea embodied in
it was violated by the Conscription Act and that a conscript is little
better than a convict. In impassioned language it intimated that conscription was despotism in its worse form and a monstrous wrong against
humanity in the interest of Wall Street's chosen few. It said, "Do not
submit to intimidation," but in form at least confined itself to peaceful
measures such as a petition for the repeal of the act. The other and later
printed side of the sheet was headed "Assert Your Rights." It stated reasons for alleging that any one violated the Constitution when he refused

to recognize "your right to assert your opposition to the draft," and went on "If you do not assert and support your rights, you are helping to deny or disparage rights which it is the solemn duty of all citizens and residents of the United States to retain." It described the arguments on the other side as coming from cunning politicians and a mercenary capitalist press, and even silent consent to the conscription law as helping to support an infamous conspiracy. It denied the power to send our citizens away to foreign shores to shoot up the people of other lands, and added that words could not express the condemnation such cold-blooded ruthlessness deserves, etc., etc., winding up "You must do your share to maintain, support and uphold the rights of the people of this country." Of course the document would not have been sent unless it had been intended to have some effect, and we do not see what effect it could be expected to have upon persons subject to the draft except to influence them to obstruct the carrying of it out. The defendants do not deny that the jury might find against them on this point.

But it is said, suppose that that was the tendency of this circular, it is protected by the First Amendment to the Constitution. . . . We admit that in many places and in ordinary times the defendants in saying all that was said in the circular would have been within their constitutional rights. But the character of every act depends upon the circumstances in which it is done. The most stringent protection of free speech would not protect a man in falsely shouting fire in a theatre and causing a panic. It does not even protect a man from an injunction against uttering words that may have all the effect of force. The question in every case is whether the words used are used in such circumstances and are of such a nature as to create a clear and present danger that they will bring about the substantive evils that Congress has a right to prevent. It is a question of proximity and degree. When a nation is at war many things that might be said in time of peace are such a hindrance to its effort that their utterance will not be endured so long as men fight and that no Court could regard them as protected by any constitutional right. It seems to be admitted that if an actual obstruction of the recruiting service were proved, liability for words that produced that effect might be enforced. The statute of 1917 in sec. 4 punishes conspiracies to obstruct as well as actual obstruction. If the act, (speaking, or circulating a paper,) its tendency and the intent with which it is done are the same, we perceive no ground for saying that success alone warrants making the act a crime. . . .

Judgements affirmed.

33

Samuel Gompers, president of the American Federation of Labor, recommended the creation of a commission to study universal conscription—of wealth as well as manpower—in order to be better prepared in the event of a future war. His concern was widely reflected not only in the ranks of labor, but among veterans as well. The feeling that there had been an inequality of sacrifice in World War I led the American Legion to formulate a bill in 1922 to prevent a similar situation from arising again. Two years later such a bill was introduced in Congress but was never reported out of committee.

Gompers's "What About Universal Conscription for War," 1924

In theory universal conscription in time of war is correct. It is right that government should take wealth as well as men. But I am unwilling at this time to be dogmatic one way or the other. I realize that not every theory can be applied in this world of human fallibility.

The problem appeals to me as one for the most profound study. It does not appeal to me as one on which hasty judgment, based on an altruistic desire, should be formed and set down as policy.

Surely we must be spared all profiteering in the next war—if there is a next war. We must be spared the hideousness of individuals preying upon other individuals or upon the government.

I should like to be certain that universal conscription will accomplish this and that it will not be a means of destroying our economic life and running our standards of life and work after a war.

We must find a cure for such crimes as were committed in the World War, but in doing that we must be certain that we do not prepare for ourselves a worse evil.

In principle universal conscription is just. It is folly, however, to take an unqualified position in favor of universal conscription until we know definitely that we can apply universal conscription without creating a surety of greater evils that would come without universal conscription.

Universal conscription might dampen the ardor for war. But even that is not sure. We do not go stalking about the world seeking war

Reprinted from the *American Federationalist*, Vol. 31 (June, 1924), pp. 461–62.

and it is quite probable that our resentment against wrong, or our resistance against attack, would be as filled with ardor in the one case as in the other. I think the great spontaneous outburst of resentment against the sinking of the Lusitania was in no way increased by any expectation of personal gain. Profiteering came as a development, largely. It did not get us into the war.

We do not want another war. But if defense of great principles requires such a sacrifice I believe our people will respond as they always have responded. We want to be sure that in preventing injustice and profiteering we do not build up something worse, something perhaps more hampering.

Advocates of conscription of wealth leave many loose ends in their arguments. First, I have not yet seen a satisfactory definition of wealth. Does it mean factories and raw materials and railroads? Or does it mean *all* wealth? Does it mean the $1,000 savings bank account saved by the wage earner? Does it mean all money wealth? Does it mean all credit? There must be a definition of wealth.

And what of the after-war period? What guarantees can there be of restoration of standards when the soldier-standard is removed? For the duration of the war we should completely abolish democracy, down to its last vestige. We should substitute the most complete and absolute autocracy. Could democracy and our present system of private ownership be destroyed and then replaced? Or would autocracy survive, with all its powers and ramifications?

These are things to think about. I should like to see a commission, composed of men from all walks of life, representing all forms of human effort, give study to this great question. We want no more war, but if we must have war we want to be as effective as possible and we do not want abuses and profiteering at home. What are the measures to be taken? We cannot determine that question according to emotional desires, probably not according to abstract principles, and probably not according to any pre-arranged formula.

34

In 1926 a manifesto was published, signed by seventy-one leading figures from fifteen countries, calling for the universal abolition of conscription. Conscription, it alleged, was not a method of maintaining peace but rather served to perpetuate war consciousness and war itself. It was destructive of human values and constituted a "degradation of human personality." Only when conscription had been eliminated could there emerge "a new era of freedom within nations and of fraternity between them." Among the signers of the statement were Albert Einstein, M. K. Gandhi, H. G. Wells, and Bertrand Russell. The idealism expressed in this document was mirrored, two years later, in the Kellogg-Briand Pact, which also sought to eliminate war.

Manifesto for the Universal Abolition of Conscription, 1926

During the war people in all the countries determined to throw off for ever the yoke of militarism, and, when peace came, the League of Nations was welcomed as the offspring of this hope. It is our duty to see that the terrible suffering of the war does not recur.

We call for some definite step towards complete disarmament and the demilitarising of the mind of civilized nations. The most effective measure towards this would be the universal abolition of conscription. We therefore ask the League of Nations to propose the abolition of compulsory military service in all countries as a first step towards true disarmament.

It is our belief that conscript armies, with their large corps of professional officers are a grave menace to peace. Conscription involves the degradation of human personality and the destruction of liberty. Barrack life, military drill, blind obedience to commands, however unjust and foolish they may be, and deliberate training for slaughter, undermine respect for the individual, for democracy and human life.

It is debasing human dignity to force men to give up their lives, or to inflict death against their will, or without conviction as to the justice of their action. The State which thinks itself entitled to force its citizens to go to war will never pay proper regard to the value and happiness of their lives in peace. Moreover, by conscription the militarist spirit of aggressiveness is implanted in the whole male population at the most impressionable age. By training for war men come to consider war as unavoidable and even desirable.

By the universal abolition of conscription war will be made less easy. The Government of a country which maintains conscription has little difficulty in declaring war, for it can silence the whole population by a mobilization order. When Governments have to depend for support upon the voluntary consent of their peoples, they must necessarily exercise caution in their foreign policies.

In the first draft of the Covenant of the League of Nations, President Wilson proposed to make conscription illegal in all affiliated countries. It is our duty to restore the original spirit which created the League, a spirit shared by many of those who fought in the war, and professed by many of the Statesmen of the countries concerned. By the universal abolition of conscription we can take a decisive step towards peace and liberty. We therefore call upon all men and women of goodwill to help create in all countries a public opinion which will induce Governments and the League of Nations to take this definite step to rid the world of the spirit of militarism, and to open the way to a new era of freedom within nations and of fraternity between them.

1940-1965:
Conscription in War
and Cold War

THE OUTBREAK OF WAR in Europe in September, 1939, found the United States Army in a rather sorry condition—180,000 men, one of the smallest forces among the major powers. The movement to remedy this situation through the enactment of draft legislation emanated not from the War Department or the White House but rather from a civilian group, the executive committee of the Military Training Camps Association. Beginning in May, 1940, this group, consisting of many former participants in the Plattsburg movement and led by the indefatigable Grenville Clark, began to organize to secure passage of a draft bill. They received little encouragement at the outset from the president, because of the political liability of supporting a peacetime draft during an election year, or from the War Department, for an assortment of reasons: the feeling on the part of some that the department's primary responsibility was to gradually enlarge and bring to fighting trim the existing army, not to absorb a mass of draftees; the pessimism felt by others that such a bill could be passed prior to hostilities; and the general assumption that supporting such a measure would endanger congressional appropriations for more pressing military items.

Nevertheless, the Clark group won an early victory when one of their leading supporters, Henry L. Stimson, was appointed as secretary of war by President Roosevelt. Stimson then led the battle for compulsory service legislation within the administration while the Military Training Camps Association organized a highly effective educational and lobbying campaign to win public support for their bill.

A modified version of the Military Training Camps Association bill was introduced in the Senate on June 20 by Senator Edward Burke (D., Nebr.) and on the following day in the House by Congressman James Wadsworth (R., N.Y.). The headlines which might have ordinarily marked this event, however, were preempted by the news of the fall of France. This traumatic episode, culminating Hitler's relentless drive through Western Europe, undercut American confidence in remaining aloof from the war and greatly enhanced the possibilities of enacting draft legislation.[1] On July 10, President Roosevelt advocated a draft system in a message to Congress, and the issue was to be eventually removed from the presidential contest by Republican nominee Wendell Willkie's statement that "some sort of selective service is the only democratic way in which to secure the competent and trained manpower we need for national defense."[2]

The acceptance by Roosevelt and Willkie of the necessity for conscription did not, however, insure easy passage of the bill in Congress. Although many rejected, in principle, a peacetime draft, the majority of the congressional opposition consisted of those who wished to allow one final test of the adequacy of volunteering before a draft would go into operation. Walter Lippmann argued against this position, preferring a draft based upon the legal, open, and orderly action of the state to the "moral horror" of a voluntary system operating under the pressure and "undiscerning cruelty of private busy-bodies and self-appointed persecuting patrioteers."[3]

Both houses of Congress, by decisive majorities, accepted, in the summer of 1940, the necessity for implementing the first peace-

1. The Gallup poll of June 23, 1940, showed 64 percent of those questioned in favor of compulsory military training, a striking increase in support of the legislation over the 37 percent who had approved it in the fall of 1939.

2. *Campaign Textbook of the Republican Party, 1940* (Washington, D.C.: Republican National Committee, 1940), p. 8.

3. Walter Lippmann, "Today and Tomorrow," *New York Herald Tribune*, Aug. 13, 1940.

time draft in American history. The very fragility of the peace made most Americans willing to accept this break with long-standing tradition. Indeed, it could be argued that the banner headlines, the bulletins crackling over the airwaves, and the intimidating images flickering on the newsreel screens had decided the case for conscription.

The 1940 draft law, as enacted, had a clearly defensive purpose: no more than 900,000 men could be enrolled under it at any one time, they would serve for only one year, and they could not be sent outside the Western Hemisphere. The act showed a decided improvement over the 1917 version in regard to the treatment of conscientious objectors. The earlier act had limited that category to members of the historic peace churches and had failed to allow for noncombatant service under civilian direction. The 1940 act extended the right of conscientious objection to all who, because of "religious training and belief," rejected all forms of war. Such persons could perform alternative service under civilian direction.

President Roosevelt signed the bill into law on September 16 and set October 16 as the first registration date. The army rapidly expanded over the next several months, but this expansion created a new problem. Delays in the construction of training camps, a paucity of equipment, and the difficulty of moving large numbers of recruits from basic training up through corps maneuvers combined to impede the development of a "new" army. The War Department saw the only resolution of this problem to lie in extending the service of the new draftees. In seeking approval for this, the army initiated a major congressional battle in the summer of 1941.

The vote on the Service Extension Act of 1941 has been frequently misconstrued. Many commentators have assumed that the continuance of the draft itself, rather than the extension of service of the initial selectees, was at stake. The real issue was whether Congress would accept the War Department's judgment that it was vitally necessary that an eighteen-month extension of service be voted. The opponents of this legislation—those who felt that the crisis was overblown, those perturbed by the increasing bellicosity of American foreign policy, and those who insisted that voting for such a bill would violate the "contract" that had been made with the draftees—nearly carried the day. The bill passed by fifteen votes in the Senate, but earned only a razor's-edge, one-vote passage in the House. If it had failed, however, there was little chance that the nation would be "armed only with the tongues of its Congressmen."[4] A bill with a shorter term of extension would have been immediately introduced and passed.

The achievement of the Selective Service System during the years of World War II, measured purely in quantitative terms, was overwhelming. Almost 6,500 local boards, staffed by uncompensated members, registered nearly 50,000,000 men and helped raise a fighting force of approximately 15,000,000.[5] This record furnishes a significant index of America's capacity to organize and mobilize her resources under duress.

The passage of the 1940 draft act represented an emergency response to a threatening situation. Congress and the American people acknowledged the necessity of departing from national tradition and adopting peacetime conscription. The War Department, however, saw compulsory military training not as an extraordinary condition but as a logical requirement for the protection of the national interest. The general staff, therefore, began planning almost immediately to transform selective service, in the postwar period, into a permanent program of universal military training.[6]

The War Department sought to have such a program enacted before the end of the war, thereby avoiding the danger of public apathy and the "return to normalcy" reaction; this attempt met with the expected resistance. Peace groups, church organizations, and labor unions opposed the recommendation—some absolutely, others arguing against undue haste and claiming that our defense needs could be more readily determined once a peace settlement had been made. Norman Thomas charged that "for America to accept postwar military conscription now is to lose the peace. It is to sentence our sons and their sons to a new war."[7]

The advocates of compulsory military training rejected such reasoning. Secretary of the Navy James Forrestal insisted that the "preparedness of the United States is our inescapable contribution to world peace."[8] General Lewis B. Hershey, director of the Selective Service System, warned that "this time we must not, dare not, go through the national throwing down of arms we passed through at the close of World War I."[9]

4. *Time*, Vol. 38 (Aug. 18, 1941), p. 12.
5. U.S., Bureau of the Budget, *The United States at War* (Washington, D.C.: Government Printing Office, 1946), p. 462.
6. Robert David Ward, "The Movement for Universal Military Training in the United States, 1942–1952" (Ph.D. diss., University of North Carolina, 1958), p. 40.
7. *Editorial Research Reports*, Vol. 1 (Apr. 15, 1944), p. 269.
8. *Congressional Digest*, Vol. 23 (Jan., 1945), p. 25.
9. *Editorial Research Reports*, Vol. 1, p. 267.

The proponents had the better of the argument. Although they were unable to have universal military training adopted, they succeeded in having selective service continued after the war. This victory can be attributed to three factors: the need to provide occupation troops for the defeated countries, the developing Cold War consciousness, and a shift in attitude on the part of the American people toward conscription.

The occupation of Germany and Japan required a sizeable force which could be raised, according to the War Department, in one of two ways: by extending the service of men already in the armed forces or by continuing inductions under the draft. Volunteering alone would not raise sufficient numbers. Presented with this option, Congress and the American people had very little choice. In the midst of tremendous public clamor for the rapid demobilization of the army, the equitable, as well as the politic, solution seemed to be the drafting of men who had not as yet served their turn.

The developing chill in Soviet-American relations also served to undercut the movement to end the draft. The *Christian Century* insisted that "conscription, which must be accepted as a regrettable but unavoidable necessity in time of war, is repugnant to peace-time America. It can be tolerated only if it is proved to be necessary because of a clear and present danger."[10] Many Americans were, indeed, being persuaded that our recent ally had now become a threat not only to America's interests but more immediately to the independence of Western Europe.

The argument for continuing compulsory military training in the aftermath of the Second World War proved remarkably similar to the case for its introduction in 1940. The country, it was said, faced an external threat which could only be offset by maintaining its state of preparedness. Congressman Sol Bloom, chairman of the House Foreign Affairs Committee, described in his autobiography the process of readying the American people for the Second World War in terms that may be used, with no substantial change, for the postwar era as well:

> It was the instillation of an attitude in the American people that would cause them to accept the possibility, and, gradually, the likelihood, of their direct participation in the war. It was not a question of overcoming a normal human antipathy towards war. It was a problem of education, of how to make the Montana wheat

10. *Congressional Digest*, Vol. 23, p. 29.

farmer . . . understand that invisible forces beyond the seas were of vital concern to him; of how to prepare millions for the possibility that the European or Asiatic cauldrons could spill over suddenly on us—precisely as one of them eventually did; of how to get all of us ready in mind and spirit.[11]

Such a program, Bloom noted, could not be achieved overnight: "It had to be accomplished step by step, and as our people grew more accustomed to preparing, at an increasing pace. The technique of preparation resembled somewhat the "technique" of an individual in increasing his tolerance for strong drink. Just as an inexperienced drinker literally cannot stomach a substantial dose, so the American people could not have stomached strong legislation before they learned to accustom their system to it."[12]

The Second World War did, indeed, accustom the American people to compulsory military service. Samuel Huntington writes that the war produced "fundamental changes in the environments of American military policy."[13] One of these "fundamental changes" was the acceptance of the necessity of maintaining a large standing army.[14] The continuation of the draft became a corollary of that decision.

The period 1940–45 marked a clear shift in American attitudes toward conscription. In December, 1938, George Gallup reported that only 37 percent of his sample thought that every able-bodied man twenty years old should be made to serve for one year in the military. That same question the following October, right on the heels of the German invasion of Poland, received only the same 37 percent affirmative response.[15] During the period 1942–46, seventeen readings were taken on a similar proposition by the Gallup organization, the National Opinion Research Center, and by *Fortune* magazine. They show a dramatic transformation of American opin-

11. Sol Bloom, *The Autobiography of Sol Bloom* (New York: G. P. Putnam's Sons, 1948), p. 246.
12. *Ibid.*
13. Samuel P. Huntington, *The Common Defense: Strategic Programs in National Politics* (New York: Columbia University Press, 1961), p. 14.
14. During the first 170 years of the nation's history, only in actual wartime, or in the year or two immediately afterward, did the armed forces ever employ as much as 1 percent of the working-age male population. Since 1941 the figure has always exceeded 3 percent; since the Korean War it has not fallen below 5 percent. (Bruce M. Russett, *What Price Vigilance? The Burdens of National Defense* [New Haven: Yale University Press, 1970], p. 2.)
15. *The Annals of the American Academy of Political and Social Science*, Vol. 241 (Sept., 1945), p. 87.

ion. The Gallup poll of November, 1943, registered the lowest proportion supporting compulsory military training, 63 percent. The
National Opinion Research Center findings the following September marked the high point of approbation, 79 percent. In the immediate postwar months, September, October, November, and
December, 1945, Gallup reported the affirmative percentages as
65, 70, 75, and 70, respectively. One year later, in November, 1946,
the figure stood at 66 percent.[16] The period of World War II clearly
marks, then, a fundamental alteration in American attitudes toward compulsory military training in peacetime. Less than 40 percent accepted such a proposition at the outbreak of the war. By
1945, between two-thirds to three-quarters of the nation had come
to accept it.

The reasons for this about-face can be readily understood. The
draft had proved an instrument of victory in World War II. It had
insured the successful prosecution of a war that had virtually universal backing. In addition, the worst fears expressed by the opponents of the draft in 1940 had not been realized. Most Americans
felt that the Selective Service System had operated fairly and had
not moved the nation in a militaristic or totalitarian direction. Finally, the sense of continuing threat discouraged attempts to dis-
mantle a system which seemed a necessary guarantee of security.

Nevertheless, the draft act of 1940, after two one-year extensions,
was allowed to expire on March 31, 1947, and all that remained of
the Selective Service System was an Office of Selective Service
Records. President Truman and the army had not pressed Congress
for an extension of the act, preferring instead to work for a replacement of selective service by universal military training. On
December 20, 1946, the president had appointed an Advisory Commission on Universal Training, chaired by Dr. Karl Compton of
the Massachusetts Institute of Technology, which issued a 445-
page report entitled *A Program for National Security* that called
for the military training of every qualified male for a period of not
less than six months. Many in Congress, however, saw this period
as an opportunity to return to a volunteer system, but adequate
numbers of volunteers did not come forward (due, in part, to the
army's raising its acceptable intelligence test scores on two occasions).[17] The House Armed Services Committee reported out a

16. Ward, "Universal Military Training," p. 199.
17. John M. Swomley, Jr., *The Military Establishment*, p. 69; Richard Gillam,
"The Peacetime Draft: Voluntarism to Coercion," *The Yale Review*, Vol. 57 (Summer, 1968), p. 507.

bill for universal military training, but its counterpart in the Senate delayed acting on the issue. President Truman renewed his call for universal military training in his 1948 state-of-the-Union message, but it failed to evoke a congressional response.

Finally, in March, 1948, the president called upon Congress to enact both a peacetime draft and universal military training. Congress, responding to the president's claim of increasing Cold War tensions, accepted the necessity for reenacting selective service, but refused to go along with universal military training. The Selective Service Act of 1948 was signed into law by the president on June 24. Its two-year tenure was about to lapse when hostilities broke out in Korea; Congress extended the legislation for an additional year.

The following year, 1951, Congress placed the Selective Service System on a permanent basis. The induction authority of the president would be renewable every four years, but the draft system would continue indefinitely. In addition, Congress accepted the principle of universal military training. The Universal Military Training and Service Act, approved on June 19, 1951, provided for a six-month training period for males between the ages of eighteen and nineteen. This program would go into operation whenever the president, by executive order, or Congress, by concurrent resolution, reduced or eliminated the existing requirement for two years of military service. The 1951 law also created a National Security Training Commission to outline a program of universal military training. The commission carried out this responsibility, and Congress held hearings on the proposed program early in 1952 but failed to enact any such proposal. In the face of much resistance to universal military training, Congress chose, instead, to continue relying upon selective service for military manpower requirements.

Throughout the 1950's and early 1960's the draft continued as an accepted part of the realities of American life. The Democratic presidential nominee in 1956, Adlai Stevenson, questioned its necessity without winning much public support for his position. The quadrennial renewals of the legislation by Congress provoked only brief, cursory debate. It was not until the escalation of the war in Vietnam, and the intensified opposition and resistance to that venture, that the legitimacy of the draft faced serious political challenge.

35

On May 8, 1940, a group of private citizens, the Military Training Camps Association, met in New York City to mark the twenty-fifth anniversary of the Plattsburg movement, the voluntary military training program which operated prior to America's involvement in World War I. One of their topics for discussion was how best to take advantage of prevailing public sentiment in order to institute a peacetime draft and reinvigorate the army. Their decision to draw up a compulsory military service bill, have it introduced in Congress, and commit their substantial resources to securing its enactment proved to be a major step in the eventual passage of the Selective Training and Service Act of 1940.

Military Training Camps Association's Proposal, 1940

THE REASONS FOR THE PROPOSED BILL

I.   We need not argue in this hour that no step should be omitted which substantially contributes to the safety of our country.

II.   We cannot insure ourselves against attack by neglecting our arms and practicing an inoffensive isolation. The strictest neutrality in the case of other nations has not kept the Nazis from attacking when self-interest indicated such a course. Once the European war is ended, there are salient on the very surface of our situation elements which might provoke attack. The sweeping claims of the Monroe Doctrine applied to the South American and West Indian possessions of the defeated adversaries of Germany present an obvious possibility of conflict. The problem of Canada may become insoluble except by force of arms. At the end of the present war we may find on one side the Germans, armed and powerful beyond any other people in the history of mankind, presiding over a lean and impoverished Europe, and on the other side the Americas ill-prepared for conflict, but abounding in living room, in wealth, in food, in all those things which Europe lacks and covets. Could any danger sign be clearer than the prospect of such a situation?

Reprinted from Military Training Camps Association, *A Proposed Bill to Protect the Integrity and Institutions of the United States Through a System of Selective Compulsory Military Training and Service* (New York, 1940).

III.   We have long thought of our navy and the oceans which divide our country from Europe and Asia as constituting a first line of defense so strong that the development of a powerful army was unnecessary. Recent events have shown that we cannot safely rely on that defense alone. Norway has been conquered and her great shipbuilding industry has passed into German hands; Holland has been conquered and her great shipping industry has passed into German hands; France has been defeated and her shipyards and her navy will presumably pass into German hands; Italy, with her fleet and her shipbuilding capacity, is subject to German disposition; and we cannot any longer wave aside the possibility that Britain may be conquered and that her shipyards and even her fleet, will come under German control.

If that occurs, Germany will at once outrank us in all the classes of fighting craft from the capital ship to the submarine and, what is worse, will outrank us in the number of ways available for the building of ships, with the machinery and skilled labor which go with them, in the ratio of approximately six to one. We can no longer count on control of the sea. Even if we assume an abandonment of the Pacific and a naval effort restricted to the North Atlantic Coast, the Caribbean and the Canal Zone, and take into account all the advantages which may be derived from fighting near our own bases, it becomes clear that we can not long rely with confident assurance on the power of the Navy to bar an aggressor from our shores.

IV.   If this be so, then we must have a second line of defense in the form of an army. If it is to be adequate to meet and turn back an aggressor, at our border, it will have to be much greater in numbers than our present establishment. The President talks of a force of 50,000 planes. The Navy has stated that the 10,000 planes which they desire would require a personnel of 300,000 men to operate and service them. We understand that the ratio of personnel to planes in the Army is somewhat lower, but it is clear that the air force alone, on the scale which the President has suggested, would require a personnel of a million men and probably somewhat more. No good army can be made entirely of an air force. There must be tanks, artillery, special services and infantry. Splendid mechanical equipment can to some extent take the place of numbers, but it is hard to see how an air force such as we contemplate, with a reasonable backing in the other arms, can be arrived at without bringing the total personnel of the Army and its trained reserves up to something in the neighborhood of 4,000,000 men. The very vastness of our territory, our double coast line and the delays necessarily incident to the movement of great forces of men and equipment over thousands of miles, make it impossible to concentrate all our power at a single predictable point of attack and give emphasis to the need for numbers.

V.   There is no prospect whatever of getting the number of men required for defense, or anything like a sufficient number, by voluntary enlistment. . . .

VI.   The only practicable way of procuring the requisite number of trained men for our land and naval forces is through a system of compulsory selective training in time of peace, and service in time of war.

(1)   To meet the requirement of modern warfare armies must be raised not haphazard and at the eleventh hour, but in advance of conflict by a systematic plan so designed that each man may serve in the capacity where he will be most effective, and the operation of basic industry, of agriculture and of the arts and sciences essential to war may be disrupted as little as possible. This can be accomplished only under an obligatory plan where the state determines who should serve and where and in what capacity. The voluntary system is not only utterly inadequate to raise modern armies, but is disruptive of industry and agriculture and of the specialties and sciences which are the allies of armies. Every democratic nation in every great modern war has gone ultimately to the obligatory system, and it has been our experience and the experience of the British in the World War and in this war, that volunteering after a while had to be prohibited on account of the confusion and disturbance which it produced.

(2)   The obligatory system, reasonably administered through the familiar system of local boards, is the closest approximation to practical justice which can be arrived at. It is as unjust to leave to the whim of the individual the question of whether he will or will not render the service which his country needs, as it would be to leave the payment of taxes to a like method of determination.

VII.   We need not argue at length that if there is to be an army, the training of its personnel cannot be safely delayed until the outbreak of war. The experience of England, which with her vast resources of men has found herself unable to put an effective army in the field because her compulsory service law and training of recruits were only initiated a year ago, is the most immediate and effective answer to the idea that a large and good army can be created on the spur of the moment. The business of the soldier has grown more complex. The modern developments of technique have placed an emphasis on the time required for training. If men are to fight for the safety of their country we owe it to them that they shall not fight ill trained. For the sake of conserving life as well as for the sake of victory we should see to it that our training is systematic, adequate and unhurried and that our armies go into battle fortified and protected by real skill in arms.

There are only two courses open to us. We can neglect our defenses and live with a sense of insecurity and panic always just under the surface, watching the temper and fearing the reactions of the strong and aggressive, or we can tighten our belts, arm ourselves in full against possible conflict and live, not on sufferance and in fear but with the steady integrity of conscious strength. The first course is demoralizing and wretched; the second course alone is possible, and an essential link in the pursuit of that course is the obligatory training of an adequate, justly chosen portion of our manhood.

SUMMARY OF THE PROPOSED BILL

The essential features of the Bill are:

1.   The registration of all male citizens and male aliens between the ages of 18 and 65, with certain exceptions for members of the Army, the Navy, the National Guard, etc.

2.   The division of the registrants into two main categories:
    a) Men between 21 and 45, who are liable for eight months' military training and for service.
    b) Men between 18 and 21, and between 45 and 65 who are liable only for home defense training and service in or near their home communities.

3.   From the great pool formed by registrants between 21 and 45, provision is made for the selection by lot of men subject to training and service, and for a careful selective process from among these men, whereby such numbers of men as are required for the land and naval forces will be chosen for training and service, having due regard for the needs of industry and agriculture, the status of the registrant with respect to persons dependent upon him and other factors. The provisions for registration and liability for training and service, which are sweeping in nature, are to be carefully distinguished from the provisions as to induction for training and service, which would, in practice, be put into effect with as little economic disruption as possible. . . .

5.   Other features include provision for the punishment of any per-

son evading registration or service or abetting any such evasion, and provision for the vocational and educational training of men inducted for training and service.

6. The proposed law would become inoperative on May 15, 1945, unless continued in effect by Congress.

36

One of the bitterest opponents, and most articulate critics, of the pending draft legislation was the isolationist senator from Montana, Burton K. Wheeler. In a radio address delivered on August 15, 1940, Wheeler warned against enacting peacetime compulsory military training and thereby hastening the march toward war.

Burton K. Wheeler against Draft Legislation, 1940

MARCHING DOWN THE ROAD TO WAR

I have said in recent weeks that the United States is marching down the road to war. Peace time conscription is not only another step in that direction but it is the greatest step toward regimentation and militarism ever undertaken by the Congress of the United States. The General Staff has advocated it before, Secretary of War Stimson advocated it as far back as 1916 but the Congress never adopted it in peace time.

Those who advocate peace time conscription generally predicate their advocacy on two contentions. These contentions are: first, that large numbers of additional men are immediately needed for the army and navy and that this large number cannot be obtained by the traditional American method of voluntary enlistment; second, that conscription is the method of raising the needed men most consonant with a democratic form of government.

I challenge both of those contentions. . . .

That the military events of the last year and the existing world situation generally bespeak a need on the part of this nation for increased and more effective defense—only the most foolhardy would deny. But common sense also dictates the magnitude and imminence of the dangers.

Nothing is so certain in the life of man as death. Because of this most

From a radio address, National Broadcasting Company, August 15, 1940.

of our citizens carry insurance against death; yet, despite its certainty, few of us deem it wise to purchase so much insurance that in order to pay the premium we must starve ourselves and our families. The people desire to take out and pay for an adequate amount of insurance against a foreseeable danger, but they do not wish to assume a load of obligation so heavy that it will bring about the very event they seek to insure against.

I believe that while avoiding hysteria and foolish excesses, adequate sums of money should be appropriated to provide the army and navy with the most modern and efficient equipment obtainable, in ample quantity, and that steps should be taken to insure efficient production of military supplies by the nation's industry. I believe, however, and on this all expert opinion is in agreement, that it is more important for our troops to be thoroughly trained and expert in the new mechanical warfare, and ably commanded, than that they be merely numerous. A small but expert force of Germans seized all of Norway, a small but expert Finnish army held the Russian Goliath at bay for many months. But a large French army was quickly crushed—less by the enemy than by its own incompetent and, in many instances, traitorous generals.

How large an army do we want? Today our army stands at a strength of 255,000 officers and men and will soon be at its full authorized strength of 375,000. The National Guard stands at 230,000 men with the number increasing rapidly. The Navy has 146,000 men and officers and is increasing the number to 170,000. This does not take into consideration our other armed forces.

How much of an increase is desirable to provide for the national safety?

Outside the army, all the most eminent military authorities—Hanson W. Baldwin of the New York *Times*, Major George Fielding Eliot, Col. Frederick Palmer, Basil Walker, and many others—agree that a force of 400,000 to 600,000 would be entirely adequate.

In view of what has been printed in the press, it is surprising to find on turning to the statements of our highest army authorities that their views do not differ materially from the quoted views of the military experts. At the recent hearings before the Senate Military Affairs Committee, General Marshall, Chief of Staff of the War Department, testified that the Army wanted a peace-time strength of 375,000 men.

When the full testimony of General Marshall is supplemented by the testimony of General Shedd, Colonel Twaddle, and Major Hershey, all of whom testified for the General Staff, the following facts are ascertained:

1. The General Staff and the War Department see no need for millions of soldiers and freely confess that it would be both unwise and impossible to attempt to induct into the army any such huge force as the public is accustomed to hear named.

2. What the General Staff testified to was that it is necessary at the present time to increase the army's strength immediately from 255,000 to 375,000—and to increase the strength of the National Guard from 230,000 to 400,000—a total increase of 290,000 men. Thereafter, it may wish to step up the strength of the army further to 500,000 in order to place the army on a *full war footing*.

In other words, without conscription, we shall soon have an army of 900,000 men. General Marshall definitely stated that they could be obtained by enlistment but not, he thought, as quickly as necessary. I ask, for what purpose is it proposed to draft an additional 1,200,000 men? . . .

I believe that the testimony of the General Staff itself and the figures I have quoted definitely disprove the first and major contention of the proponents of conscription—that only by conscription can the men needed to meet the demands of national defense be secured.

But we are told that another reason why we should abandon all American traditions and adopt peace time conscription is because it is *so* fair and *so* democratic.

How can one say that conscription constitutes the essence of the democratic concept and is at the same time the chief hallmark of all those dictator regimes from which democracy has been completely and shamelessly banished. Where is conscription found in its fullest flower, where is it ennobled and glorified as the highest honor of the citizen, if not in those lands where militarism and totalitarianism have blanketed the populace, and stifled democracy, most completely?

Every nation must defend itself from invasion—that is the universal law of self-preservation. Every inhabitant of the land must be ready to contribute to its defense, even to laying down his life if need be.

To say, however, that every resident of a country must be prepared to defend the country from invasion even at the cost of his life if need be, is something very different from the proposition to turning over to one man the power to compel free citizens to spend part of their lives in the army, when men are available who are perfectly willing to make a career of this work.

To use a homely illustration no one can doubt that keeping the streets of our cities clean, free from pestilential and disease-breeding dirt, is a matter of the most immediate and vital concern to the inhabitants of every city and to the state. No one would dispute, either, that if some unforeseeable emergency arose every citizen in the city or state would be commanded to clean them if necessary to safeguard the public welfare. Yet, because this obligation is inherent in citizenship, no one has come forward to advocate that it is undemocratic to permit our streets to be cleaned by those who are willing to make this their work, nor would it be contended that street-cleaning should be performed by citizens conscripted for such purpose.

What has been said of street-cleaning is, of course, equally applicable to the occupations of firemen, policemen, transport workers and the like. The performance of all these tasks is vital to the functioning of our society and the welfare of our nation; in the absence of volunteers they would fall upon the general body of citizenry, but we have never found it necessary on democratic grounds to require every citizen to spend a year of his life cleaning streets.

The democracy which we hail in our country, and which we all seek jealously to guard, no doubt means different things to different people, but it is certain that to every one of us democracy means at least the right to choose freely our own occupations and to conduct our lives with the greatest amount of freedom consistent with the general welfare. I recognize that where the defense of the nation and the public weal are concerned, the rights of the individual must yield. But conversely, I believe that if the public necessity does not require, the essence of democracy is to leave the individual unmolested in the enjoyment of "the inalienable rights of life, liberty and the pursuit of happiness."

It is significant to point out here that the English guard their liberties more jealously than we do. In the World War, it was not until after the Battle of the Marne that England resorted to conscription. And while they were at war Australia and New Zealand defeated conscription in a public referendum. And *today*, Canada and Australia only resorted to conscription months after they entered this war, and even then with the provision that no conscript could be sent out of Canada or Australia.

Certainly, to many millions of Americans it will seem that if conscription in peace time is democracy, then democracy has reached its fullest flowering in lands across the waters which surround us—in Japan, in Germany, in Italy, in Russia.

Many sincere persons who view conscription with mistrust and dislike, nevertheless withhold their opposition on the ground that "it does not seem right that only the jobless and the low-paid worker should be obliged to join the Army." General Shedd probably referred to this aspect of the question when he said "they [the principles of conscription] spread the requirements of military service over the entire personnel in such a just and proper way. . . ."

In almost the next breath, however, General Shedd was explaining that if we had the compulsory selective service recommended by the General Staff it would be designed to select the "unimportant" men, while the important ones would not be inducted into the Army.

Said General Shedd, I quote, "Well, I believe it [voluntary enlistment] would tend more to disrupt the country, because you cannot pick and choose the *unimportant* man. I do not mean unimportant from his point of view; but unimportant in the whole economic life of our country." . . .

Is there anything democratic about a conscription law that grabs the unimportant man—the unskilled farm laborer—and sends him off to the trenches at $21 per month while the skilled man or the important man gets from $15 to $20 a day in the factory or draws down huge bonuses as president of a corporation? The son of a captain of industry is obviously "important" to business; he must prepare to take over his father's place. Mrs. Jones' son, an unemployed worker, is important only to the army. It is to Mrs. Jones' son that the army looks for recruits now, and it will be to him they will turn for conscription. The only question is: shall young Jones be induced to join the army voluntarily by offering him a decent rate of pay and a fair chance of promotion, or shall he be forced to join the army at $21 a month, whether he likes it or not? If there is any doubt about what the answer is, just ask young Jones.

But another reason for conscription was advanced by Secretary of War Stimson. Said Mr. Stimson:

"Conscription is necessary to impress upon the country the gravity of the world situation."

For Secretary Stimson it is not enough that the American people should arrive at its opinion of the world situation on the basis of free, open and rational consideration of the situation; it must be stampeded into a militaristic frame of mind, and made ready for any adventures the Secretary thinks necessary.

"Government by persuasion," said Secretary Stimson, "is very much slower than government by arbitrary force." . . . There are, however, still a few of us who believe "government by persuasion" still has virtues for which increased speed cannot compensate. Maybe Hitler made the trains run on time—but the German people are now paying the price in tears and blood and life.

I have suggested the reasons why the General Staff wants conscription. From the beginning of time the General Staffs of every country in the world have wanted conscription. That is part of militarism. I now ask, why do high administration officials and financiers with international connections urge it upon us? I am afraid that only the future will reveal this to us—but I say to you now that is NOT because they believe our shores or skies are in danger of invasion. For these men there is an entire hemisphere to be "defended." When men begin to envisage the defense of their country in terms of entire hemisphere, then, of course, millions upon millions of men are necessary.

It was in the name of *defense* of Germany that Hitler invaded Czecho-Slovakia. It was in the name of defense that Hitler invaded Poland, Belgium, Holland and Norway. In the name of *defense* Russia invaded little Finland. To what corners of the world is it now proposed or intended to send these millions of our men—in the name of defense? . . .

Some senators say the people want conscription. I challenge them to go to the country on that issue. I would like to have the New York lawyers, the Army General Staff, and any others who are advocating the passage of this Bill stand before the farmers, the workers, the mothers and fathers and tell them what a fine thing peace time conscription is for their boys. I would like to see a national referendum on the question of conscription. I would like to see those who will have to do the fighting and the dying decide this question.

The original Burke-Wadsworth Bill recited in its preamble that, I quote, "the Congress hereby declares that the integrity and institutions of the United States are gravely threatened." The Military Affairs Committee has stricken this clause from the revised Bill. I deeply deplore its omission from the present Bill.

For I say to you, and I say it to you with all the solemity of which I am capable: the integrity and institutions of the United States are indeed gravely threatened, and it is the Bill now before Congress and the hysteria which bred it which creates that threat.

If this Bill passes, it will slit the throat of the last Democracy still living, it will accord to Hitler his greatest and cheapest victory. On the headstone of American Democracy he will inscribe: "Here Lies The Foremost Victim Of The War Of Nerves."

37

John L. Lewis, president of the Congress of Industrial Organizations, was a fervent opponent of draft legislation. In the following statement of August 14, 1940, presented on the floor of the Senate by Senator Rush Holt of West Virginia, Lewis warned against our overreacting to a moment of crisis. There was no need to violate our traditions by enacting peacetime conscription; voluntarism, under the proper incentives, would suffice to develop an adequate fighting force.

John L. Lewis and the C.I.O. Position, 1940

The Congress of Industrial Organizations stands second to no one in its desire for effective national defense. It has, therefore, pledged itself to the fullest cooperation with proper defense measures.

In the establishment of adequate national defense, however, it is just as essential that unsound and unwise proposals be defeated as it is that proper measures be taken. In the excitement of a period of crisis measures are sometimes advanced so fundamentally in opposition to our national democratic traditions that their proponents would not dare propose them at any other time. It is our belief that peacetime military conscription is just such a measure.

The very genesis of the measure for peacetime conscription is open to serious question.

1.   The proposed bill was drawn up under unofficial auspices by private citizens, although no measure could be more affected with the public interest.

2.   The bill was launched by a group of prominent New York corporation lawyers and other wealthy persons. Neither these persons nor the Congressional sponsors of the bill have been notable in their support of legislation for the welfare of the common people of this country.

3.   The measure was not formally requested of Congress by the President of the United States, the responsible head of preparation for national defense.

4.   At their recent national conventions both of the major political parties gave the proposal for conscription consideration, but neither saw fit to give endorsement to the proposal.

Briefly, these are the reasons which have impelled the C.I.O. to oppose the pending measures:

1.   There is a better way to recruit a proper army for defense than conscription.

Reprinted from the *Congressional Record*, 76th Cong., 2d sess., Vol. 86 (August 22, 1940), p. 10722.

Voluntary enlistment under terms which have real concern for the needs of the individual would quickly provide a suitable army. The period of enlistment should be shortened to one year. The pay should be raised at least to compare with that of the self-respecting workman. The right to return to private employment should be protected. Provision should be made for the continuation of social security protection during the period of such enlistment. Private debts should be either assumed or suspended. Officers' commissions should be more freely open to enlisted men, so that an army career is open to men from the ranks. Under such circumstances the most effective and loyal kind of an army could be raised, with much less cost to the nation than the enormous expenditures necessary for conscription.

2. Military conscription now would establish the principle in this nation that the lives of our young men are less privileged than the profit rights of dollars.

Today the Nation is watching the shameful spectacle of our Government yielding to the imperious demands of corporate industry for vast tax concessions and enormous loans as a precondition to manufacturing arms. The same interests who thus strangle our national defense call loudly for the forcible conscription of our young men. They claim in one breath that no dollar will be turned to the defense of our nation without a fat and untaxed profit being assured, while almost at the same moment they call upon our young men, most of them workers, to cast aside their liberty and sacrifice their ambitions or suffer punishment as a felon. It would be a terrible day in American history should our young men be forced to the draft while industry is free to lay down its ultimatums to the government.

3. Forced military service in peacetime would be an alarming departure from the basic principles of our democracy. It is the first step toward the break-down of those free institutions which we seek to protect.

Citizens who become subject to conscription lose a substantial part of those civil rights and liberties which distinguish a free democracy from a totalitarian state.

Such conscription would further establish in the minds of the young people of the Nation the idea that voluntary loyalty to the Nation is no longer a necessary virtue. It would introduce them to the principle of compulsion, a principle native to the Fascist state and alien to our own.

4. The production of equipment for an army has lagged far behind the enlistments into the military service.

Already there are more men available to the Army and the National

Guard than can be equipped for some time to come. The present speed of enlistments is far more rapid than the provision of equipment. From the point of effective defense, an efficient, loyal, and highly trained army, highly mechanized, is many times more efficient than a sullen, ill-equipped, poorly trained, conscript army of three times the size. Conscription now would be an enormous waste of money and manpower.

5. The entire fabric of the nation, both industrial and social, would be torn by conscription. The dislocations in industrial production and in community life caused by conscription would take years to heal.

Therefore, the C.I.O. is opposed to provision for peacetime conscription as a measure inimical to the most effective kind of national defense and alien to the democratic way of life.

38

The House vote on the draft bill came ten days after its success in the Senate, and, once again, the bill was approved—this time by a vote of 263–149. The bill was then signed by the president on September 16, 1940; America, for the first time, had peacetime conscription. The law required that all males between the ages of twenty-one and thirty-six register for the draft. The period of service was to be for one year unless the Congress were to declare the national interest to be imperiled, in which case the term of service might be extended. No more than 900,000 men could be in training under the act at any one time, and no draftees could be sent outside the Western Hemisphere. October 16 was selected as the registration date, and over 16,000,000 men signed up on that day.

Through the implementation of this legislation, the government developed a well-functioning process of inducting manpower and thus was able, after Pearl Harbor, to shift from a peacetime to a wartime footing, in this area at least, without much difficulty.

World War II Draft Law, 1940

AN ACT

To provide for the common defense by increasing the personnel of the armed forces of the United States and providing for its training.

Reprinted from Public Law Number 783, 76th Cong., 2d sess.

Be it enacted by the Senate and House of Representatives of the United States of America in Congress assembled, That (a) the Congress hereby declares that is imperative to increase and train the personnel of the armed forces of the United States.

(b) The Congress further declares that in a free society the obligations and privileges of military training and service should be shared generally in accordance with a fair and just system of selective compulsory military training and service.

(c) The Congress further declares, in accordance with our traditional military policy as expressed in the National Defense Act of 1916, as amended, that it is essential that the strength and organization of the National Guard, as an integral part of the first-line defenses of this Nation, be at all times maintained and assured. To this end, it is the intent of the Congress that whenever the Congress shall determine that troops are needed for the national security in excess of those of the Regular Army and those in active training and service under section 3 (b), the National Guard of the United States, or such part thereof as may be necessary, shall be ordered to active Federal service and continued therein so long as such necessity exists.

Sec. 2. Except as otherwise provided in this Act, it shall be the duty of every male citizen of the United States, and of every male alien residing in the United States, who, on the day or days fixed for the first or any subsequent registration, is between the ages of twenty-one and thirty-six, to present himself for and submit to registration at such time or times and place or places, and in such manner and in such age group or groups, as shall be determined by rules and regulations prescribed hereunder.

Sec. 3 (a) Except as otherwise provided in this Act, every male citizen of the United States, and every male alien residing in the United States who has declared his intention to become such a citizen, between the ages of twenty-one and thirty-six at the time fixed for his registration, shall be liable for training and service in the land or naval forces of the United States. The President is authorized from time to time, whether or not a state of war exists, to select and induct into the land and naval forces of the United States for training and service, in the manner provided in this Act, such number of men as in his judgment is required for such forces in the national interest: *Provided,* That within the limits of the quota determined under section 4 (b) for the subdivision in which he resides, any person, regardless of race or color, between the ages of eighteen and thirty-six, shall be afforded an opportunity to volunteer for induction into the land or naval forces of the United States for the training and service prescribed in subsection (b), but no person who so volunteers shall be inducted for such training and service so long as he is deferred after classification: *Provided further*, That no man shall be inducted for training and service under this Act unless and until he is acceptable to the land or naval forces for such training and service and his physical and mental fitness for such training and service has been satisfactorily determined: *Provided further*, That no men shall be inducted for such training and service until adequate provision shall have been made for such shelter, sanitary facilities, water supplies, heating and lighting arrangements, medical care, and hospital accommodations, for such men, as may be determined by the Secretary of War or the Secretary of the Navy, as the case may be, to be essential to public and personal health: *Provided further*, That except in time of war there shall not be in active training or service in the land forces of the United States at any one time under subsection (b) more than nine hundred thousand men inducted under the provisions of this Act. The men inducted into the land or naval forces for training and service under this Act shall be assigned to camps or units of such forces.

(b) Each man inducted under the provisions of subsection (a) shall serve for a training and service period of twelve consecutive months, unless sooner discharged, except that whenever the Congress has declared that the national interest is imperiled, such twelve-month period may be extended by the President to such time as may be necessary in the interests of national defense.

(c) Each such man, after the completion of his period of training and service under subsection (b), shall be transferred to a reserve component of the land or naval forces of the United States; and until he attains the age of forty-five, or until the expiration of a period of ten years after such transfer, or until he is discharged from such reserve component, whichever occurs first, he shall be deemed to be a member of such reserve component and shall be subject to such additional training and service as may now or hereafter be prescribed by law: *Provided*, That any man who completes at least twelve months' training and service in the land forces under subsection (b), and who thereafter serves satisfactorily in the Regular Army or in the active National Guard for a period of at least two years, shall, in time of peace, be relieved from any liability to serve in any reserve component of the land or Naval forces of the United States and from further liability for the training and service under subsection (b), but nothing in this subsection shall be construed to prevent any such man, while in a reserve component of such forces, from being ordered or called to active duty, in such forces.

(d) With respect to the men inducted for training and service under this Act there shall be paid, allowed, and extended the same pay, allowances, pensions, disability and death compensation, and other benefits as are provided by law in the case of other enlisted men of like grades and length of service of that component of the land or naval forces to which they are assigned, and after transfer to a reserve component of the land or naval forces as provided in subsection (c) there shall be paid, allowed, and extended with respect to them the same benefits as are provided by law in like cases with respect to other members of such reserve component. Men in such training and service and men who have been so transferred to reserve components shall have an opportunity to qualify for promotion.

(e) Persons inducted into the land forces of the United States under this Act shall not be employed beyond the limits of the Western Hemisphere except in the Territories and possessions of the United States, including the Philippine Islands.

(f) Nothing contained in this or any other Act shall be construed as forbidding the payment of compensation by any person, firm, or corporation to persons inducted into the land or naval forces of the United States for training and service under this Act, or to members of the reserve components of such forces now or hereafter on any type of active duty, who, prior to their induction or commencement of active duty, were receiving compensation from such person, firm, or corporation.

Sec. 4 (a) The selection of men for training and service under section 3 (other than those who are voluntarily inducted pursuant to this Act) shall be made in an impartial manner, under such rules and regulations as the President may prescribe, from the men who are liable for such training and service and who at the time of selection are registered and classified but not deferred or exempted: *Provided,* That in the selection and training of men under this Act, and in the interpretation and execution of the provisions of this Act, there shall be no discrimination against any person on account of race or color.

(b) Quotas of men to be inducted for training and service under this Act shall be determined for each State, Territory, and the District of Columbia, and for subdivisions thereof, on the basis of the actual number of men in the several States, Territories, and the District of Columbia, and the subdivisions thereof, who are liable for such training and service but who are not deferred after classification, except that credits shall be given in fixing such quotas for residents of such subdivisions who are in the land and naval forces of the United States on the date fixed for determining such quotas. After such quotas are fixed, credits shall be given in filling such quotas for residents of such subdivisions who subsequently become members of such forces. Until the actual numbers necessary for determining the quotas are known, the quotas may be based on estimates, and subsequent adjustments therein shall be made when such actual numbers are known. All computations under this subsection shall be made in accordance with such rules and regulations as the President may prescribe. . . .

Sec. 5

(d) Regular or duly ordained ministers of religion, and students who are preparing for the ministry in theological or divinity schools recognized as such for more than one year prior to the date of enactment of this Act, shall be exempt from training and service (but not from registration) under this Act.

(e) The President is authorized, under such rules and regulations as he may prescribe, to provide for the deferment from training and service under this Act in the land and naval forces of the United States of those men whose employment in industry, agriculture, or other occupations or employment, or whose activity in other endeavors, is found in accordance with section 10 (a) (2) to be necessary to the maintenance of the national health, safety, or interest. The President is also authorized, under such rules and regulations as he may prescribe, to provide for the deferment from training and service under this Act in the land and naval forces of the United States (1) of those men in a status with respect to persons dependent upon them for support which renders their deferment advisable, and (2) of those men found to be physically, mentally, or morally deficient or defective. No deferment from such training and service shall be made in the case of any individual except upon the basis of the status of such individual, and no such deferment shall be made of individuals by occupational groups or of groups of individuals in any plant or institution.

(f) Any person who, during the year 1940, entered upon attendance for the academic year 1940–1941—

(1) at any college or university which grants a degree in arts or science, to pursue a course of instruction satisfactory completion of which is prescribed by such college or university as a prerequisite to either of such degrees; or

(2) at any university described in paragraph (1), to pursue a course of instruction to the pursuit of which a degree in arts or science is pre-

scribed by such university as a prerequisite; and who, while pursuing such course of instruction at such college or university, is selected for training and service under this Act prior to the end of such academic year, or prior to July 1, 1941, whichever occurs first, shall, upon his request, be deferred from induction into the land or naval forces for such training and service until the end of such academic year, but in no event later than July 1, 1941.

(g) Nothing contained in this Act shall be construed to require any person to be subject to combatant training and service in the land or naval forces of the United States who, by reason of religious training and belief, is conscientiously opposed to participation in war in any form. Any such person claiming such exemption from combatant training and service because of such conscientious objections whose claim is sustained by the local board shall, if he is inducted into the land or naval forces under this Act, be assigned to noncombatant service as defined by the President, or shall, if he is found to be conscientiously opposed to participation in such noncombatant service, in lieu of such induction, be assigned to work of national importance under civilian direction. Any such person claiming such exemption from combatant training and service because of such conscientious objections shall, if such claim is not sustained by the local board, be entitled to an appeal to the appropriate appeal board provided for in section 10 (a) (2). Upon the filing of such appeal with the appeal board, the appeal board shall forthwith refer the matter to the Department of Justice for inquiry and hearing by the Department or the proper agency thereof. After appropriate inquiry by such agency, a hearing shall be held by the Department of Justice with respect to the character and good faith of the objections of the person concerned, and such person shall be notified of the time and place of such hearing. The Department shall, after such hearing, if the objections are found to be sustained, recommend to the appeal board (1) that if the objector is inducted into the land or naval forces under this Act, he shall be assigned to noncombatant service as defined by the President, or (2) that if the objector is found to be conscientiously opposed to participation in such noncombatant service, he shall in lieu of such induction be assigned to work of national importance under civilian direction. If after such hearing the Department finds that his objections are not sustained, it shall recommend to the appeal board that such objections be not sustained. The appeal board shall give consideration to but shall not be bound to follow the recommendation of the Department of Justice together with the record on appeal from the local board in making its decision. Each person whose claim for exemption from combatant training and service because of conscientious objections is sustained shall be listed by the local board on a register of conscientious objectors.

(h) No exception from registration, or exemption or deferment from training and service, under this Act, shall continue after the cause therefor ceases to exist.

Sec. 6 The President shall have authority to induct into the land and naval forces of the United States under this Act no greater number of men than the Congress shall hereafter make specific appropriation for from time to time.

Sec. 7 No bounty shall be paid to induce any person to enlist in or be inducted into the land or naval forces of the United States: *Provided,* that the clothing or enlistment allowances authorized by law shall not be regarded as bounties within the meaning of this section. No person liable for service in such forces shall be permitted or allowed to furnish a substitute for such service; no substitute as such shall be received, enlisted, enrolled, or inducted into the land or naval forces of the United States; and no person liable for training and service in such forces under section 3 shall be permitted to escape such training and service or be discharged therefrom prior to the expiration of his period of such training and service by the payment of money or any other valuable thing whatsoever as consideration for his release from such training and service or liability therefor. . . .

Sec. 8

(b) In the case of any such person who, in order to perform such training and service, has left or leaves a position, other than a temporary position, in the employ of any employer and who (1) receives such certificate, (2) is still qualified to perform the duties of such position, and (3) makes application for reemployment within forty days after he is relieved from such training and service—

(A) if such position was in the employ of the United States Government, its Territories or possessions, or the District of Columbia, such person shall be restored to such position or to a position of like seniority, status, and pay;

(B) if such position was in the employ of a private employer, such employer shall restore such person to such position or to a position of like seniority, status, and pay unless the employer's circumstances have so changed as to make it impossible or unreasonable to do so;

(C) if such position was in the employ of any State or political subdivision thereof, it is hereby declared to be the sense of the

Congress that such person should be restored to such position or to a position of like seniority, status, and pay.

(c) Any person who is restored to a position in accordance with the provisions of paragraph (A) or (B) of subsection (b) shall be considered as having been on furlough or leave of absence during his period of training and service in the land or naval forces, shall be so restored without loss of seniority, shall be entitled to participate in insurance or other benefits offered by the employer pursuant to established rules and practices relating to employees on furlough or leave of absence in effect with the employer at the time such person was inducted into such forces, and shall not be discharged from such position without cause within one year after such restoration. . . .

Sec. 9 The President is empowered, through the head of the War Department or the Navy Department of the Government, in addition to the present authorized methods of purchase or procurement, to place an order with any individual, firm, association, company, corporation, or organized manufacturing industry for such product or material as may be required, and which is of the nature and kind usually produced or capable of being produced by such individual, firm, company, association, corporation, or organized manufacturing industry.

Compliance with all such orders for products or material shall be obligatory on any individual firm, association, company, corporation, or organized manufacturing industry or the responsible head or heads thereof and shall take precedence over all other orders and contracts theretofore placed with such individual, firm, company, association, corporation, or organized manufacturing industry, and any individual, firm, association, company, corporation, or organized manufacturing industry or the responsible head or heads thereof owning or operating any plant equipped for the manufacture of arms or ammunition or parts of ammunition, or any necessary supplies or equipment for the Army or Navy, and any individual, firm, association, company, corporation, or organized manufacturing industry or the responsible head or heads thereof owning or operating any manufacturing plant, which, in the opinion of the Secretary of War or the Secretary of the Navy shall be capable of being readily transformed into a plant for the manufacture of arms or ammunition, or parts thereof, or other necessary supplies or equipment, who shall refuse to give to the United States such preference in the matter of the execution of orders, or who shall refuse to manufacture the kind, quantity, or quality of arms or ammunition, or the parts thereof, or any necessary supplies or equipment, as ordered by

the Secretary of War or the Secretary of the Navy, or who shall refuse
to furnish such arms, ammunition, or parts of ammunition, or other
supplies or equipment, at a reasonable price as determined by the
Secretary of War or the Secretary of the Navy, as the case may be, then
and in either such case, the President, through the head of the War or
Navy Departments of the Government, in addition to the present authorized methods of purchase or procurement, is hereby authorized
to take immediate possession of any such plant or plants, and through
the appropriate branch, bureau, or department of the Army or Navy to
manufacture therein such product or material as may be required, and
any individual, firm, company, association, or corporation, or organized
manufacturing industry or the responsible head or heads thereof, failing
to comply with the provisions of this section shall be deemed guilty of
a felony, and upon conviction shall be punished by imprisonment for
not more than three years and a fine not exceeding $50,000. . . .

Sec. 10. (a) The President is authorized—

(1) to prescribe the necessary rules and regulations to carry out
the provisions of this Act;

(2) to create and establish a Selective Service System, and shall
provide for the classification of registrants and of persons who volunteer for induction under this Act on the basis of availability for
training and service, and shall establish within the Selective Service
System civilian local boards and such other civilian agencies, including appeal boards and agencies of appeal, as may be necessary
to carry out the provisions of this Act. There shall be created one
or more local boards in each county or political subdivision corresponding thereto of each State, Territory, and the District of Columbia. Each local board shall consist of three or more members
to be appointed by the President, from recommendations made by
the respective Governors or comparable executive officials. No
member of any such local board shall be a member of the land or
naval forces of the United States, but each member of any such
local board shall be a civilian who is a citizen of the United States
residing in the county or political subdivision corresponding thereto
in which such local board has jurisdiction under rules and regulations prescribed by the President. Such local boards, under rules
and regulations prescribed by the President, shall have power
within their respective jurisdictions to hear and determine, subject
to the right of appeal to the appeal boards herein authorized, all
questions or claims with respect to inclusion for, or exemption or

deferment from, training and service under this Act of all individuals within the jurisdiction of such local boards. The decisions of such local boards shall be final except where an appeal is authorized in accordance with such rules and regulations as the President may prescribe. Appeal boards and agencies of appeal within the Selective Service System shall be composed of civilians who are citizens of the United States. No person who is an officer, member, agent, or employee of the Selective Service System, or of any such local or appeal board or other agency, shall be excepted from registration, or deferred from training and service, as provided for in this Act, by reason of his status as such officer, member, agent, or employee;

(3) to appoint by and with the advice and consent of the Senate, and fix the compensation at a rate not in excess of $10,000 per annum, of a Director of Selective Service who shall be directly responsible to him and to appoint and fix the compensation of such other officers, agents, and employees as he may deem necessary to carry out the provisions of this Act. . . .

Sec. 11. Any person charged as herein provided with the duty of carrying out any of the provisions of this Act, or the rules or regulations made or directions given thereunder, who shall knowingly fail or neglect to perform such duty, and any person charged with such duty, or having and exercising any authority under said Act, rules, regulations, or directions who shall knowingly make, or be a party to the making, of any false, improper, or incorrect registration, classification, physical or mental examination, deferment, induction, enrollment, or muster, and any person who shall knowingly make, or be a party to the making of, any false statement or certificate as to the fitness or unfitness or liability or nonliability of himself or any other person for service under the provisions of this Act, or rules, regulations, or directions made pursuant thereto, or who otherwise evades registration or service in the land or naval forces or any of the requirements of this Act, or who knowingly counsels, aids, or abets another to evade registration or service in the land or naval forces or any of the requirements of this Act, or of said rules, regulations, or directions, or who in any manner shall knowingly fail or neglect to perform any duty required of him under or in the execution of this Act, or rules or regulations made pursuant to this Act, or any person or persons who shall knowingly hinder or interfere in any way by force or violence with the administration of this Act or the rules or regulations made pursuant thereto, or conspire to do so, shall, upon conviction in the district court of the United States having jurisdiction thereof, be punished by imprisonment for not more than five years or a fine of not more than $10,000, or by both such fine and imprisonment, or if subject to military or naval law may be tried by court martial, and, on conviction, shall suffer such punishment as a court martial may direct. No person shall be tried by any military or naval court martial in any case arising under this Act unless such person has been actually inducted for the training and service prescribed under this Act or unless he is subject to trial by court martial under laws in force prior to the enactment of this Act. Precedence shall be given by courts to the trial of cases arising under this Act. . . .

Sec. 18. This Act may be cited as the "Selective Training and Service Act of 1940."

39

The 1940 draft act provided that conscientious objectors could serve either in a noncombatant status in the army or in work of national importance under civilian direction. Although the act still retained a rather limited definition of conscientious objection, it was an advance over its predecessor in that it provided an option of alternative service not under military direction. The Civilian Public Service Camps were established, and over twelve thousand conscientious objectors made up the work force. Another six thousand objectors, two-thirds of whom were Jehovah's Witnesses seeking exemption as ministers, were convicted of violations of the draft act and sentenced to prison.

Arle Brooks, an ordained minister of the Disciples of Christ, refused to even register for the draft. Tried and found guilty, Brooks made the following statement to the court prior to sentencing.

Arle Brooks on Being Convicted for Draft Evasion

My conscience forbade me to register under the Selective Service Training Act of 1940.

The present wars are the natural product of our economic system and our way of living. Preparation for war is easier than going through the

Reprinted from *Christian Century*, Vol. 58, (Feb. 5, 1941), p. 181.

painful process of reconstructing our social and economic system and improving our own lives.

Wars destroy human lives. Individuals have the right to give their lives for a cause. They have no right to take the life of another. Wars are destructive, futile and immoral. Wars have failed to solve the basic problems of the world. Participation in war to settle international or national differences does not do justice to man's intelligence.

The people of America are filled with fear of an invasion. Are we so morally weak that the power of one man could control 130,000,000 free people? Free people cannot be enslaved unless they allow it. Are we too lethargic to find a better method of settling international affairs? The people of India have almost won their freedom from Great Britain without firing a shot. They are willing to give their lives but refuse to take the lives of the British soldiers.

Democracy does not mean a blind following of the will of the majority. In a democracy the minority has a right and a duty to follow its ideals. Sometimes the ideals of the minority have eventually been adopted by the majority. Gandhi said: "We are sunk so low that we fancy that it is our duty and our religion to do what the law lays down. If man will only realize that it is unmanly to obey laws that are unjust no man's tyranny will enslave him. . . . It is a superstition and an ungodly thing to believe that an act of a majority binds a minority."

I believe in and have worked for the brotherhood of man, which is the highest form of democracy and which recognizes no national boundaries. I have worked with children of the slums of Chicago, with transients, relief people, prisoners in Texas, and with sharecroppers in Mississippi.

⌈Conscription is a denial of the democracy for which I have worked. Under conscription the individual is required blindly to obey his superior officer even when the superior officer is wrong. Hitler could not wage his war if the people of Germany had not granted him the power to conscript them. The United States is adopting a system of conscription which may produce tyranny instead of freedom.⌋

I cannot agree with those who believe that registration is a mere census. Registration is the first and necessary step in conscription. My conscience will not permit me to take this first step.

As a minister I could have received complete exemption. I felt it my moral duty to do all within my power to protest against conscription which will eventually weaken and destroy democracy. I am not evading the draft. I am opposing it. I am defending democracy.

40

While the Second World War was still raging, plans were being made to extend the draft into peacetime and insure universal military training. As early as 1943 a bill to that effect had been introduced in the Congress, and, with the end of the war in sight, a number of groups began to organize to further this proposal. President Franklin Roosevelt, in his first message to the Seventy-ninth Congress on January 6, 1945, gave his unqualified support to a system of universal military training in peacetime.

One of the principal opponents of this growing movement was Senator Robert Taft. In a speech delivered at Gettysburg National Cemetery, he argued the case against universal military training, claiming it would have a dire effect upon our society. "Military conscription is essentially totalitarian," Taft charged, and it would be a fundamental error for America to institutionalize such an alien phenomenon.

Robert Taft's Speech against Universal Military Training, 1945

It seems improbable to me that the training of a million and a quarter boys a year would ever be necessary. The vast reserve provided could only be needed for a great overseas expedition like that in which we are now engaged. For such an expedition, it would take several years to organize ships, planes, and munitions, just as it did in this war. We would surely have to have new modern equipment in many fields, and it would take longer to build it than it would to train the men, as we found in this war. It would seem that for sudden attack, or for attack from the air or from attack by rockets the great mass of millions of reserves would be of little value. I should think we rather need an expert army with the most modern weapons. In the event of a sudden attack, our main reliance would have to be a regular army of highly trained and technically trained men, and during such an attack they would not be much aided by 10,000,000 reserves. The argument that we can save in the size of a professional army by having many millions of reserves

Reprinted from a speech presented at Gettysburg National Cemetery, May 30, 1945; reprinted in the *Congressional Record*, 79th Cong., 1st sess., Vol. 91, pp. A2814–16.

bears all the earmarks of a propaganda argument instead of one based on common sense.

Having determined that we need an army of a certain size, with certain reserves, we could then decide whether we could get it by voluntary means in the American tradition. Suppose we need a million men in the armed forces. We expect to have at last 50,000,000 people working at civilian jobs in this country. Surely we can make the army sufficiently attractive as an occupation for 2 per cent of these to be willing to volunteer. With good pay, reasonable treatment for men and their families, and provision for retraining and retirement when a man is too old to stay in the army, I don't see why army life cannot be made just as attractive as working daily on a machine, mining coal, or engaging in hundreds of other occupations. Many jobs in the army should give highly technical training with interesting knowledge which makes the trainees capable of advancement in other activities in life.

To provide the necessary reserves, it could be made worth the while of many boys to take the necessary training. Many alternative plans have been suggested to a year's conscription. For instance, adequate reserves might be provided by training 200,000 boys in each age group. It would be possible to obtain volunteers in that number for a three months course and basic training during one summer, courses in school and a later three months summer course in the field. The boys could be paid a sum which would assist them in their regular education during the winter. Additional courses could be provided for those who wish to become reserve officers. What I have suggested is only one idea and there may be many others. The army will immediately criticize any plan, because they are determined to have conscription. They want the boys for twelve months consecutively because they want to change their habits of thought, to make them soldiers, if you please, for the rest of their lives. Nothing less will do. We are indeed bankrupt of ideas if we cannot provide a method by which necessary military forces and reserves are provided by an American voluntary system.

The other arguments for conscription seem to me almost too trivial to discuss. It is said that it will teach the boys discipline and that they need it. My own opinion is that we need more initiative and original thinking and less discipline rather than more. Our present army is not the most disciplined army in the world, but there isn't any better army for the simple reason that the boys do some thinking for themselves.

It is said that the army will improve their health, and that they need it because so many failed to pass the strict health requirements of the army. As a matter of fact, the great bulk of defects were those relating to teeth, eyes, nerves, mental and heart conditions, all of which had arisen long before the age of conscription. There is nothing to show that the army would conscript any of these boys. To improve their health, we must reach them at a much younger age.

The argument that it would improve the morals of our boys has almost been dropped because of its foolishness. If there is one place where morals will not be improved, it is in the vicinity of army camps.

It is true that there are some boys who are benefited by army control, but to improve a few, let us not change the whole character of the American life which I believe has been the cause of success in this war.

It is said that we are going to teach the boys citizenship in the camps. This argument makes clear a real danger in the whole system. By handing boys over for twelve months to the arbitrary and complete domination of the government, we put it in the power of the government to indoctrinate them with the political doctrines then popular with the government. It has all the dangers of federal education and none of its advantages. Attempts along this line have been made with the present army, and a large amount of propaganda sent out to be taught to the soldiers. In wartime it is bad enough; in peacetime, it would be intolerable.

Some have supported this project on the ground that the training is only to be part military and a considerable amount of it is to be character training along other lines. We have already a complete school system in this country. If it isn't adequate and does not give education in citizenship, we can well spend our time and money in trying to improve that system. As a matter of fact, it is already the finest system of education the world has ever seen.

Military conscription is essentially totalitarian. It has been established for the most part by totalitarian countries and their dictators led by Napoleon and Bismarck. It has heretofore been established by aggressor countries. It is said it would insure peace by emphasizing the tremendous military potential of this country. Surely we have emphasized that enough in this war. No one can doubt it. On the contrary, if we establish conscription every other nation in the world will feel obliged to do the same. It would set up militarism on a high pedestal throughout the world as the goal of all the world. Militarism has always led to war and not to peace. Conscription was no insurance of victory in France, in Germany, or in Italy. The countries with military conscription found that it was only an incident and not the determining factor in defense or in victory.

Military training by conscription means the complete regimentation of the individual at his most formative period for a period of twelve months. If we admit that in peacetime we can deprive a man of all liberty and voice and freedom of action, if we can take him from his family and his home, that we can do the same with labor, we can order the farmer to produce and we can take over any business. If we can draft men, it is difficult to find an argument against drafting capital. Those who enthusiastically orate of returning to free enterprise and at the same time advocate peacetime conscription are blind to the implications of this policy. They are utterly inconsistent in their position. Because of its psychological effect on every citizen, because it is the most extreme form of compulsion, military conscription will be more the test of our whole philosophy than any other policy. Some say it is unconstitutional. It makes very little difference whether it actually violates the terms of the Constitution. It is against the fundamental policy of America and the American nation. If adopted, it will color our whole future. We shall have fought to abolish totalitarianism in the world, only to set it up in the United States.

Government by the people can only exist if the people are individuals who think. It can only exist if the individual is free to rule the state and if he is not ruled by the state. We must be constantly vigilant to keep alive the thinking of freemen, and there is no such threat to that thinking as the course which would impose on the nation compulsory military training.

41

A House Select Committee on Postwar Military Policy, chaired by Congressman Clifton A. Woodrum of Virginia, held a series of hearings in June, 1945, on the question of the structure of the nation's peacetime military establishment. Appearing before the committee, Chief of Staff General George C. Marshall argued strenuously for the enactment of universal military training, "a supremely democratic procedure." The following excerpt is from General Marshall's prepared statement and his questioning by Chairman Woodrum.

George C. Marshall on Universal Military Training, 1945

The problem of the maintenance of the future peace of the world directly involves the problem of the postwar military policy of the United States. The decision regarding the military policy of the United States is directly related to the democratic processes of the government, really meaning the reactions of the people to the services the individual citizen might be required to render the government.

Another factor is heavily though indirectly involved and that is consideration of the taxes to be imposed on the citizen for the maintenance of the military policy, to which must be added the very positive reaction of the citizen regarding the taxes to which he must submit to meet the huge existing war debt.

Any fixed legal demand on the citizen for services to the community, the state, or the Federal Government, is quite naturally questioned by the majority and is usually bitterly opposed by at least an articulate minority.

The question of universal military training involves all of the foregoing factors, and the great difficulty, as I see it, in reaching a correct decision, will be to avoid details and to get clearly focused in our minds what are the real necessities of the situation, and what will be the best method for meeting them, having in mind our traditions, our national characteristics and the military experience of this government during its short life of 156 years among the nations of the world.

I think it would be best for me to state in the briefest possible form my own personal conclusions in the matter, which are as follows:

A decision regarding the general military policy of this government is a matter of urgent necessity at this time.

A large standing army is not an acceptable solution for three reasons: Its cost would be prohibitive; the necessary men to fill its ranks could not be hired in time of peace; and it would be repugnant to the American people. Therefore some other solution must be found.

To support our determination to maintain the peace, the world must recognize our military powers as realistic and not as a remote potential.

Whatever military system we plan we must have a thorough understanding of the practicability of obtaining the annual appropriations necessary.

I know of no system other than universal military training which will meet the requirements I have just outlined, together with an effective

Reprinted from *Hearings of the House Select Committee on Postwar Military Policy*, 79th Cong., 1st sess., 1945, pp. 567–71.

program for industrial mobilization and continuous scientific research.

Until the settlement of the terms of the peace it will be impossible to determine the strength of the postwar military forces to be maintained on an active status. We shall not know until then just what our military obligations or requirements are to be. But it is clear to me that whatever the terms of peace, the fundamental basis of our defense must be universal military training. No other practical solution has been offered.

The acceptance at the present time of a general policy recognizing the necessity for universal military training would in my opinion have a far-reaching effect in obtaining a satisfactory international agreement for the terms of the peace. It would certainly be in keeping with the tragic lessons of our history. It would be a supremely democratic procedure, and would not involve the individual in military service except by further act of Congress and approval of the President. It would be far more economical than any other method for maintaining military power. If we are to have an effective and economical transition from our vast war establishment to our peace establishment, we must now decide on the fundamental basis on which we are to proceed. . . .

It appears to me that those who object to compulsory military training have offered no practical solution for obtaining what is in all our minds today, and that is some guaranty for the future peace of the world.

Whether or not army training methods would have an unfortunate influence on the individual can be determined I think from the experience of this war. I assert that we have produced a democratic army, one composed of self-respecting soldiers whose spirit has not been crushed and who have shown splendid evidence of high morale. I submit that the army has demonstrated that it can efficiently and expeditiously instruct men and that it does this without detriment to the mind and character of the individual, rather the contrary. I firmly believe that universal training would be a stimulant to education rather than a deterrent. It would be a perfect demonstration of democracy, with rich and poor alike, side by side, rendering a common service.

Mr. Woodrum: General, we appreciate very much that statement, and, if you do not object, I would like to ask you to elaborate just a little on one very significant statement . . . to the effect that, "The acceptance at the present time of a general policy recognizing the necessity for universal military training would in my opinion have a far-reaching effect in obtaining a satisfactory international agreement for the terms of the peace."

Now, any number of individuals and organizations appearing before this committee have insisted that any action now, and even any discussion now of military preparedness in the postwar period, would indicate our lack of faith and confidence in the efforts made to build a world organization for peace; that it would be an overt act in the minds of other nations of the earth, and that it probably would lead us into difficulties.

Now, the committee of course knows that, above most other American citizens, you not only have had such a rich experience in your high capacity as Chief of Staff, but have been present at any number of these international conferences and have had an opportunity to contact personally the leaders of other nations.

I wish you would elaborate just a little on that statement and tell us what you think of the logic of such form of reasoning.

General Marshall: Mr. Woodrum, I realize that from a certain point of view I am stepping a little out of my purely military status as Chief of Staff. However, as you have just said, during the past three years it has been given to me to have many opportunities for dealing with—not only meeting, but directly dealing with—a great many of the senior officials of the various governments of the Allies.

My own reaction to the statement that you make of those who fear that some such action by this country would defeat, rather than assist us, in obtaining the character of peace that we would want—my own reaction is exactly the opposite of that.

In many conversations I have had with officials, leading officials of other countries, I find always the fear that we will withdraw into our shell and at the same time endeavor, as they put it, to inflict on the world an idealistic policy without, on our own part, showing any basis for maintaining or backing up such policy of idealism.

It seems to me very clear that if the United States takes a leading part, as I presume it will, in at least proposing stipulations and terms for the final peace, we must either depend completely on a new, and I might well say, unheard-of idealism among European nations or we must be prepared to back up what we put into the terms of the peace....

Mr. Woodrum: General, if I may follow this with one other question: We assume that our national policy, as well as our high hopes and fervent prayers, support the establishment of a world organization that will minimize and, if possible, prevent future wars; if we may assume that, in addition thereto—or rather to implement that policy—it is going to be necessary for us to have a very much larger military establishment in the post-war period than we have had in the past, then as I understand your statement, we are confronted with the alternatives of either

a larger standing professional army or this means of raising the reserve.
Now, would you just say a word on that.

General Marshall: I don't think that is quite an accurate statement of my point of vew, Mr. Chairman, for this reason: I regard a large standing army as an impossibility, frankly, both from the standpoint of obtaining the personnel in time of peace, and—of course this is your side of it—because of the repugnance of our people toward a large standing force. I don't think you could raise a large standing army in time of peace, nor do I think you could possibly afford it, unless you go deeper into our financial resources than the American people would permit. That leaves us with just one course for the rapid creation of a trained dependable organization, universal military training.

I will repeat that, perhaps in better English: I think a large standing army is not of the question. Even though you were to recommend it here, I think you would find it would be an impracticable proposition. I think I can speak with some authority on the matter of obtaining men for such an army, because I have been on that end of it for most of my life. You cannot obtain many men in time of peace, except maybe in the midst of a tragic depression, and even then you do not get exactly what you want.

So, the problem boils down to some system that is within our financial possibilities and still is an acceptable procedure. Other than a large standing army, I know of no other system except one based fundamentally on universal military training. In other words, if you do not have that, you cannot, in my opinion, expect to maintain before the world a respectable military posture, and you must go ahead on the basis that we went before; that is, on the hope, the slender hope, that we will again be given time, and a long time, to organize an army.

As you know, I went through all the long agony of the creation of the present armies and the losses that we suffered during that period of delay. I remember the close calls that we had, which might well have been tragic in their consequence to this country.

I hesitate to emphasize the thought that we will not again be given the opportunity because it has been said often, but I think you have to face frankly two things: Either universal military training or the hope—that is all you can possibly have—the hope that you will have better than a year for preparation. Of course, if you decide to repeat the policies of the past and rest our security on a hope, it means that your lack of readiness would, in my opinion, encourage the very thing you wish so earnestly to avoid.

I might add one further comment: From the viewpoint of the Japanese rather than the Germans, I have come to the conclusion—that they were seriously misled, and to that extent encouraged into this war, by hearing so much of the views or statements of our young men in college that "they were not going to fight," and that "they would not participate in any other war even in defense of their country."

To the Japanese, hungering for the riches of China and Malasia, that was almost an invitation to war, and they accepted it.

42

President Harry S Truman addressed a joint session of Congress on October 23, 1945, calling for a program of universal training. The military phase of this program, Truman indicated in his memoirs, was "incidental" to what he had in mind—a program "to develop skills that could be used in civilian life, to raise the physical standards of the nation's manpower, to lower the illiteracy rate, to develop citizenship responsibilities, and to foster the moral and spiritual welfare of our young people."[18] Congress proved unwilling to implement the president's proposal for universal training and decided instead to extend the life of the Selective Service System.

Truman on Universal Training, 1945

In my message to the Congress of September 6, 1945, I stated that I would communicate further with respect to a long range program of national military security for the United States. I now present to the Congress my recommendations with respect to one essential part of this program—universal training.

The United States now has a fighting strength greater than at any other time in our history. It is greater than that of any other nation in the world.

We are strong because of many things: our natural resources which we have so diligently developed; our great farms and mines, our fac-

Reprinted from *Public Papers of the Presidents of the United States: Harry S Truman, 1945* (Washington, D.C., 1961), pp. 404–13.

18. Harry S Truman, *Memoirs*, Vol. 1: *Year of Decisions* (Garden City, N.Y.: Doubleday and Co., Inc., 1955), p. 511.

tories, shipyards and industries which we have so energetically created and operated. But above all else, we are strong because of the courage and vigor and skill of a liberty loving people who are determined that this nation shall remain forever free.

With our strength comes grave responsibility. With it must also come a continuing sense of leadership in the world for justice and peace.

For years to come the success of our efforts for a just and lasting peace will depend upon the strength of those who are determined to maintain that peace. We intend to use all our moral influence and all our physical strength to work for that kind of peace. We can ensure such a peace only so long as we remain strong. We must face the fact that peace must be built upon power, as well as upon good will and good deeds.

Our determination to remain powerful denotes no lack of faith in the United Nations Organization. On the contrary, with all the might we have, we intend to back our obligations and commitments under the United Nations Charter. Indeed, the sincerity of our intention to support the Organization will be judged partly by our willingness to maintain the power with which to assist other peace-loving nations to enforce its authority. It is only by strength that we can impress the fact upon possible future aggressors that we will tolerate no threat to peace or liberty.

To maintain that power we must act now. The latent strength of our untrained citizenry is no longer sufficient protection. If attack should come again, there would be no time under conditions of modern war to develop that latent strength into the necessary fighting force.

Never again can we count on the luxury of time with which to arm ourselves. In any future war, the heart of the United States would be the enemy's first target. Our geographical security is now gone—gone with the advent of the robot bomb, the rocket, aircraft carriers and modern airborne armies.

The surest guaranty that no nation will dare again to attack us is to remain strong in the only kind of strength an aggressor understands— military power.

To preserve the strength of our nation, the alternative before us is clear. We can maintain a large standing Army, Navy, and Air Force. Or we can rely upon a comparatively small regular Army, Navy and Air Force, supported by well trained citizens, who in time of emergency could be quickly mobilized.

I recommend the second course—that we depend for our security upon a comparatively small professional armed force, reinforced by a well trained and effectively organized citizen reserve. The backbone of our military force should be the trained citizen who is first and foremost a civilian, and who becomes a soldier or a sailor only in time of danger—and only when Congress considers it necessary. This plan is obviously more practical and economical. It conforms more closely to long-standing American tradition.

In such a system, however, the citizen reserve must be a trained reserve. We can meet the need for a trained reserve in only one way—by universal training.

Modern war is fought by experts—from the atomic scientist in his laboratory to the fighting man with his intricate modern weapons. The day of the minute man who sprang to the flintlock hanging on his wall is over. Now it takes many months for men to become skilled in electronics, aeronautics, ballistics, meteorology, and all the other sciences of modern war. If another national emergency should come, there would be no time for this complicated training. Men must be trained in advance.

The sooner we can bring the maximum number of trained men into service, the sooner will be the victory and the less tragic the cost. Universal training is the only means by which we can be prepared right at the start to throw our great energy and our tremendous force into the battle. After two terrible experiences in one generation, we have learned that this is the way—the only way—to save human lives and material resources.

The importance of universal training has already been recognized by the Congress, and the Congress has wisely taken the initiative in this program.

The Select Committee of the House of Representatives on Postwar Military Policy has organized hearings and has heard extended testimony from representatives of churches and schools, labor unions, veterans organizations, the armed services, and many other groups. After careful consideration the Committee has approved the broad policy of universal military training for the critical years ahead. I concur in that conclusion, and strongly urge the Congress to adopt it.

In the present hour of triumph, we must not forget our anguish during the days of Bataan. We must not forget the anxiety of the days of Guadalcanal. In our desire to leave the tragedy of war behind us, we must not make the same mistake that we made after the first World War when we sank back into helplessness.

I recommend that we create a postwar military organization which will contain the following basic elements:

First—A comparatively small regular Army, Navy, and Marine Corps;

Second—A greatly strengthened National Guard and Organized Reserve for the Army, Navy and Marine Corps;

Third—A General Reserve composed of all the male citizens of the United States who have received training.

The General Reserve would be available for rapid mobilization in time of emergency, but it would have no obligation to serve, either in this country or abroad, unless and until called to the service by an Act of Congress.

In order to provide this General Reserve, I recommend to the Congress the adoption of a plan for Universal Military Training.

Universal Military Training is not conscription. The opponents of training have labeled it conscription, and by so doing, have confused the minds of some of our citizens. "Conscription" is compulsory service in the Army or Navy in time of peace or war. Trainees under this proposed legislation, however, would not be enrolled in any of the armed services. They would be civilians in training. They would be no closer to membership in the armed forces than if they had no training. Special rules and regulations would have to be adopted for their organization, discipline and welfare.

Universal training is not intended to take the place of the present Selective Service System. The Selective Service System is now being used to furnish replacements in the armed forces for the veterans of this war who are being discharged.

Only the Congress could ever draw trainees under a Universal Training Program into the Army or the Navy. And if that time ever came, these trainees could be inducted only by a selective process, as they were inducted for World War I and World War II. The great difference between having universal training and no training, however, is that, in time of emergency, those who would be selected for actual military service would already have been basically trained.

That difference may be as much as a year's time. That difference may be the margin between the survival and the destruction of this great nation.

The emphasis in the training of our young men will not be on mere drilling. It will be on the use of all the instruments and weapons of modern war. The training will offer every qualified young man a chance to perfect himself for the service of his country in some military specialty.

Under the plan which I propose, provisions should be made within the armed services to help trainees improve their educational status. The year of universal training should provide ample opportunity for self-improvement. Some part of the training could be used to develop skills which would be useful in future civilian life just as such skills have been developed during the present war.

The period of training could well be used to raise the physical standards of the nation's manpower, to lower its illiteracy rate, and to develop in our young men the ideals of responsible American citizenship.

Medical examinations of the young trainees would do much toward removing some of the minor disabilities which caused the rejection of so many men during this war by the Selective Service System.

The moral and spiritual welfare of our young people should be a consideration of prime importance, and, of course, facilities for worship in every faith should be available.

But the basic reason for universal training is a very simple one—to guarantee the safety and freedom of the United States against any potential aggressor. The other benefits are all by-products—useful indeed, but still by-products. The fundamental need is, and always will be, the national security of the United States, and the safety of our homes and our loved ones.

Since training alone is involved, and not actual military service, no exemptions should be allowed for occupation, dependency, or for any other reason except total physical disqualification.

All men should be included in the training, whether physically qualified for actual combat service or not. There should be a place into which every young American can fit in the service of our country. Some would be trained for combat, others would be trained for whatever war service they are physically and mentally qualified to perform.

I recommend that the training should be for one year. Each young man should enter training either at the age of eighteen or upon his graduation from high school—whichever is later; but in any event before his twentieth birthday. A trainee who completes his high school education in his seventeenth year should be eligible, with parental consent, to enter the course of training.

After the first few months of training, selected trainees who are not physically qualified for military service could be trained in certain skills so that if war came, they could take their places in shipyards, munitions factories and similar industrial plants.

Upon completion of a full year's training, the trainee would become a member of the General Reserve for a period of six years. After that he should be placed in a secondary reserve status.

Present personnel in the Army and Navy Reserves would, of course, be retained, and the new trainees would provide the source from which Reserves of the future would draw their personnel.

Commissions would be granted to qualified men who complete the course of training and who then take additional instruction in Officer Candidate Schools, in the Reserve Officers Training Corps or Naval Reserve Officers Training Corps. Outstanding trainees could be selected after an adequate period of training, and sent to college with Government financial aid, on condition that they return, after graduation and with ROTC training, as junior officers for a year or more of additional training or service.

Such a system as I have outlined would provide a democratic and efficient military force. It would be a constant bulwark in support of our ideals of government. It would constitute the backbone of defense against any possible future act of aggression.

It has been suggested in some quarters that there should be no universal training until the shape of the peace is better known, and until the military needs of this country can be estimated and our commitments under the United Nations Organization can be determined. But it is impossible today to foresee the future. It is difficult at any time to know exactly what our responsibilities will require in the way of force. We do know that if we are to have available a force when needed, the time to begin preparing is right now.

The need exists today—and must be met today.

If, at some later time, conditions change, then the prorgam can be reexamined and revalued. At the present time we have the necessary organization, the required camp installations, and the essential equipment and training grounds immediately available for use in a training program. Once we disband and scatter this set-up, it will be much harder and more expensive to reestablish the necessary facilities.

The argument has been made that compulsory training violates traditional American concepts of liberty and democracy, and even that it would endanger our system of government by creating a powerful military caste. The purpose of the program, however, is just the contrary. And it will have just the contrary result. The objective is not to train professional soldiers. It is to train citizens, so that if and when the Congress should declare it necessary for them to become soldiers, they could do so more quickly and more efficiently. A large trained reserve of peace-loving citizens would never go to war or encourage war, if it could be avoided.

It is no valid argument against adopting universal training at this time that there are now millions of trained veterans of this war. No fair minded person would suggest that we continue to rely indefinitely upon those veterans. They have earned the heartfelt gratitude of us all—and they have also earned the right to return promptly to civilian life. We must now look to our younger men to constitute the new reserve military strength of our nation.

There are some who urge that the development of rocket weapons and atomic bombs and other new weapons indicates that scientific research, rather than universal training, is the best way to safeguard our security. . . .

But research, new materials, and new weapons will never, by themselves, be sufficient to withstand a powerful enemy. We must have men trained to use these weapons. As our armed forces become more and more mechanized, and as they use more and more complicated weapons, we must have an ever-increasing number of trained men. Technological advances do not eliminate the need for men. They increase that need. . . .

Any system which is intended to guarantee our national defense will, of course, cause some inconvenience—and perhaps even some hardship —to our people. But we must balance that against the danger which we face unless we are realistic and hard-headed enough to be prepared. Today universal training is the only adequate answer we have to our problem in this troubled world.

There will be better answers, we hope, in the days to come. The United States will always strive for those better answers—for the kind of tried and tested world cooperation which will make for peace and harmony among all nations. It will continue to strive to reach that period quickly. But that time has not yet arrived.

Even from those who are loudest in their opposition to universal training, there has come no other suggestion to furnish the protection and security which we must have—nothing but pious hope and dangerous wishful thinking.

I urge that the Congress pass this legislation promptly—while the danger is still fresh in our minds—while we still remember how close we came to destruction four years ago—while we can vividly recall the horrors of invasion which our Allies suffered—and while we can still see all the ravages and ruin of war.

Let us not by a short-sighted neglect of our national security betray those who come after us.

It is our solemn duty in this hour of victory to make sure that in the years to come no possible aggressor or group of aggressors can endanger the national security of the United States of America.

43

Congressman Joseph Martin (R., Mass.) sought, by introducing the following bill, to have America lead a movement for the international abolition of conscription. Senator Clyde Hoey (D., N.C.) presented a similar resolution in the Senate, but neither man could secure sufficient support on the issue from his colleagues. The resolutions and their lack of success were reminiscent of President Wilson's attempt to end conscription after the First World War. Wilson had included a provision to that effect in his first draft of the League of Nations covenant, but he was later led to remove it on appeals from the French and Italian delegations.[19]

Bill to Abandon Peacetime Conscription Universally, 1945

I have introduced a resolution urging President Harry S Truman, Secretary of State James F. Byrnes, and the personal representative of the President on the United Nations Organization, Edward R. Stettinius, Jr., to begin immediately efforts to secure an agreement by the nations of the world to abandon peacetime conscription of youth for military service.

If mutual understanding can be reached between nations and peoples that the policy of gigantic systems of universal compulsory military service should be eliminated, it would relieve the United States and all other nations of the necessity to assume this great new burden at a time when we must build, reconstruct, and readjust the world to peace.

The elimination of compulsory military service as a policy of nations would be the greatest single act of statesmanship that could be accomplished in the immediate present. The system which has long been the practice of European nations has never prevented war. It is always viewed with suspicion and fear by other countries, forcing them to adopt the same policy. It becomes an insupportable burden, a constant drain on the people of the world, and a further incentive to war.

In view of the world's hope of peace and the ultimate destruction of the military power of Germany and Japan, an effort to eliminate compulsory military service as a policy of all peoples cannot come too soon.

Reprinted from the *Congressional Record*, 79th Cong., 1st sess., Vol. 91 (1945), p. A3808.

19. Arthur A. Ekirch, Jr., *The Civilian and the Military*, p. 196.

A world-wide agreement toward that end is certainly a goal no reasonable person can object to.

The text of the resolution follows:

Whereas the first concern of every American is the security of the nation; and

Whereas the American people are determined that their government shall henceforth make proper provision for the continuous maintenance of such security; and

Whereas in accordance with this firm determination, it has become necessary to consider a system of compulsory military service in the United States as a permanent part of our insurance against unpreparedness in the event of sudden war; and

Whereas compulsory military service would result in greater restrictions over the lives and activities of our people, would impose heavy burdens on them, causing greater taxes, and profound changes in their way of life; and

Whereas compulsory military service has long been customary in many European states and elsewhere, but has been contrary to American tradition since the founding of our republic; and

Whereas compulsory military service has never prevented war in Europe or elsewhere, but on the contrary, causes suspicion and fears to grow between nations and inclines the rulers of men to war rather than to peace; and

Whereas 50 nations, having expressed their desire for peace, met at San Francisco and resolved to make greater efforts than ever before to abate the fear and likelihood of war in the years to come; and

Whereas the people of the United States and their leaders in all sections and parties have in good faith approved the San Francisco Charter and desire our President to take a leading part in fulfilling the great purpose for which it was formed; and

Whereas with the ultimate destruction of the military power of Germany and Japan there will never be a better time than now to secure international agreement looking to permanent peace; and

Whereas an agreement between the nations of the world to eliminate systems of compulsory military service would itself be greatly conducive to that restoration of peace which is so profoundly desired by all the

plain peoples of the world, and would release their energies and resources for rebuilding their war devasted countries; and

Whereas world-wide abolition of compulsory military service in no way
precludes the maintenance of national or international military forces
adequate for safeguarding national or collective security: Therefore be it

Resolved, That before the United States adopts compulsory military
service, the President of the United States, the Secretary of State, and
the personal representative of the President on the United Nations Organization, Edward R. Stettinius, Jr., be and hereby are urged to work
unceasingly for an immediate international agreement whereby compulsory military service shall be wholly eliminated from the policies and
practices of all nations.

44

The Truman administration, after securing two extensions of the
1940 draft act, gave up the battle for continuation of selective service in 1947. The decision to acquiesce in the ending of the draft
reflected the administration's continuing desire to enact universal
military training.

Speaking before an emergency joint session of Congress on
March 17, 1948, Truman restated the case for universal military
training, bracketing his appeal with a call for passage of the Marshall Plan and a "temporary reenactment" of selective service legislation. The universal military training proposal, once again, failed
to win congressional approval, but a selective service bill was signed
into law on June 24, 1948.

Truman's Address to Congress, 1948

. . . Second, I recommend prompt enactment of universal training
legislation.

Until the free nations of Europe have regained their strength, and so
long as communism threatens the very existence of democracy, the
United States must remain strong enough to support those countries of

Reprinted from *Public Papers of the Presidents of the United States: Harry S
Truman, 1948* (Washington, D.C., 1964), pp. 185–86.

Europe which are threatened with communist control and police-state rule.

I believe that we have learned the importance of maintaining military strength as a means of preventing war. We have found that a sound military system is necessary in time of peace if we are to remain at peace. Aggressors in the past, relying on our apparent lack of military force, have unwisely precipitated war. Although they have been led to destruction by their misconception of our strength, we have paid a terrible price for our unpreparedness.

Universal training is the only feasible means by which the civilian components of our armed forces can be built up to the strength required if we are to be prepared for emergencies. Our ability to mobilize large numbers of trained men in time of emergency could forestall future conflict and, together with other measures of national policy, could restore stability to the world.

The adoption of universal training by the United States at this time would be unmistakable evidence to all the world of our determination to back the will to peace with the strength for peace. I am convinced that the decision of the American people, expressed through the Congress, to adopt universal training would be of first importance in giving courage to every free government in the world.

Third, I recommend the temporary reenactment of selective service legislation in order to maintain our armed forces at their authorized strength.

Our armed forces lack the necessary men to maintain their authorized strength. They have been unable to maintain their authorized strength through voluntary enlistments, even though such strength has been reduced to the very minimum necessary to meet our obligations abroad and is far below the minimum which should always be available in the continental United States.

We cannot meet our international responsibilities unless we maintain our armed forces. It is of vital importance, for example, that we keep our occupation forces in Germany until the peace is secure in Europe.

There is no conflict between the requirements of selective service for the regular forces and universal training for the reserve components. Selective service is necessary until the solid foundation of universal training can be established. Selective service can then be terminated and the regular forces may then be maintained on a voluntary basis.

The recommendations I have made represent the most urgent steps toward securing the peace and preventing war.

We must be ready to take every wise and necessary step to carry out this great purpose. This will require assistance to other nations. It will require an adequate and balanced military strength. We must be prepared to pay the price of peace, or assuredly we shall pay the price of war. . . .

45

On September 21, 1950, in the midst of the Korean War, President Truman issued another appeal for universal military training. Congress accepted his proposal in principle with its passage of the 1951 draft act, entitled the Universal Military Training and Service Act. This law created a National Security Training Commission, which was to explore the implementation of a universal military training program. The commission, chaired by James Wadsworth, sponsor of the 1940 draft act and long a proponent of universal military training, issued its report on October 29, 1951.

Report of the National Security Training Commission, 1951

SUMMARY OF THE REPORT

By giving approval to the principle of universal military training, through the enactment of Public Law 51, the United States has laid a foundation for enduring military strength. This solemn and far-reaching action reflects a realization that the major problems which this Nation faces in the world will be of long duration, that no tidy or decisive conclusion is to be expected soon; and that in consequence our basic and long-term military policies much provide for swift adjustment between periods of acute crisis which demand large standing forces, and periods of relative calm which require smaller standing forces, plus a large, trained, and ready reserve. This national decision further reflects the reality that all free society is engaged in mortal struggle with Soviet Communism—a movement aimed as a world dominated by the will of the Kremlin—and that such struggle will continue until the basic conflict is resolved or reconciled. It underlines our awareness that democracy must be durable if it is to survive.

Dictators' hopes for world domination have always been rooted in

Reprinted from National Security Training Commission, *First Report to the Congress* (Washington, D.C.: Government Printing Office, 1951), pp. 68–69.

the conviction that democracies would eventually allow their defenses to sag into impotence. So long as the military power of the United States has been represented almost entirely by its forces in being, there has been a basis for confidence on the part of our enemies that we would allow our strength to slip away with the years, for we have an ingrained suspicion of standing forces and have cut them back at every apparent opportunity, with small regard for the real dangers confronting us. Moreover, the economic and social dangers of maintaining large standing forces *ad infinitum* have always been real. Even an economy as dynamic as our own would be perhaps gravely strained if required to continue its present contribution to the American armed forces, and to the economic and military support of the balance of the free world, for a decade or more.

Universal military training provides our country with an insurance policy against these two dangers. By transferring a significant portion of the responsibility for security to a continually vitalized citizens' reserve, it provides us with depth in trained military manpower, which depth is a basic precondition for any significant reduction of our standing forces; it provides a method for achieving reasonable protection at a cost that can be borne over an extended period. With an efficient universal military training program operating in combination with other vital elements of our security, we may hope to remain strong enough over the years to deter or repel any military threat, without undermining the mainstays of our greatness—our industries, our scientific and educational pre-eminence, our freedoms and democratic institutions. . . .

46

The draft became a charged campaign issue during the presidential election of 1956, when Democratic nominee Adlai Stevenson raised the possibility of its eventual abolition. The following four selections from the *New York Times* trace and evaluate the debate over the issue, which generated far more heat than light. The fact that simply raising the question of the draft should provoke such an amazing degree of concern indicates the position that the peacetime draft had come to occupy in the nation's life.

Since Stevenson's margin of defeat in the election was so wide, it is impossible to isolate one issue and label that the cause of his lack of success. It appears, however, that his position on the elimination of the draft damaged his campaign and contributed to his widespread public image of being naïve and overly idealistic. The fact that he was debating what many Americans regarded as a military question with a man with a substantial military reputation accentuated the damage. It is of some interest that one of the people attacking Stevenson's proposal in the campaign was Barry Goldwater, who later, as a candidate in 1964, himself came out for the gradual termination of the draft.

Stevenson and Eisenhower on the Draft, 1956

Adlai Stevenson addressed an American Legion convention on September 5 and remarked:

It is clear that we must rethink the problems of military strategy and military requirements in this atomic age. Many military thinkers believe that the armies of the future, a future now upon us, will employ mobile, technically trained and highly professional units equipped with tactical atomic weapons. Already it has become apparent that our most urgent need is to encourage trained men to re-enlist rather than to multiply the number of partly trained men as we are currently doing.

We can now anticipate the possibility hopefully but responsibly that within the forseeable future we can maintain the military forces we need without the draft.

President Eisenhower's response to Stevenson's claim came during a television speech on September 19:

We cannot prove wise and strong by hinting that our military draft might soon be suspended, even though every family naturally hopes for the day when it might be possible. This I state categorically cannot be done under world conditions of today. It would weaken our armed forces, it would propagate neutralist sentiments everywhere. It would shock our allies, who are calling upon their people to shoulder arms in our common cause.

We cannot, in short, face the future simply by walking into the past backwards.

We cannot salute the future with bold words while we surrender it with feeble deeds.

Support for Stevenson's plan came in a letter to the *New York Times* from economist John Kenneth Galbraith:

You expressed editorially on Oct. 8 the hope that President Eisenhower's recent statement on the draft has taken this issue out of the present campaign.

By implication, as more specifically in an earlier editorial, you criticized Adlai Stevenson for having introduced the subject.

It does seem to me that Mr. Stevenson has rendered a signal service in bringing this subject into discussion. I, for one, would be very sorry were it not further debated. May I add that, while I am a supporter of Mr. Stevenson and not unaware of the tendency in this season to make one's views conform to one's politics, my convictions on this subject extend back to my service some years ago on General Hershey's committee on the provision of technical and trained manpower.

The use of the draft to supply military manpower is based on two assumptions, both of which I believe we must agree are now obsolete. The first is that military manpower must be procured cheaply; to do otherwise will make national defense infinitely expensive. The second is that the physical hazards of military service should be distributed equally among all members of the community and not confined to those who, for economic reasons, are led to seek a livelihood in the armed forces.

ERA OF MASS DEFENSE

These assumptions were once above challenge. In the days when defense depended on mass armies and when governments were poor, military manpower had to be procured at low cost. Without the draft the armies of France, Germany or Russia circa World War I would have been economically quite out of question. And one of the scandals of our own Civil War experience was that well-to-do young men were able to get out of the army by buying a substitute. But plainly these basic conditions no longer apply. While I support the view that we still need sizable land forces, we are not talking of mass armies. One cannot be certain what scale of pay and allowances would attract, say, the present numbers to the armed forces, but the amounts would not be astronomic. What is well within our capacity would have been far beyond the capacity of a European government of fifty years ago.

The conditions of service have also changed. We are speaking of peacetime service, which is not more dangerous than ordinary civilian existence. Indeed it is by no means certain now that in the event of war service in the armed forces would involve much more risk of death than residence in Manhattan. In the last war London civilians faced the dangers comparable to those of many members of Britain's armed forces.

COST OF MILITARY SERVICE

Thus the traditional justifications for compulsory service have disappeared. We could pay what is necessary for voluntary service. Danger is now widely distributed, anyway. As a result the draft survives principally as a device by which we use compulsion to get young men to serve at less than the market rate of pay. We shift the cost of military service from the well-to-do taxpayer, who benefits by lower taxes, to the impecunious young draftee. This is a highly regressive arrangement which we would not tolerate in any other area. Presumably freedom of choice here as elsewhere would be worth paying for.

As an important added benefit a shift from compulsion to fully paid service would give us a better trained force—something that modern weapons make most desirable. We would not, as now, have a force which consists of partly trained men who leave about as soon as their training is complete.

One purpose of an election campaign, hopefully, is to get debate on new issues as well as old ones. It seems to me that Mr. Stevenson has performed a service in starting a debate on a subject where attitudes have been largely frozen since World War I.

Arthur Krock, writing in the *New York Times* of October 21, evaluated the question of the draft as a leading campaign issue and discussed Stevenson's presentation of the controversial idea:

DRAFT ISSUE

The question of the duration of the military draft, also raised by Stevenson, has moved from the vague to something more specific. The Democratic candidate's first discussion of the draft was merely an expression of the view that conceivably it could be terminated in "the forseeable future" without injury to national security. This was attacked by the President and other Republicans on these grounds: (1) to intrude the thought in the campaign tended to create in families of the world a hope that international conditions do not support; (2) it gave a new argument to out-of-power politicians in the anti-Communist nations who are opposing military establishments that have been erected at the urging of the United States; (3) Soviet Russia will turn this to its own advantage, not only in these nations but in the neutral areas; (4) Stevenson proposed no effective substitute.

This week he met the last named point. A professional, specially trained, highly paid career military force of volunteers, he said, would be free of the basic defect in the draft that, at huge annual cost, gives youths only brief training and then turns them back into civilian life. He did not espouse the additional proposal of his chief counselor on this subject—Chester Bowles—that the military career men whom his plan would produce after service from the age of 18 to 30 be given $25,000 each to balance the advantage of persons in the same age bracket who had remained in civilian life. But this facet may appear as the debate develops over Stevenson's bomb-test and draft stoppage position that the President called "pie-in-the-sky promises and wishful thinking."

LAYMEN UNQUALIFIED

On the volunteer-career corps versus draft proposition, the layman again is unqualified for the expert judgment sought of him through his vote, although, as with the H-bomb tests, he would like to see an end of the business. And, since the draft enters most American homes, it is much higher in the public consciousness than the deadly mushroom clouds in the distant Pacific or the wilds of Siberia.

Yet ideas for the termination and replacement of the draft also belong primarily in the expert realm. The armed forces may split over Stevenson's proposals as the nuclear scientists have—though in this instance the degree and quality of the disputants will be easier for laymen to calculate. In an effort to begin such a calculation this correspondent today sought the views of Admiral Thomas C. Kincaid because, as a commander of large American forces in the second World War and a member of the National Training Security Commission, he is an outstanding authority.

ARGUMENT NOT NEW

"The argument in behalf of an enlarged permanent military service is not new," he said. "But it could be no effective substitute for the draft. When universal military training was omitted from national policy we were obliged to depend on the draft for any reserve at all. We couldn't do without it in time of war, and no sound fiscal plan that I can envisage would build a career corps to the essential size. Also I think a proposal encouraging hope of a forseeable end of the draft is, in present world circumstances, psychologically injurious to progress toward our foreign policy goals."

The Republicans charge that Stevenson introduced the draft and bomb test topics in the campaign because he had been unable to rally the voters on other issues, and concluded that these would appeal particularly to women, whose vote could be decisive in the election. But the Republicans are confident that all population groups will be guided in such matters by the views of the President, especially since he happens to have been a general once himself.

47

In the following document, former President Dwight D. Eisenhower makes a case for universal military training. There are many who support Eisenhower's proposal, among them former Selective Service System Director General Lewis B. Hershey, but there is also a significant amount of opposition—much of it, surprisingly, from the military. They see the program as involving a tremendous expense with only a minimal improvement in our military efficiency. General Hershey, in commenting upon the military's response to the proposal, has said: "I'm as popular as a bastard at a family reunion with the military because they don't want to run a correctional institution. But they have the know-how to teach discipline. Authority is just a method of getting things done without being reduced to chaos. What I'm proposing isn't like Hitler. If this country decided to do this kind of thing, it would be the people who decided to do it and not some dictator."[20]

A great many outside the military had an even stronger reaction to universal military training. An editorial in *The Christian Century*, commenting on the Eisenhower recommendation, said in summary: "Whatever his intentions, Eisenhower's proposal would be vicious in its effect on human beings, on American traditions and on the nation's soul."[21]

20. Lieutenant General Lewis B. Hershey, quoted in Keith R. Johnson, "Who Should Serve?" *Atlantic Monthly*, Vol. 87 (Feb., 1966), p. 66.
21. *Christian Century*, Vol. 63 (Sept. 7, 1966), p. 1073.

Eisenhower for Universal Military Training

During the years in which I served as Chief of Staff of the Army, I tried hard but unsuccessfully to persuade Congress to establish a sound system of Universal Military Training in this country. I felt that UMT was desirable not only from the standpoint of military preparedness, but for reasons of fitness and discipline among our youth. I also believed that it would provide the fairest approach to the always thorny problem of manpower procurement.

War, of course, is always unfair to youth. Some young men have to fight and others do not, and I see no complete cure for that until the blessed day arrives when men have learned to live in peace, and there will no longer be need for military force. That day is not here, however, and it cannot come so long as an implacable enemy of human freedom strives to enslave the world. Today more than ever, therefore, I think that this country should adopt, as the cornerstone of its defense establishment, a workable plan of universal training—and I mean *universal*, with a minimum of really essential exceptions.

First, let's take a look at what our present manpower-procurement system is doing to this country.

During the past year, I have watched with dismay the rising tide of rancor engendered by our draft system. Yet it is not hard to understand why this clamorous dissent should exist. At one end of the manpower spectrum we have had the college students, who until recently were deferred almost automatically. At the other end, we have had the young men whom the military authorities deemed unfit because of physical, mental, educational or moral deficiencies. Thus, as regards military exemption, we have had two large, privileged classes.

It is from the middle of the spectrum that the Selective Service has drawn the bulk of its manpower in recent years. These are the boys who are physically fit and possess sufficient education to make good soldiers, but who for various reasons have not gone on from high school to college. With harsh irony, they refer to themselves as the "sitting ducks." They feel, and justly, that they are a highly important segment of the nation's work force and are entitled to the same consideration as our future scientists and engineers, doctors, and lawyers, professors and industrial managers.

Now, I believe implicitly in the necessity of higher education for great numbers of our young people. Yet I also look back to World War II and the postwar years, and I remember vividly what happened to that generation of students. Before that conflict ended, we necessarily were taking nearly all of our able-bodied young men for military service; hundreds of thousands of college careers were delayed or interrupted. Yet when peace came, the boys who really wanted an education returned to college and in most cases finished their courses of study with a determination and maturity that were heartening to behold. Education and military service certainly are not mutually exclusive.

There have been other inequities in the draft. For several years young married men were deferred, and when our growing commitment in Vietnam necessitated increased quotas we had for a time the spectacle of many youths rushing into marriage—before they were ready to undertake the establishment of a home—in order to avoid military service. That rule is now changed. Others, by their own admission, have started fathering children as quickly as possible after marriage. This, I am told, is called "babying out."

Many graduate schools have experienced substantial recent increases in enrollment—considerably beyond natural year-to-year growth—because some young men preferred to prolong their education rather than do their stint for their country. Deferments have also been given for so-called critical occupations, and this unquestionably has influenced some boys in the choice of careers.

All of this has resulted not only in unfairness to those young men who *are* called, but also in a state of mind which I think is very bad for America. We still have in this country, thank the Lord, a great majority of young people who do have a strong sense of patriotism, who understand and believe in the United States' effort to contain communism before it engulfs the world. But we also have a minority who use every legal loophole to avoid their obligations, who seem willing to accept the splendid opportunities that this country offers without lifting a hand to preserve our way of life. And on the outer fringe we have a few who even use deceit and other illegal means to avoid the draft. The latter should be dealt with sternly and with dispatch.

It is my hope that out of this frustrating and humiliating experience will come a better way of providing the military manpower that we must have—a system which will help revive among *all* our young people a deep sense of "duty, honor, country." It is surely one of the fundamentals of our democratic system that every young person should love and believe in his country and feel a conscientious obligation to *do something* for his country—in peace and in war. Patriotism is not only a noble emotion but an emotion that is necessary to national survival. It is also an emotion which can be diluted by bitterness engendered by a system that is deemed unfair by so many.

In hammering out any new system of manpower procurement and training, therefore, we must keep certain objectives firmly in mind:

1. It must be a system which will provide the men we must have for our worldwide commitments.

2. It must have sufficient flexibility to permit us, in times of emergency, to bring additional men into our armed forces quickly and in substantial numbers.

3. It must, as far as possible, eliminate present unfairness.

4. It should bring to every young man an understanding of his obligation to his country and a sense of participation in its affairs.

5. It should be a builder of physical fitness, self-discipline and decent personal habits.

6. It should include the vast numbers of boys who are now exempted because of educational deficiencies or moderate physical disabilities such as trick knees, overweight problems and a host of other minor and often correctable infirmities.

I realize that to accomplish these objectives will take a lot of doing. But, looking back at the miracles that were achieved in World War II, I am convinced that it can be done—once we understand the need and go about the task with determination. . . .

Under the system that I envision, every young male American, no matter what his status in life or his plans for the future, would spend 49 weeks—one year minus three weeks' vacation—in military training. Only the barest minimum of exemptions would be permitted: obvious mental incompetents, those with some drastic physical defect, perhaps a few extreme-hardship cases.

Basically, I have always felt that 19 is about the right age to begin military service. Boys of 19 are young enough to be flexible, and in most cases they are more mature than those of 18. There are, however, other considerations. Eighteen is usually the age at which a boy finishes high school and is ready to enter college or go to work. It is a natural break in his life. If we were to enlist boys at 18 rather than 19 or any other age, it would cause less disruption in our schools and in working careers. Therefore, all things considered, I think 18 should be the age at which our young men should begin their year of UMT.

This year should be considered not only as their contribution to country but as part of their education. The government would, of course, provide sustenance, clothing and other necessaries, but the trainees would be paid only a small stipend—say five or ten dollars a month—in order to have a bit of pocket change for incidentals.

At the beginning of the year, each UMT trainee would be offered the option of enlisting immediately in our regular forces for a two-year term of duty, with all the pay, advances and benefits pertaining thereto, including later education under the G.I. bill of rights. A great many, I believe, would choose this course.

For the large number who *remained* in UMT, the year would be spent primarily in military training. It would include regular daily stints on the training base, athletics, remedial education for those who need it, building vigorous bodies and learning the wisdom of discipline, cleanliness and good personal habits. Youngsters with correctable physical weaknesses—and we have millions of them in this favored land—would benefit from good nutrition, a year of disciplined life, and special medical attention if they needed it.

The boys in UMT could and should be used in times of emergency such as floods, storms and fires. They could be useful in helping to maintain order and in assisting the victims of misfortune. On the other hand, they should not be impressed into any regular work program outside their base. We want no semblance of forced labor in America.

Almost two million boys now reach the age of 18 each year, and in times of peace or small wars we certainly could not use that many in our regular military forces. Consequently, many of our young men would complete their period of service with the 49 weeks of UMT. They would then be free to go on to college or vocational school or to begin their careers without interruption—except in the case of a major war, when all our potential military manpower would be needed.

If the inducements of full pay and later education at government expense did not produce the volunteers that we need for our regular forces, then it would be necessary to draft the added men. To do this in the fairest way, we should employ the lottery. In the beginning, we would have to include in the lottery the large pool of youths who were past UMT age but were still liable to military service. This pool would diminish each year, and after five or six years would cease to exist. From then on, the lottery would apply only to the boys in UMT.

This basic plan is by no means original with me. I have merely selected what I regard as the best parts of many suggested plans and put them together in an integrated whole. It is impossible within the compass of a short article to fill in all the details. For example, how would we fit the R.O.T.C. units, the National Guard and our reserves into the UMT system? I do not believe that these worthwhile services would have to be abandoned. All such complex matters can be worked out through careful study.

A suggested variant is that we adopt a system of universal service but offer each young man the choice of military training or of serving in some civilian group such as the Peace Corps, a hospital cadre or a conservation corps. I strongly doubt the wisdom of this plan, because (1) it would be almost impossible to provide enough useful civilian duties for those who elected this course; (2) the scheme would still be unfair to the boys who have to fight our wars; (3) the important benefits of a year of military education would not reach those who chose civilian service.

I am fully aware that the plan I suggest is not perfect. There are difficulties to be surmounted in putting it into operation.

One is that there would be some disruption of normal procedures on college campuses and in vocational schools. During the first year of UMT, these institutions would have virtually no male freshman classes; the second year, few sophomores; and so on until the end of the fourth year. After that, conditions would return to normal, the only difference being that first-year college students would average a year older—which could be a good thing.

The second obstacle—and this is a tough one—is the cost. Nobody really knows the price tag of UMT, but estimates run from three to six billion dollars a year above present military expenditures. If we wished to cut the training period to six months, costs could be sharply reduced, but I think that this would also seriously dilute the benefits. In the begining, we would also have to build and equip many new military camps, thus increasing the early costs.

I have no ready-made plan for financing UMT. I wish only to say that a big, powerful country such as ours could surely find a way to pay the bill. Personally, I think the program is far more important than some of the public efforts on which we are now spending so much.

Still another problem is the procurement of training personnel—military instructors, teachers, doctors, and so on. I do not regard this problem as insurmountable. We could call in reserve officers for a time if needed, and I am confident that we could find the other necessary people if we had to—just as we did during World War II.

Opposed to these obstacles are the enormous benefits that our country would reap from such a system.

First, there are the long-term military advantages. After a few years of UMT, we would have always a huge reserve of young men with sound basic military training. The R.O.T.C. would turn out better officers; the National Guard would be far more efficient. In case of a great emergency, all these men would be ready for combat after a brief refresher course, and in the event of a nuclear attack—the Lord forbid!—a disciplined body of young men in every community would be a priceless asset.

Second, although I certainly do not contend that UMT would be a cure for juvenile delinquency, I do think it could do much to stem the growing tide of irresponsible behavior and outright crime in the United States. To expose all our young men for a year to discipline and the correct attitudes of living inevitably would straighten out a lot of potential troublemakers. In this connection—although I am sure that in saying this I label myself as old-fashioned—I deplore the beatnik dress, the long, unkempt hair, the dirty necks and fingernails now affected by a minority of our boys. If UMT accomplished nothing more than to produce cleanliness and decent grooming, it might be worth the price tag—and I am not altogether jesting when I say this. To me a sloppy appearance has always indicated sloppy habits of mind.

But above and beyond these advantages of UMT is the matter of attitude toward country. If a UMT system were to become a fixture of our national life, I think that resentment against military obligation would die away, that virtually every young man would take pride and satisfaction in giving a year of his life to the United States of America. After all, the good instincts lie near the surface in the young. Patriotism, a sense of duty, a feeling of obligation to country are still there. They are the noblest and the most necessary qualities of any democratic system, and I am convinced that UMT would help call them to the surface once more.

I am aware, of course, that many Congressmen regard Universal Military Training as political poison. I think they are being unduly timid. I am convinced that most Americans believe in the value of such a system, and that many others could be persuaded by an enlightened educational campaign. Most of all, I urge that we act *now*.

1965-the Present:
The Draft: Institution
in Crisis

BY THE EARLY 1960's, it appeared that a permanent peacetime draft had, in fact, become the new American tradition. The Cold War stood as an ever-present justification for military preparedness. In addition, most Americans had become acclimated to selective service; once operational, the draft benefitted from the essentially uncritical attitude accorded the agencies of the government. Even many of those subject to its authority did not feel particularly threatened by its existence. As long as monthly calls remained low, they could frequently manipulate educational and occupational deferments to avoid induction. Only those who lacked academic or vocational opportunities faced immediate classification as I-A, and they constituted the least vocal and least powerful groups in society.

This climate of acceptance began to disintegrate in 1965. With the large-scale commitment of ground combat troops in Vietnam, the war became a concern of increasing numbers of Americans. The escalating involvement was matched by growing doubts about the legitimacy and morality of the nation's policy in Indochina. As uncertainty hardened into opposition, the draft became the focus of resistance to the war effort.

President Johnson responded to the growing antagonism being

directed toward the draft by creating, on July 2, 1966, the National Advisory Commission on Selective Service. The commission, chaired by former Assistant Attorney General Burke Marshall, delivered its report in February, 1967, recommending that the order of induction be reversed, with nineteen-year-olds being called first by a process of random selection (lottery); that no further student or occupational deferments be granted; and that draft policies be more uniformly developed and centrally administered.

The draft act came up for renewal in the summer of 1967, and Congress extended the law with only two opposing votes in the Senate and nine in the House. None of the commission's recommendations were accepted, leading Burke Marshall to complain that "the new bill makes the system worse than it was before."[1]

One section of the 1967 act that had received an exceptional amount of attention was the conscientious objector clause. Congress, responding to the Supreme Court's 1965 decision in the Seeger case, had sought to narrow access to that classification.

The Selective Service Act of 1948 had defined "religious training and belief" as "an individual's belief in a relation to a Supreme Being involving duties superior to those arising from any human relation, but [it] does not include essentially political, sociological, or philosophical views or a merely personal moral code." Daniel A. Seeger, in applying for conscientious objector status, had placed quotation marks around the word "religious" on the Selective Service form and then stricken the words "training and." His local draft board, narrowly defining the eligibility requirement, had dismissed his claim as based upon a position that was merely ethical and therefore unacceptable. The Supreme Court, on March 8, 1965, unanimously ruled that Seeger, in fact, was entitled to deferment. In an opinion which cited Paul Tillich's *Systematic Theology*, Bishop John A. T. Robinson's *Honest to God*, and David Saville Muzzey's *Ethics as a Religion*, the Court stated as the test of religious belief whether it occupied "in the life of its possessor a place parallel to that filled by the God of those admittedly qualified for the exemption." While broadening the criteria for conscientious objection, the Court failed to act on Justice Douglas's contention that any religious requirement violated the First Amendment's "establishment of religion" clause.

Congress, in enacting the 1967 draft act, sought to cut back on

1. Richard Gillam, "The Peacetime Draft: Voluntarism to Coercion," *The Yale Review*, Vol. 57, p. 517.

the Court's broader interpretation. The act, in deleting the required belief in a Supreme Being as a basis for conscientious objection, offered merely a negative definition of "religious training and belief" as not including "essentially political, sociological or philosophical views, or a merely personal moral code."

The Supreme Court responded to this attempt to narrow access to conscientious objector status in a decision handed down on June 15, 1970. The case involved Elliott Welsh II, who, after having his claim for exemption rejected, refused induction and received a three-year prison sentence. His position represented a step beyond Seeger's in that he was far more insistent in denying that his views were religious. Welsh had struck the word "religious" from the Selective Service form and had characterized his beliefs as formed from readings in history and sociology. The Court, in a 5–3 decision, reversed Welsh's conviction. It argued that the test of belief is that it must be "deeply held" and not based solely upon "considerations of policy, pragmatism or expediency." Justice Black insisted that the law's exclusionary principle should not be read to eliminate those "whose conscientious objection to participation in all wars is founded to a substantial extent upon consideration of public policy." The Court's new standard included "all those whose consciences, spurred by deeply held moral, ethical, or religious beliefs, would give them no rest or peace if they allowed themselves to become a part of an instrument of war."[2] The *New York Times* applauded this decision as properly eliminating the implication "that only those who subscribe to formal religions are to be credited with a fundamental aversion to war and killing."[3]

The draft board of Kosciusko County, Indiana, had a different response to the Welsh decision. With a parting blast at the Supreme Court for allowing a "loophole to unpatriotic and non-religious boys," the entire board resigned. There was no point in staying in operation, one member insisted, when they can "thumb their noses at you and say they aren't going to go. You can't get the bite on anybody now. I don't know how we're going to get anybody drafted."[4]

Despite the reaction of the Kosciusko County board, the Seeger and Welsh decisions did not pose any major threat to the system. An issue which could, however, have wreaked havoc with the draft

2. *New York Times*, June 16, 1970.
3. *Ibid.*
4. *New York Post*, June 26, 1970.

had yet to be decided by the Court—what Gordon Zahn has described as the "explosive principle" of selective conscientious objection.[5] The selective service law stated that only those who were opposed to participation in every war are entitled to exemption. With the growing moral revulsion toward the war in Vietnam, an increasing number of young men felt that they could not conscientiously enter the military. However, since they were unable to categorically state that they would not serve in any war, the law offered them no relief. Their hope, then, lay in an affirmation of selective objection by the Court.

The National Advisory Commission on Selective Service considered the possibility of allowing selective conscientious objection. In its report, the majority came out against the proposition on several grounds: that support or nonsupport of a war is essentially a political position which should be expressed through the democratic process; that it would be disruptive of the morale and effectiveness of the armed forces; and that legal recognition of such a principle could eventuate in a "general theory of selective disobedience to law, which could quickly tear down the fabric of government."[6]

The Supreme Court finally handed down a judgment on this issue on March 8, 1971. Two similar cases were involved. The first appellant, Guy Gillette, had advised his draft board that he opposed serving in Vietnam although he would be willing to fight in defense of the United States or in a United Nations peacekeeping effort. His claim for exemption was denied, and he was eventually convicted for refusing to report for induction. The second appellant, Louis Negre, had applied for a discharge from the army after he had been drafted. Negre argued that the war in Vietnam failed to fulfill the traditional Catholic criteria for a just war, and he should not, therefore, be obliged to participate in it. His application was denied by the army, a lower court sustained the denial, and Negre was sent to Vietnam. The Supreme Court decided, by an 8–1 margin, that opposition to a particular war was not sufficient basis for exemption and that denial of the just war argument did not violate the appellant's First Amendment rights. Justice Thurgood Marshall, speaking for the majority, concluded that "the nature of conscription, much less war itself, requires the personal

5. *Worldview*, Mar., 1967.
6. U.S., National Advisory Commission on Selective Service, *In Pursuit of Equity*, pp. 50–51.

desires and perhaps the dissenting views of those who must serve
to be subordinated to some degree to the pursuit of public purposes."[7] Justice William Douglas, in his minority opinion, reiterated a sentiment from an earlier case: "Freedom to differ is not
limited to things that do not matter much. The test of its substance
is the right to differ as to the things that touch the heart of the
existing order."[8]

If the Supreme Court had legitimated selective objection, it
would have added significantly to the already expanding rolls of
conscientious objectors. The number of men holding this classification had doubled between 1967 and 1970 from twenty thousand to
forty thousand.

The Selective Service System did not respond enthusiastically to
this upsurge in petitions. Frank M. Adams, the seventy-six-year-old
chairman of a local draft board in Denver, took a rather jaundiced
view: "So many of these C.O.'s—you could tell they were so clev-
erly coached. We could tell outside forces were directing those
boys. Personally I had sympathy if they were truthful, but there
were not many of them."[9]

During the last six months of 1970, any potential conscientious
objector who wrote to the national headquarters of Selective Service requesting information received a form letter which spoke of
an "inherent inequity" when anyone sought to avoid "the common
defense." It warned that "too much tolerance has been the cause
of destruction of strong nations," and that "no consideration will be
given to those who attempt to escape service" on moral grounds if
the number of objectors grows too large.[10]

While those applying for exemption on conscientious grounds
have shown a willingness to cooperate with the Selective Service
System, there are two other groups who have refused to accom-
modate themselves to the requirements of the draft law: those who
have fled the country to avoid induction, and those who have remained behind to resist the draft. The exodus of young men from
America to Canada and, to a lesser extent, to Western Europe, constitutes one of the saddest ironies of the recent past. A nation which
had once welcomed men fleeing from conscription now found herself losing some of her finest young men for the same reason. Sup-

7. *New York Times*, Mar. 9, 1971.
8. *Ibid.*
9. *New York Times*, May 23, 1971.
10. *Ibid.*, Feb. 18, 1971.

port groups in Canada have estimated that there are about eighty thousand draft-age Americans there.[11]

Those who stayed behind to challenge the authority of the Selective Service System utilized a variety of strategies: burning and turning in draft cards, refusing induction, and engaging in attacks on draft board files.[12] Beginning with the public burning of draft cards in the summer and fall of 1965, the resistance movement steadily enlarged its base. In December, 1966, one hundred student leaders from various universities sent an open letter to President Johnson. Their statement, which received front-page coverage in the *New York Times*, warned the administration that unless the government changed its war policy, more and more of its young men would choose jail rather than bear arms.

The following fall "A Call to Resist Illegitimate Authority" was issued. Sponsored by individuals who were not subject to the draft but wished to support and share risks with those who were, the statement was signed by Robert McAfee Brown, Noam Chomsky, Herbert Marcuse, Bishop James Pike, and hundreds of other academics, clergymen, and writers.

Shortly after the publication of this call, a group including Reverend William Sloane Coffin, Jr., and Dr. Benjamin Spock visited the Justice Department to deliver draft cards that had recently been collected at meetings across the country. Before entering, Coffin addressed a rally which had gathered in support of the event. Insisting that "the dictates of government must be tested on the anvil of individual conscience," he accepted, along with his colleagues, complicity in the act of refusal of those men whose cards he was turning in: "If they are now arrested for failing to comply with a law that violates their consciences, we too must be arrested, for in the sight of the law we are as guilty as they."[13] Less than three months later, the government indicted Reverend Coffin and four others for conspiring to aid, abet, and counsel resistance to the draft.

If the government hoped that this prosecution would have a chilling effect on the resistance movement, events soon proved otherwise. The Church of the Brethren, at its annual conference in

11. Thomas Lee Hayes, *American Deserters in Sweden: The Men and Their Challenge* (New York: Association Press, 1971), p. 21.

12. For the most complete account of the draft resistance movement, see Michael Ferber and Staughton Lynd, *The Resistance.*

13. Jessica Mitford, *The Trial of Dr. Spock,* p. 269.

June, 1970, endorsed by an overwhelming vote a statement which commended to draft-aged men and their parents "open nonviolent noncooperation with the system of conscription."[14] A Selective Service System report, dated August 29, 1970, indicated that prosecutions for draft evasion had increased ten times over their level in 1965.[15] In addition, the sentences meted out were steadily lengthening, proving, as one commentator noted, that "draft resisters seemed to have hit a sensitive nerve."[16] One federal judge in San Francisco, defending his stiff sentences in draft cases, insisted that he "didn't become a judge to preside over the decline and fall of the American republic."[17]

Such warnings seemed to have little deterrent effect. The Oakland Induction Center, which processes draftees from all of northern California and part of Nevada, issued a report in May, 1970, covering the six months ending on March 31 of that year. The results were astounding. Of those ordered to report for induction, more than half did not even show up. Of those that did, 11 percent refused induction.[18] Although a certain portion of those who did not appear when ordered eventually reported, and although California has a higher proportion of draft refusals than most other states, the figures would certainly give pause to anyone who saw draft resisters as a small, highly visible group of publicity seekers.

The resistance movement described so far consisted of individuals and later more highly organized acts of refusal to comply with the draft law. However, at the same time a different pattern of opposition, or what Francine Gray has described as the "ultra resistance,"[19] was developing—assaults on the Selective Service System itself. Although the first use of this tactic is associated in the public's mind with the Berrigan brothers, it had a far less dramatic beginning. On Washington's birthday, 1966, Barry Bondhus entered his local draft board in Minnesota and dumped two buckets of his own and his family's excrement over the I-A files. His action attracted little national attention, so the pouring of blood over the files in a Baltimore board by Reverend Phillip Berrigan in October,

14. *New York Times*, June 28, 1970.
15. *Ibid.*, Aug. 30, 1970.
16. John Poppy, "The Draft: Hazardous to Your Health?" *Look*, Aug. 12, 1969.
17. *Miami Herald*, Apr. 18, 1971.
18. *New Haven Journal-Courier*, May 4, 1970.
19. Francine du Plessix Gray, *Divine Disobedience: Profiles in Catholic Radicalism* (New York: Alfred A. Knopf, Inc., 1970).

1967, seemed like a new direction in the movement. Berrigan was joined by his brother, Daniel, seven months later in an action involving a board in Catonsville, Maryland. In this case the files were incinerated by napalm produced from a formula in an army manual. The dramatic, almost liturgical, quality of the event, plus Daniel Berrigan's gift for defining it in moving, almost poetic terms, helped launch a series of similar actions organized mainly by Catholic priests, nuns, and laymen. Over the next two years draft-board raids took place in Boston, Milwaukee, Washington, Chicago, New York, and many smaller cities. In September, 1970, the Selective Service System announced that there had been 271 "antidraft occurrences" in the first eight months of that year. The episodes ranged from minor harassments such as sit-ins and bricks thrown through windows to attacks on draft files.[20] In May, 1969, fifteen persons invaded the central draft depository in Chicago and destroyed all the records of twelve local boards and some files of eight others. It required four months of work plus forty additional workers to reconstruct the files, a process that cost the government more than $60,000.[21]

Opposition to the draft had not been confined, however, to antiwar activists. A number of career army officers have begun to view the draft as a burden rather than an advantage. The escalation of the war in Vietnam, with its consequent demand for increased manpower, required expanded use of draftees and draft-induced volunteers. The army discovered, to its dismay, that the negative feelings some of these men felt about the war did not disappear once they donned a uniform. The desertion rate rose 300 percent from 1966 to 1970.

The Army experienced equal difficulty with many of the men who served out their time. The breakdown of military discipline, the racial confrontations, the "fraggings" (actual or attempted murders of superior officers and noncoms), and widespread heroin addiction have all been generally publicized. For many career army officers, this unprecedented situation seemed the result of having to wage an "unwinnable" war while assimilating large numbers of alienated young men who were simply not good military material. Hugh Mulligan, concluding an Associated Press series on changes in military life, captured the mood of these officers who viewed "the

20. *New York Times*, Sept. 8, 1970.
21. *Ibid.*

end of the draft as the end of the line, finally, of the problem kids, leaving the ranks hopefully open for those who want in rather than out."[22]

President Nixon began to discuss the feasibility of ending the draft during the 1968 presidential campaign. In an address on October 17, he stated that "we have lived with the draft so long, in fact, that too many of us now accept it as normal and necessary. I say it's time we took a new look at the draft—at the question of permanent conscription in a free society."[23]

Many "new looks" have been given the draft in recent years. Some, such as Robert McNamara and Margaret Mead, advocated an expansion of selective service into national service, enlisting all the young people of the society for a year or two of their lives. Others argued for a reorganization of the draft in pursuit of equity while still retaining the premise of compulsion. The lottery, instituted by Congress on November 26, 1969, was an example of such an improvement from within. Still others, pressing an increasingly popular position, called for an end to the draft and the creation of a volunteer army.

President Nixon's commission on a volunteer army, chaired by former Secretary of Defense Thomas S. Gates, Jr., made a strong case for such a proposition. The administration set July 1, 1973, as the target date for a "zero draft," and the Pentagon, in preparation for that event, planned pay increases in the lower ranks, new servicemen's housing, and an increased advertising budget for recruiting. Congress, faced with the expiration of the draft law on June 30, 1971, accepted the administration's timetable and voted a two-year extension.

Congressman F. Edward Hebert, chairman of the House Armed Services Committee and long-time supporter of the Selective Service System, remarked with jovial cynicism that "the only way to get a volunteer army is to draft it."[24] Hebert's assumption is now being tested, since Secretary of Defense Melvin Laird announced on January 27, 1973, that the armed forces would henceforth depend exclusively on volunteer enlistments. The draft has not ended, since the Selective Service System remains intact and the process of registration and classification goes on, but zero draft calls are

22. *New York Post*, May 27, 1971.
23. Gerald Leinwand, *The Draft* (New York: Washington Square Press, Inc., 1970), p. 97.
24. *New York Times*, Mar. 23, 1971.

now the policy. The issue is now joined: Can, as Congressman Hebert suggests, the nation only maintain its military manpower requirements by conscription, or will the nation be able to restore a tradition that disappeared in the past generation—voluntary military service in peacetime?

48

One of the landmark decisions in the area of compulsory military service was handed down in 1965 by the Supreme Court in the case of *United States* v. *Seeger*. Daniel Seeger, a pacifist, had filed a claim with his local draft board as a conscientious objector, but the claim was denied on the grounds that it was not based on an explicit belief in God. Seeger's appeal of that decision eventually progressed to the Supreme Court and found support there. The Court, in its decision, broadened the basis for conscientious objection by defining the permissible framework to include an ethical or humanistic concern, without an explicit belief in God.

United States v. Seeger, 1965

THE FACTS IN THE CASE

No. 50: Seeger was convicted in the District Court for the Southern District of New York of having refused to submit to induction to the armed forces. He was originally classified 1–A in 1953 by his local board, but this classification was change in 1955 to 2–S (student) and he remained in this status until 1958 when he was reclassified 1–A. He first claimed exemption as a conscientious objector in 1957 after successive annual renewals of his student classification. Although he did not adopt verbatim the printed Selective Service System form, he declared that he was conscientiously opposed to participation in war in any form by reason of his "religious" belief; that he preferred to leave the question as to his belief in a Supreme Being open, "rather than answer 'yes' or 'no'"; that his "skepticism or disbelief in the existence of God" did "not necessarily mean lack of faith in anything whatsoever"; that his was a "belief in and devotion to goodness and virtue for their own sakes, and a

Reprinted from *United States* v. *Seeger*, 380 U.S. 163 [citations deleted].

religious faith in a purely ethical creed." He cited such personages as Plato, Aristotle and Spinoza for support of his ethical belief in intellectual and moral integrity "without belief in God, except in the remotest sense." His belief was found to be sincere, honest, and made in good faith; and his conscientious objection to be based upon individual training and belief, both of which included research in religious and cultural fields. Seeger's claim, however, was denied solely because it was not based upon a "belief in a relation to a Supreme Being" as required by Section 6(j) of the Act. At trial Seeger's counsel admitted that Seeger's belief was not in relation to a Supreme Being as commonly understood, but contended that he was entitled to the exemption because "under the present law Mr. Seeger's position would also include definitions of religion which have been stated more recently," and could be "accommodated" under the definition of religious training and belief in the Act. He was convicted and the Court of Appeals reversed, holding that the Supreme Being requirement of the section distinguished "between internally derived and externally compelled beliefs" and was, therefore, an "impermissible classification" under the Due Process Clause of the Fifth Amendment. . . .

BACKGROUND OF SECTION 6 (j)

Chief Justice Hughes, in his opinion in *United States* v. *Macintosh*, 283 U.S. 605 (1931), enunciated the rationale behind the long recognition of conscientious objection to participation in war accorded by Congress in our various conscription laws when he declared that "in the forum of conscience, duty to a moral power higher than the States has always been maintained." In a similar vein Harlan Fiske Stone, later Chief Justice, drew from the Nation's past when he declared that

> "both morals and sound policy require that the state should not violate the conscience of the individual. All our history gives confirmation to the view that liberty of conscience has a moral and social value which makes it worthy of preservation at the hands of the state. So deep in its significance and vital, indeed, is it to the integrity of man's moral and spiritual nature that nothing short of the self-preservation of the state should warrant its violation; and it may well be questioned whether the state which preserves its life by a settled policy of violation of the conscience of the individual will not in fact ultimately lose it by the process." Stone, "The Conscientious Objector," 21 Col. Univ. Q. 253, 269 (1919).

Governmental recognition of the moral dilemma posed for persons of certain religious faiths by the call to arms came early in the history of this country. Various methods of ameliorating their difficulty were adopted by the Colonies, and were later perpetuated in state statutes and constitutions. Thus by the time of the Civil War there existed a state pattern of exempting conscientious objectors on religious grounds. In the Federal Militia Act of 1862 control of conscription was left primarily in the States. However, General Order No. 99, issued by the Adjutant General pursuant to that Act, provided for striking from the conscription list those who were exempted by the States; it also established a commutation or substitution system fashioned from earlier state enactments. With the Federal Conscription Act of 1863, which enacted the commutation and substitution provisions of General Order No. 99, the Federal Government occupied the field entirely, and in the 1864 Draft Act, 13 Stat. 9, it extended exemptions to those conscientious objectors who were members of religious denominations opposed to the bearing of arms and who were prohibited from doing so by the articles of faith of their denominations. *Selective Service System Monograph No. 11*, Conscientious Objection 40–41 (1950). In that same year, the Confederacy exempted certain pacifist sects from military duty.

The need for conscription did not again arise until World War I. The Draft Act of 1917, 40 Stat. 76, 78, afforded exemptions to conscientious objectors who were affiliated with a "well-recognized religious sect or organization [then] organized and existing and whose existing creed or principles [forbade] its members to participate in war in any form. . . ." The Act required that all persons be inducted into the armed services, but allowed the conscientious objectors to perform noncombatant service in capacities designated by the President of the United States. Although the 1917 Act excused religious objectors only, in December 1917, the Secretary of War instructed that "personal scruples against war" be considered as constituting "conscientious objection." Selective Service System Monograph No. 11, Conscientious Objection 54–55 (1950). This Act, including its conscientious objector provisions, was upheld against constitutional attack in the *Selective Draft Law Cases*, 245 U. S. 366, 389–390 (1918).

In adopting the 1940 Selective Training and Service Act Congress broadened the exemption afforded in the 1917 Act by making it unnecessary to belong to a pacifist religious sect if the claimant's own opposition to war was based on "religious training and belief." 54 Stat. 889. Those found to be within the exemption were not inducted into the armed services but were assigned to noncombatant service under the supervision of the Selective Service System. The Congress recognized that one might be religious without belonging to an organized church just as surely as minority members of a faith not opposed to war might through religious reading reach a conviction against participation in war. *Congress Looks at the Conscientious Objector* (National Service Board for Religious Objectors, 1943) 71, 79, 83, 87, 88, 89. Indeed, the consensus of the witnesses appearing before the congressional committees was that individual belief—rather than membership in a church or sect—determined the duties that God imposed upon a person in his everyday conduct; and that "there is a higher loyalty than loyalty to this country, loyalty to God." *Id.*, at 29–31. See also the proposals which were made to the House Military Affairs Committee but rejected. Thus, while shifting the test from membership in such a church to one's individual belief the Congress nevertheless continued its historic practice of excusing from armed service those who believed that they owed an obligation, superior to that due the state, of not participating in war in any form.

Between 1940 and 1948 two courts of appeals held that the phrase "religious training and belief" did not include philosophical, social or political policy. Then in 1948 the Congress amended the language of the statute and declared that "religious training and belief" was to be defined as "an individual's belief in a relation to a Supreme Being involving duties superior to those arising from any human relation, but [not including] essentially political, sociological, or philosophical views or a merely personal moral code." The only significant mention of this change in the provision appears in the report of the Senate Armed Services Committee recommending adoption. It said simply this: "This section reenacts substantially the same provisions as were found in subsection 5 (g) of the 1940 act. Exemption extends to anyone who, because of religious training and belief in his relation to a Supreme Being, is conscientiously opposed to combatant military service or to both combatant and noncombatant military service. . . ."

INTERPRETATION OF SECTION 6 (j)

1. The crux of the problem lies in the phrase "religious training and belief" which Congress has defined as "belief in a relation to a Supreme Being involving duties superior to those arising from any human relation." In assigning meaning to this statutory language we may narrow the inquiry by noting briefly those scruples expressly excepted from the definition. The section excludes those persons who, disavowing

religious belief, decide on the basis of essentially political, sociological or economic considerations that war is wrong and that they will have no part of it. These judgments have historically been reserved for the Government, and in matters which can be said to fall within these areas the conviction of the individual has never been permitted to override that of the state. *United States* v. *Macintosh, supra* (dissenting opinion). The statute further excludes those whose opposition to war stems from a "merely personal moral code," a phrase to which we shall have occasion to turn later in discussing the application of Section 6 (j) to these cases. We also pause to take note of what is not involved in this litigation. No party claims to be an atheist or attacks the statute on this ground. The question is not, therefore, one between theistic and atheistic beliefs. We do not deal with or intimate any decision on that situation in these cases. Nor do the parties claim the monotheistic belief that there is but one God; what they claim (with the possible exception of Seeger who bases his position here not on factual but on purely constitutional grounds) is that they adhere to theism, which is the "Belief in the existence of a god or gods; . . . Belief in superhuman powers or spiritual agencies in one or many gods," as opposed to atheism. Our question, therefore, is the narrow one: Does the term "Supreme Being" as used in Section 6 (j) mean the orthodox God or the broader concept of a power or being, or a faith, "to which all else is subordinate or upon which all else is ultimately dependent"? *Webster's New International Dictionary* (Second Edition). In considering this question we resolve it solely in relation to the language of Section 6 (j) and not otherwise.

2. Few would quarrel, we think, with the proposition that in no field of human endeavor has the tool of language proved so inadequate in the communication of ideas as it has in dealing with the fundamental questions of man's predicament in life, in death or in final judgment and retribution. This fact makes the task of discerning the intent of Congress in using the phrase "Supreme Being" a complex one. Nor is it made easier by the richness and variety of spiritual life in our country. Over 250 sects inhabit our land. Some believe in a purely personal God, some in a supernatural deity; others think of religion as a way of life envisioning as its ultimate goal the day when all men can live together in perfect understanding and peace. There are those who think of God as the depth of our being; others, such as the Buddhists, strive for a state of lasting rest through self-denial and inner purification; in Hindu philosophy, the Supreme Being is the transcendental reality which is truth, knowledge and bliss. Even those religious groups which have traditionally opposed war in every form have splintered into various

denominations: from 1940 to 1947 there were four denominations using the name "Friends," *Selective Service System Monograph No. 11*, Conscientious Objection 13 (1950); the "Church of the Brethren" was the official name of the oldest and largest church body of four denominations composed of those commonly called Brethren, *id.*, at 11; and the "Mennonite Church" was the largest of 17 denominations, including the Amish and Hutterites, grouped as "Mennonite bodies" in the 1936 report on the Census of Religious Bodies. This vast panoply of beliefs reveals the magnitude of the problem which faced the Congress when it set about providing an exemption from armed service. It also emphasizes the care that Congress realized was necessary in the fashioning of an exemption which would be in keeping with its long-established policy of not picking and choosing among religious beliefs.

In spite of the elusive nature of the inquiry, we are not without certain guidelines. In amending the 1940 Act, Congress adopted almost intact the language of Chief Justice Hughes in *United States* v. *Macintosh, supra*:

> "The essence of religion is belief in a relation to *God* involving duties superior to those arising from any human relation." At 633–634 (Emphasis supplied.)

By comparing the statutory definition with those words, however, it becomes readily apparent that the Congress deliberately broadened them by substituting the phrase "Supreme Being" for the appellation "God." And in so doing it is also significant that Congress did not elaborate on the form or nature of this higher authority which it chose to designate as "Supreme Being." By so refraining it must have had in mind the admonitions of the Chief Justice when he said in the same opinion that even the word "God" had myriad meanings for men of faith:

> "[P]utting aside dogmas with their particular conceptions of deity, freedom of conscience itself implies respect for an innate conviction of paramount duty. The battle for religious liberty has been fought and won with respect to religious beliefs and practices, which are not in conflict with good order, upon the very ground of the supremacy of conscience within its proper field."

Moreover, the Senate Report on the bill specifically states that Section 6 (j) was intended to re-enact "substantially the same provisions as were found" in the 1940 Act. That statute, of course, refers to "religious training and belief" without more. Admittedly, all of the parties

here purport to base their objection on religious belief. It appears, therefore, that we need only look to this clear statement of congressional
intent as set out in the report. Under the 1940 Act it was necessary only
to have a conviction based upon religious training and belief; we believe that is all that is required here. Within that phrase would come
all sincere religious beliefs which are based upon a power or being, or
upon a faith, to which all else is subordinate or upon which all else is
ultimately dependent. The test might be stated in these words: A sincere and meaningful belief which occupies in the life of its possessor a
place parallel to that filled by the God of those admittedly qualifying
for the exemption comes within the statutory definition. This construction avoids imputing to Congress an intent to classify different religious
beliefs, exempting some and excluding others, and is in accord with
the well-established congressional policy of equal treatment for those
whose opposition to service is grounded in their religious tenets.

3. The Government takes the position that since *Berman v. United
States, supra,* was cited in the Senate Report on the 1948 Act, Congress
must have desired to adopt the *Berman* interpretation of what constitutes "religious belief." Such a claim, however, will not bear scrutiny.
First, we think it clear that an explicit statement of congressional intent
deserves more weight than the parenthetical citation of a case which
might stand for a number of things. Congress specifically stated that it
intended to re-enact substantially the same provisions as were found
in the 1940 Act. Moreover, the history of that Act reveals no evidence
of a desire to restrict the concept of religious belief. On the contrary the
Chairman of the House Military Affairs Committee which reported out
the 1940 exemption provisions stated:

> "We heard the conscientious objectors and all of their representa-
> tives that we could possibly hear, and, summing it all up, their
> whole objection to the bill, aside from their objection to compulsory
> military training, was based upon the right of conscientious objec-
> tion and in most instances to the right of the ministerial students to
> continue in their studies, and we have provided ample protection
> for those classes and those groups." 86 *Cong. Rec.* 11368 (1940).

During the House debate on the bill, Mr. Faddis of Pennsylvania
made the following statement:

> "We have made provision to take care of conscientious objectors.
> I am sure the committee has had all the sympathy in the world with
> those who appeared claiming to have religious scruples against

rendering military service in its various degrees. Some appeared
who had conscientious scruples against handling lethal weapons,
but who had no scruples against performing other duties which did
not actually bring them into combat. Others appeared who claimed
to have conscientious scruples against participating in any of the
activities that would go along with the Army. The committee took
all of these into consideration and has written a bill which, I believe,
will take care of all the reasonable objections of this class of people." 86 *Cong. Rec.* 11418 (1940).

Thus the history of the Act belies the notion that it was to be restrictive
in application and available only to those believing in a traditional God.

As for the citation to *Berman*, it might mean a number of things. But
we think that Congress' action in citing it must be construed in such a
way as to make it consistent with its express statement that it meant
substantially to re-enact the 1940 provision. As far as we can find, there
is not one word to indicate congressional concern over any conflict between *Kauten* and *Berman*. Surely, if it thought that two clashing
interpretations as to what amounted to "religious belief" had to be
resolved, it would have said so somewhere in its deliberations. Thus, we
think that rather than citing *Berman* for what it said "religious belief"
was, Congress cited it for what it said "religious belief" was not. For both
Kauten and *Berman* hold in common the conclusion that exemption
must be denied to those whose beliefs are political, social or philosophical in nature, rather than religious. Both, in fact, denied exemption on that very ground. It seems more likely, therefore, that it was this
point which led Congress to cite *Berman*. The first part of the Section 6
(j) definition—belief in a relation to a Supreme Being—was indeed set
out in *Berman*, with the exception that the court used the word "God"
rather than "Supreme Being." However, as the Government recognizes,
Berman took that language word for word from *Macintosh*. Far from
requiring a conclusion contrary to the one we reach here, Chief Justice
Hughes' opinion, as we have pointed out, supports our interpretation.

Admittedly, the second half of the statutory definition—the rejection
of sociological and moral views—was taken directly from *Berman*. But,
as we have noted, this same view was adhered to in *United States* v.
Kauten, supra. Indeed the Selective Service System has stated its view
of the cases' significance in these terms: "The *United States* v. *Kauten*
and *Herman Berman* v. *United States* cases ruled that a valid conscientious objector claim to exemption must be based solely on 'religious
training and belief' and not on philosophical, political, social, or other

grounds. . . ." *Selective Service System Monograph No. 11*, Conscientious Objection 337 (1950). That the conclusions of the Selective Service System are not to be taken lightly is evidenced in this statement by Senator Gurney, Chairman of the Senate Armed Services Committee and sponsor of the Senate bill containing the present version of Section 6 (j):

> "The bill which is now pending follows the 1940 act, with very few technical amendments, worked out by those in Selective Service who had charge of the conscientious-objector problem during the war." 94 *Cong. Rec.* 7305 (1948).

Thus we conclude that in enacting Section 6 (j) Congress simply made explicit what the courts of appeals had correctly found implicit in the 1940 Act. Moreover, it is perfectly reasonable that Congress should have selected *Berman* for its citation, since this Court denied certiorari in that case, a circumstance not present in *Kauten*.

Section 6 (j), then, is no more than a clarification of the 1940 provision involving only certain "technical amendments," to use the words of Senator Gurney. As such it continues the congressional policy of providing exemption from military service for those whose opposition is based on grounds that can fairly be said to be "religious." To hold otherwise would not only fly in the face of Congress' entire action in the past; it would ignore the historic position of our country on this issue since its founding. . . .

These are but a few of the views that comprise the broad spectrum of religious beliefs found among us. But they demonstrate very clearly the diverse manners in which beliefs, equally paramount in the lives of their possessors, may be articulated. They further reveal the difficulties inherent in placing too narrow a construction on the provisions of Section 6 (j) and thereby lend conclusive support to the construction which we today find that Congress intended.

5. We recognize the difficulties that have always faced the trier of fact in these cases. We hope that the test that we lay down proves less onerous. The examiner is furnished a standard that permits consideration of criteria with which he has had considerable experience. While the applicant's words may differ, the test is simple of application. It is essentially an objective one, namely, does the claimed belief occupy the same place in the life of the objector as an orthodox belief in God holds in the life of one clearly qualified for exemption?

Moreover, it must be remembered that in resolving these exemption problems one deals with the beliefs of different individuals who will articulate them in a multitude of ways. In such an intensely personal area, of course, the claim of the registrant that his belief is an essential part of a religious faith must be given great weight. . . . The validity of what he believes cannot be questioned. Some theologians, and indeed some examiners, might be tempted to question the existence of the registrant's "Supreme Being" or the truth of his concepts. But these are inquiries foreclosed to Government. . . . Local boards and courts in this sense are not free to reject beliefs because they consider them "incomprehensible." Their task is to decide whether the beliefs professed by a registrant are sincerely held and whether they are, in his own scheme of things, religious.

But we hasten to emphasize that while the "truth" of a belief is not open to question, there remains the significant question whether it is "truly held." This is the threshold question of sincerity which must be resolved in every case. . . .

APPLICATION OF SECTION 6 (j)

As we noted earlier, the statutory definition excepts those registrants whose beliefs are based on a "merely personal moral code." The records in these cases, however, show that at no time did any one of the applicants suggest that his objection was based on a "merely personal moral code." Indeed at the outset each of them claimed in his application that his objection was based on a religious belief. We have construed the statutory definition broadly and it follows that any exception to it must be interpreted narrowly. The use by Congress of the words "merely personal" seems to us to restrict the exception to a moral code which is not only personal but which is the sole basis for the registrant's belief and is in no way related to a Supreme Being. It follows, therefore, that if the claimed religious beliefs of the respective registrants in these cases meet the test that we lay down then their objections cannot be based on a "merely personal" moral code.

In *Seeger*, the Court of Appeals failed to find sufficient "externally compelled beliefs." However, it did find that "it would seem impossible to say with assurance that [Seeger] is not bowing to 'external commands' in virtually the same sense as is the objector who defers to the will of a supernatural power." . . .

The Court of Appeals also found that there was no question of the applicant's sincerity. He was a product of a devout Roman Catholic home; he was a close student of Quaker beliefs from which he said "much of [his] thought is derived"; he approved of their opposition to war in any form; he devoted his spare hours to the American Friends Service Committee and was assigned to hospital duty.

In summary, Seeger professed "religious belief" and "religious faith." He did not disavow any belief "in a relation to a Supreme Being"; indeed he stated that "the cosmic order does, perhaps, suggest a creative intelligence." He decried the tremendous "spiritual" price man must pay for his willingness to destroy human life. In light of his beliefs and the unquestioned sincerity with which he held them, we think the Board, had it applied the test we propose today, would have granted him the exemption. We think it clear that the beliefs which prompted his objection occupy the same place in his life as the belief in a traditional deity holds in the lives of his friends, the Quakers. We are reminded once more of Dr. Tillich's thoughts:

> "And if that word [God] has not much meaning to you, translate it, and speak of the depths of your life, of the source of your being, of your ultimate concern, *of what you take seriously without any reservation*. Perhaps, in order to do so, you must forget everything traditional that you have learned about God. . . ." Tillich, *The Shaking of the Foundations*, 57 (1948). (Emphasis supplied.)

It may be that Seeger did not clearly demonstrate what his beliefs were with regard to the usual understanding of the term "Supreme Being." But as we have said Congress did not intend that to be the test. We therefore affirm the judgment. . . .

49

In July, 1965, the Selective Service System issued to its employees an orientation kit including a document entitled "Channeling," which was soon to receive a great deal of notoriety. "Channeling" was essentially a discussion of how the Selective Service System "channeled" young men into jobs or professions which were in the national interest. Pointing out that the line separating its primary function—military manpower procurement—from "the process of channeling manpower into civilian support" is often finely drawn, the document went on to discuss in detail how the system asserted itself in this other area. By granting occupational deferments, the government attached a premium to certain professions and thus greatly increased the possibility that they would be adequately staffed. In this way the Selective Service System had an impact on American society far beyond the simple procurement of military personnel.

Many persons who read "Channeling" were taken aback by such statements such as: "The psychology of granting wide choice under pressure to take action is the American or indirect way of achieving what is done by direction in foreign countries where choice is not permitted." Such assertions provoked a series of attacks on "Channeling"[25] and led to its eventually being withdrawn from circulation.

"Channeling," 1965

One of the major products of the Selective Service classification process is the channeling of manpower into many endeavors, occupations, and activities that are in the national interest. . . .

The line dividing the primary function of armed forces manpower procurement from the process of channeling manpower into civilian support is often finely drawn. The process of channeling by not taking men from certain activities who are otherwise liable for service, or by giving deferment to qualified men in certain occupations, is actual procurement by inducement of manpower for civilian activities which are manifestly in the national interest.

While the best known purpose of Selective Service is to procure manpower for the armed forces, a variety of related processes take place outside delivery of manpower to the active armed forces. Many of these may be put under the heading of "channeling manpower." Many young men would not have pursued higher education if there had not been a program of student deferment. Many young scientists, engineers, tool and die makers, and other possessors of scarce skills would not remain in their jobs in the defense effort if it were not for a program of occupational deferments. Even though the salary of a teacher has historically been meager, many young men remain in that job, seeking the reward of a deferment. The process of channeling manpower by deferment is entitled to much credit for the large number of graduate students in technical fields and for the fact that there is not a greater

25. For a detailed analysis of the social implications of "Channeling," see Thomas Reeves and Karl Hess, *The End of the Draft*, pp. 45–65.

shortage of teachers, engineers and other scientists working in activities which are essential to the national interest. . . .

The System has also induced needed people to remain in these professions and in industry engaged in defense activities or in the support of national health, safety or interest. . . .

This was coupled with a growing public recognition that the complexities of future wars would diminish further the distinction between what constitutes military service in uniform and a comparable contribution to the national interest out of uniform. Wars have always been conducted in various ways, but appreciation of this fact and its relationship to preparation for war has never been so sharp in the public mind as it is now becoming. The meaning of the word "service," with its former restricted application to the armed forces, is certain to become widened much more in the future. This brings with it the ever increasing problem of how to control effectively the service of individuals who are not in the armed forces.

In the Selective Service System the term "deferment" has been used millions of times to describe the method and means used to attract to the kind of service considered most important, the individuals who were not compelled to do it. The club of induction has been used to drive out of areas considered to be less important to the areas of greater importance in which deferments were given, the individuals who did not or could not participate in activities which were considered essential to the defense of the Nation. The Selective Service System anticipates further evolution in this area. . . .

No group deferments are permitted. Deferments are granted, however, in a realistic atmosphere so that the fullest effect of channeling will be felt, rather than be terminated by military service at too early a time.

Registrants and their employers are encouraged and required to make available to the classifying authorities detailed evidence as to the occupations and activities in which registrants are engaged. . . . Since occupational deferments are granted for no more than one year at a time, a process of periodically receiving current information and repeated review assures that every deferred registrant continues to contribute to the overall national good. This reminds him of the basis for his deferment. . . .

Patriotism is defined as "devotion to the welfare of one's country." It has been interpreted to mean many different things. Men have always been exhorted to do their duty. But what that duty is depends upon a variety of variables, most important being the nature of the threat to national welfare and the capacity and opportunity of the individual. Take, for example, the boy who saved the Netherlands by plugging the dike with his finger.

At the time of the American Revolution the patriot was the so-called "embattled farmer" who joined General Washington to fight the British. The concept that patriotism is best exemplified by service in uniform has always been under some degree of challenge, but never to the extent that it is today. In today's complicated warfare, when the man in uniform may be suffering far less than the civilians at home, patriotism must be interpreted far more broadly than ever before.

This is not a new thought, but it has had a new emphasis since the development of nuclear and rocket warfare. Educators, scientists, engineers and their professional organizations, during the last ten years particularly, have been convincing the American public that for the mentally qualified man there is a special order of patriotism other than service in uniform—that for the man having the capacity, dedicated service as a civilian in such fields as engineering, the sciences and teaching constitutes the ultimate in their expression of patriotism. A large segment of the American public has been convinced that this is true.

It is in this atmosphere that the young man registers at age 18 and pressure begins to force his choice. He does not have the inhibitions that a philosophy of universal service in uniform would engender. The door is open for him as a student to qualify if capable in a skill badly needed by his nation. He has many choices and he is prodded to make a decision.

The psychological effect of this circumstantial climate depends upon the individual, his sense of good citizenship, his love of country and its way of life. He can obtain a sense of well-being and satisfaction that he is doing as a civilian what will help his country most. This process encourages him to put forth his best effort and removes to some degree the stigma that has been attached to being out of uniform.

In the less patriotic and more selfish individual it engenders a sense of fear, uncertainty and dissatisfaction which motivates him, nevertheless, in the same direction. He complains of the uncertainty which he must endure; he would like to be able to do as he pleases; he would appreciate a certain future with no prospect of military service or civilian contribution, but he complies. . . .

Throughout his career as a student, the pressure—the threat of loss of deferment—continues. It continues with equal intensity after graduation. His local board requires periodic reports to find out what he is up to. He is impelled to pursue his skill rather than embark upon some less important enterprise and is encouraged to apply his skill in an essential activity in the national interest. The loss of deferred status is the consequence for the individual who has acquired the skill and either does not use it or uses it in a nonessential activity.

The psychology of granting wide choice under pressure to take action is the American or indirect way of achieving what is done by direction in foreign countries where choice is not permitted. Here, choice is limited but not denied, and it is fundamental that an individual generally applies himself better to something he has decided to do rather than something he has been told to do.

The effects of channeling are manifested among student physicians. They are deferred to complete their education through school and internship. This permits them to serve in the armed forces in their skills rather than in an unskilled capacity as enlisted men.

The device of pressurized guidance, or channeling, is employed on Standby Reservists of which more than 2½ million have been referred by all services for availability determinations. The appeal to the Reservist who knows he is subject to recall to active duty unless he is determined to be unavailable is virtually identical to that extended to other registrants.

The psychological impact of being rejected for service in uniform is severe. The earlier this occurs in a young man's life, the sooner the beneficial effects of pressured motivation by the Selective Service System are lost. He is labeled unwanted. His patriotism is not desired. Once the label of "rejectee" is upon him all efforts at guidance by persuasion are futile. If he attempts to enlist at 17 or 18 and is rejected, then he receives virtually none of the impulsion the System is capable of giving him. If he makes no effort to enlist and as a result is not rejected until delivered for examination by the Selective Service System at about age 23, he has felt some of the pressure but thereafter is a free agent.

This contributed to the establishment of a new classification of 1-Y (registrant qualified for military service only in time of war or national emergency). That classification reminds the registrant of his ultimate qualification to serve and preserves some of the benefit of what we call channeling. Without it or any other similar method of categorizing men in degrees of acceptability, men rejected for military service would be left with the understanding that they are unfit to defend their country, even in wartime.

An unprejudiced choice between alternative routes in civilian skills can be offered only by an agency which is not a user of manpower and is, therefore, not a competitor. In the absence of such an agency, bright

young men would be importuned with bounties and pirated like potential college football players until eventually a system of arbitration
would have to be established.

From the individual's viewpoint, he is standing in a room which has
been made uncomfortably warm. Several doors are open, but they all
lead to various forms of recognized, patriotic service to the Nation.
Some accept the alternatives gladly—some with reluctance. The consequence is approximately the same.

The so-called Doctor Draft was set up during the Korean episode to
insure sufficient physicians, dentists and veterinarians in the armed
forces as officers. The objective of that law was to exert sufficient pressure to furnish an incentive for application for commission. However,
the indirect effect was to induce many physicians, dentists and veterinarians to specialize in areas of medical personnel shortages and to seek
outlets for their skills in areas of greatest demand and national need
rather than of greatest financial return.

Selective Service processes do not compel people by edict as in foreign systems to enter pursuits having to do with essentiality and progress. They go because they know that by going they will be deferred.

The application of direct methods to effect the policy of every man
doing his duty in support of national interest involves considerably more
capacity than the current use of indirection as a method of allocation
of personnel. The problem, however, of what is every man's duty when
each individual case is approached is not simple. The question of
whether he can do one duty better than another is a problem of considerable proportions and the complications of logistics in attempting to
control parts of an operation without controlling all of it (in other
words, to control allocation of personnel, without controlling where people eat, where they live, and how they are to be transported), adds to
the administrative difficulties of direct administration. The organization necessary to make the decisions, even poor decisions, would, of
necessity, extract a large segment of population from productive work.
If the members of the organization are conceived to be reasonably
qualified to exercise judgment and control over skilled personnel, the
impact of their withdrawal from war production work would be severe.
The number of decisions would extend into billions. . . .

Deciding what people should do, rather than letting them do something of national importance of their own choosing, introduces many
problems that are at least partially avoided when indirect methods, the
kind currently invoked by the Selective Service System, are used.

Delivery of manpower for induction, the process of providing a few thousand men with transportation to a reception center, is not much of an administrative or financial challenge. It is in dealing with the other millions of registrants that the System is heavily occupied, developing more effective human beings in the national interest. If there is to be any survival after disaster, it will take people, and not machines, to restore the Nation.   July 1, 1965

50

President Johnson's twenty-member National Advisory Commission on Selective Service, headed by Burke Marshall, studied all facets of the draft over a seven-month period beginning in July, 1966. They examined hundreds of reports, did extensive interviewing, and recorded over 3,500 pages of testimony. The following selection is the summary section of their report, which was published in February, 1967.

Marshall Commission Report, 1967

To provide a flexible system of manpower procurement which will assure the Armed Forces' ability to meet their national security commitments under all foreseeable circumstances, the Commission recommends:

1. Continuation of a selective service system.

To make the controlling concept of that system the rule of law, rather than a policy of discretion, so as to assure equal treatment for those in like circumstances, the Commission recommends:

2. A consolidated selective service system under more centralized administration to be organized and operated as follows:

A. National headquarters should formulate and issue clear and binding policies concerning classifications, exemptions, and deferments, to be applied uniformly throughout the country.

Reprinted from U.S. National Advisory Commission on Selective Service, *In Pursuit of Equity: Who Serves when Not All Serve?* (Washington, D.C.: Government Printing Office, 1967), pp. 4–10.

B. A structure of eight regional offices (aligned for national security purposes with the eight regions of the Office of Emergency Planning) should be established to administer the policy and monitor its uniform application.

C. An additional structure of area offices should be established on a population basis with at least one in each state. At these offices men would be registered and classified in accordance with the policy directives disseminated from national headquarters. (The Commission sees the possibility of 300–500 of these offices being able to answer the national need.)

(1) The use of modern data-handling equipment, as well as the application of uniform rules, would facilitate processing, registration, and classification.

(2) Under appropriate regulations, registrants would change their registration from one area office to another as they changed their permanent residence.

D. Local boards, composed of volunteer citizens, would operate at the area office level as the registrants' court of first appeal.

E. These changes should be made in the organization of the local boards:

(1) Their composition should represent all elements of the public they serve.

(2) The maximum term of service should be 5 years.

(3) A maximum retirement age should be established.

(4) The President's power to appoint members should not be limited to those nominated by the governors of the states.

(5) Women should be eligible to serve.

F. The entire appeals process should be made uniform and strengthened in the following ways:

(1) The registrant should be able to appeal his classification to his local board within 30 days instead of the 10 days presently stipulated.

(2) Local boards should put their decisions in writing so appeal boards will have the benefit of the record in making their decisions, and the registrant will be able to know the reasons for the decision.

(3) Appeal boards should be colocated with the eight regional offices, although operate independently of them. The National Selective Service (Presidential) Appeal Board would remain as presently constituted.

(4) Appeal agents should be readily available at the area offices to assist registrants in making appeals.

(5) An adequate number of panels should be established, above the local board level, for the specific purpose of hearing conscientious objector cases on an expedited basis.

To remove widespread public ignorance concerning the operations of the Selective Service System, the Commission recommends:

3. Both the registrant and the general public should be made fully acquainted with the workings of the improved system and the registrant's rights under it, in these ways:

A. Easily understandable information should be prepared in written form and made available to all registrants each time they are classified.

B. An adviser to registrants should be readily available at the area office to inform and counsel registrants who need assistance with registration and classification problems.

C. Public information procedures regarding the entire system should be made more effective by national headquarters.

To reduce the uncertainty in personal lives that the draft creates, and to minimize the disruption it often causes in the lives of those men who are called, the Commission recommends:

4. The present "oldest first" order of call should be reversed so that the youngest men, beginning at age 19, are taken first.

To further reduce uncertainty and to insure fairness in the selection of inductees from a large pool of eligible men, when all are not needed, the Commission recommends:

5. Draft-eligible men should be inducted into service as needed according to an order of call which has been impartially and randomly determined. The procedure would be as follows:

A. At age 18, all men would register, and as soon as practicable thereafter would receive the physical, moral, and educational achievements tests and evaluations which determine their eligibility for military service according to Department of Defense standards. (This universal testing would meet social as well as military needs.)

B. Those found to be qualified for service (I-A) who would reach the age of 19 before a designated date would be included in a pool of draft eligibles. Those men reaching 19 after that date would be placed in a later draft-eligible pool.

C. The names of all men in the current draft-eligible pool would be arranged in an order of call for the draft through a system of impartial random selection.

D. For a specified period (a year, or possibly less), men in the pool would undergo their maximum vulnerability to the draft. Induction, according to the needs of the Department of Defense throughout that period, would be in the sequence determined by the impartial and random process.

E. When the specified period of maximum vulnerability had elapsed, an order of call would be determined for a new group of men, and the remaining men in the previous pool would not be called unless military circumstances first required calling all of the men in the new group.

6. No further student or occupational deferments should be granted, with these exceptions:

A. Under appropriate regulations which will safeguard against abuses, students who are in school and men who are in recognized apprentice training when this plan goes into effect will be permitted to complete the degrees or programs for which they are candidates. Upon termination of those deferments they will be entered into the random selection pool with that year's 18-year-olds.

B. Thereafter, men who are already in college when they are randomly selected for service would be permitted to finish their sophomore year before induction.

C. Men who undertake officer training programs in college should be deferred, provided they commit to serve in the Armed Forces as enlisted men if they do not complete their officer programs.
(These represent majority decisions; a minority of the Commission favors continued student deferment.)

D. Hardship deferments, which defy rigid classification but which must be judged realistically on individual merits, would continue to be granted.

7. Study should begin now to determine the feasibility of a plan which would permit all men who are selected at 18 for induction

to decide themselves when, between the ages of 19 and 23, to fulfill that obligation. Inducements would be offered to make earlier choice more attractive, and the option of choice could always be canceled if manpower needs were not met. If the feasibility of this plan is confirmed, the plan should be put into effect as soon as possible.

To broaden the opportunities for those who wish to volunteer for military service, the Commission recommends:

8. Opportunities should be made available for more women to serve in the Armed Forces, thus reducing the numbers of men who must involuntarily be called to duty.

9. The Department of Defense should propose programs to achieve the objective, insofar as it proves practicable, of accepting volunteers who do not meet induction standards but who can be brought up to a level of usefulness as a soldier, even if this requires special educational and training programs to be conducted by the armed forces.

To remove the inequities in the enlistment procedures of the Reserve and National Guard programs, the Commission recommends:

10. Direct enlistment into Reserve and National Guard forces should not provide immunity from the draft for those with no prior service except for those who enlist before receiving their I-A classification.

11. If the Reserves and National Guard units are not able to maintain their force levels with volunteers alone, they should be filled by inductions. Inductions would be determined by the same impartial random selection system which determines the order of call for active duty service.

The Commission supports recommendations presented to it by the National Advisory Commission on Health Manpower and the Department of State:

12. A national computer file of draft eligible health professionals should be established to assist selective service area offices to place their calls for doctors and dentists and allied professions so as to cause minimum disruption in the medical needs of the community.

13. Policies governing the drafting of aliens in the United States should be modified in the following ways to make those policies more equitable and bring them into closer conformity with the country's treaty arrangements:

A. All nonimmigrant aliens should be exempt from military service.

B. Resident aliens should not be subject to military service until 1 year after their entry into the United States as immigrants.

C. One year after entry, all resident aliens should be subject to military draft equally with U.S. citizens unless they elect to abandon permanently the status of permanent alien and the prospect of U.S. citizenship.

D. Aliens who have served 12 months or more in the Armed Forces of a country with which the United States is allied in mutual defense activities should be exempted from U.S. military service, and credit toward the U.S. military service obligation should be given for any such service of a shorter period.

In arriving at the recommendations presented herein, the Commission considered other propositions which it rejected. Among them were:

1. Elimination of the draft and reliance on an all-volunteer military force.

Although there are many arguments against an exclusively volunteer force, the decisive one, the Commission concluded, was its inflexible nature, allowing no provision for the rapid procurement of larger numbers of men if they were needed in times of crisis.

2. A system of universal training.

In the context in which the Commission studied it, universal training is a program designed by its proponents to offer physical fitness, self-discipline and remedial training to great numbers of young Americans—and not a substitute for the draft. The Commission concluded that:

A. Such a program cannot be justified on the grounds of military need, and

B. Compulsion is not a proper means of accomplishing the worthwhile objectives of rehabilitation.

The problem of men rejected for service for health and educational deficiencies, to which universal training is directed, is one which presents the country with a tragedy of urgent dimensions. Recommendations in this report will, the Commission hopes, help to alleviate this problem.

The proposal to examine all 18-year-old men will help in identifying the problems and obtaining assistance for those rejected. The proposal to permit men failing to meet induction standards to volunteer for service and receive special training will also be of value. But the larger part of this problem is imbedded in the conditions of the rejected men's lives, such as discrimination and poverty. It is essential to the future of the country that further steps be taken to correct those conditions before they can grow—as they are growing now—into a national shame and a threat to the nation's security.

3. A system of compulsory national service; and along with that,

4. Volunteer national service as an alternative to military service.

The Commission found first of all that there are difficult questions of public policy—and a lack of constitutional basis—involved in compulsory national service. Second, it concluded that no fair way exists to equate voluntary service programs with military service.

Volunteer national service must, then, be considered on its own merits as a separate program unrelated to military service. That there is a spirited interest in such service today is abundantly clear. But the needs which such service would meet and the way in which programs would be administered and financed are matters which are still inconclusive. The Commission received no clear or precise answers to the questions it raised concerning them. The Commission is sensitive to the spirit which motivates the desire for national service, and it suggests further research to define the issues more clearly, together with public and private experimentation with pilot programs.

5. Recognition as conscientious objectors of those opposed to particular wars (instead of war in any form).

There is support within the Commission for this proposal. However, a majority of the Commission opposes it. The Commission majority believes, moreover, that the recent Supreme Court decision in *U.S.* v. *Seeger* offers sufficient guidance in defining the standards of the conscientious objector's position. That decision interprets the statute's requirement that conscientious objection be based on religious training and belief, to include "a given belief that is sincere and meaningful [and] occupies a place in the life of its possessor parallel to that filled by the orthodox belief in God of one who clearly qualifies for the exemption."

There remains another point to be made in this summary:

The Commission gave careful study to the effect of the draft on and its fairness to the Negro. His position in the military manpower situation is in many ways disproportionate, even though he does not serve in the Armed Forces out of proportion to his percentage of the population. He is underrepresented (1.3 percent) on local draft boards. The number of men rejected for service reflects a much higher percentage (almost 50 percent) of Negro men found disqualified than of whites (25 percent). And yet, recent studies indicate that proportionately more (30 percent) Negroes of the group qualified for service are drafted than whites (18 percent)—primarily because fewer Negroes are admitted into Reserve or officer training programs. Enlistment rates for qualified Negroes and whites are about equal, but reenlistments for Negroes are higher: Department of Defense figures show that the rate of first-term reenlistments is now more than double that of white troops. Negro soldiers have a high record of volunteering for service in elite combat units. This is reflected in, but could not be said to be the sole reason for, the Negro's overrepresentation in combat (in terms of his proportion of the population): Although Negro troops account for only 11 percent of the total U.S. enlisted personnel in Vietnam, Negro soldiers comprise 14.5 percent of all Army units, and in Army combat units the proportion is, according to the Department of Defense, "appreciably higher" than that. During the first 11 months of 1966, Negro soldiers totaled 22.4 percent of all Army troops killed in action.

There are reasons to believe, the Commission finds, that many of the statistics are comparable for some other minority groups, although precise information is not available. Social and economic injustices in the society itself are at the root of inequities which exist. It is the Commission's hope that the recommendations contained in this report will have the effect of helping to correct those inequities.

51

The issue of a volunteer army has attracted an increasing amount of attention in recent years. One of the basic concerns of those interested in the proposal is the economic feasibility of such a program. Walter Y. Oi, an economist at the University of Washington, did an extensive amount of research into the economics of a volunteer army,[26] and he concluded that an army of 2.65 million men

26. Walter Y. Oi, "The Costs and Implications of an All-Volunteer Force," in Sol Tax, ed., *The Draft*, 221–51.

could be raised and maintained on a voluntary basis by an additional four billion dollars annually in military pay. Oi argued that the draft was counterproductive, causing reduced output and efficiency in the economic system, and a volunteer army, although seemingly more expensive, would actually prove a real saving.

The best general analysis of the functioning of a volunteer system has been offered by Professor Milton Friedman of the University of Chicago.

Milton Friedman: "Why Not a Voluntary Army?"

Manning our military forces currently requires the services of only a minority of young men. At most, something like one-third will have seen military service by the time they reach age 26. This percentage is scheduled to decline still further as the youngsters born in the postwar baby boom come of age. Hence, some method of "selective service"— of deciding which young man should serve and which two or three should not—is inevitable. However, the present method is inequitable, wasteful, and inconsistent with a free society.

On this point there is wide agreement. Even most supporters of a draft like the present one regard it as at best a necessary evil. And representatives of all parts of the political spectrum have urged that conscription be abolished—including John K. Galbraith and Barry Goldwater; the New Left and the Republican Ripon Society.

The disadvantages of our present system of compulsion and the advantages of a voluntary army are so widely recognized that we can deal with them very briefly (section 1). The more puzzling question is why we have continued to use compulsion. The answer is partly inertia —a carryover from a total war situation when the case for a voluntary army is far weaker (section 2). But even more, the answer is the tyranny of the status quo. The natural tendency of an administrator of a large, complex, and ongoing activity is to regard the present method of administering it as the only feasible way to do so and to object strenuously that any proposed alternative is visionary and unfeasible—even though the same man, once the change is made and it becomes the existing method, will argue just as strenuously that *it* is the only feasible method.

This bureaucratic stand-pattism has been reinforced by a confusion between the apparent and the real cost of manning the armed forces by

Reprinted from the *Congressional Record*, 90th Cong., 1st sess., Vol. 113 (March 9, 1967), pp. 6098–6100.

compulsion. The confusion has made it appear that a voluntary army would be much more expensive to the country and hence might not be feasible for fiscal reasons. In fact, the cost of a voluntary army, properly calculated, would almost surely be less than of a conscripted army (section 3a). It is entirely feasible to maintain present levels of military power on a strictly voluntary basis.

The other disadvantages that have been attributed to a voluntary army are that it might be racially unbalanced (section 3b), would not provide sufficient flexibility in size of forces (section 3c), and would enhance the political danger of undue military influence (section 3d). While the problems referred to are real, the first and third are in no way connected with the use of voluntary or compulsory means to recruit enlisted men and do not constitute valid arguments against abolishing the draft. The second has more merit but devices exist to provide moderate flexibility under a voluntary as under a compulsory system.

There is no reason why we cannot move to volunteer forces gradually —by making conditions of service more and more attractive until the whip of compulsion fades away (section 4). This, in my opinion, is the direction in which we should move, and the sooner the better.

1. THE DISADVANTAGES OF COMPULSION AND ADVANTAGES OF A VOLUNTARY ARMY

(a) *Military effectiveness.*—A volunteer army would be manned by people who had chosen a military career rather than at least partly by reluctant conscripts anxious only to serve out their term. Aside from the effect on fighting spirit, this would produce a lower turnover in the armed services, saving precious man-hours that are now wasted in training or being trained. It would permit also intensive training and a higher average level of skill of the men in the service. And it would encourage the use of more and better equipment. A smaller, but more highly skilled, technically competent, and better armed force would provide the same or greater military strength.

(b) *Individual freedom.*—A voluntary army would preserve the freedom of individuals to serve or not to serve. Or, put the other way, it would avoid the arbitrary power that now resides in draft boards to decide how a young man shall spend several of the most important years of his life—let alone whether his life shall be risked in warfare. An incidental advantage would be to raise the level and tone of political discussion.

A voluntary army would enhance also the freedom of those who now do not serve. Being conscripted has been used as a weapon—or thought by young men to be so used—to discourage freedom of speech, assembly, and protest. The freedom of young men to emigrate or to travel abroad has been limited by the need to get the permission of a draft board if the young man is not to put himself in the position of inadvertently being a lawbreaker.

A conspicuous example of the effect on freedom of a voluntary army is that it would completely eliminate the tormenting and insoluble problem now posed by the conscientious objector—real or pretended.

(c) *Arbitrary discrimination.*—A by-product of freedom to serve would be avoidance of the present arbitrary discrimination among different groups. A large fraction of the poor are rejected on physical or mental grounds. The relatively well-to-do are in an especially good position to take advantage of the possibilities of deferment offered by continuing their schooling. Hence the draft bears disproportionately on the upper lower classes and the lower middle classes. The fraction of high-school graduates who serve is vastly higher than of either of those who have gone to college or those who dropped out before finishing high school.

(d) *Removal of uncertainty for individuals subject to draft.*—A voluntary army would permit young men, both those who serve and those who do not, to plan their schooling, their careers, their marriages, and their families in accordance with their own long run interests. As it is, the uncertainty about the draft affects every decision they make and often leads them to behave differently than they otherwise would in the correct or mistaken belief that they will thereby reduce the chance of being drafted. This disadvantage could be avoided under a compulsory system by, for example, a universal lottery that at age 16, say, assigned youngsters categories such as: certain to be called, likely to be called, possibly will be called, unlikely to be called, certain not to be called. The size of each category would be determined by estimates of future military needs.

(e) *Effect on rest of community.*—Substitution of a voluntary army (or of a lottery) for the present draft would permit colleges and universities to pursue their proper educational function, freed alike from the incubus of young men—probably numbering in the hundreds of thousands—who would prefer to be at work rather than in school but who now continue their schooling in the hope of avoiding the draft and from controversy about issues strictly irrelevant to their educational function. We certainly need controversy in the universities—but about intellectual and educational issues, not whether to rank or not to rank.

Similarly, the community at large would benefit from the reduction of unwise earlier marriages contracted at least partly under the whip of the draft and from the probable associated reduction in the birth rate. Industry and government would benefit from being able to hire young men on their merits, not their deferments.

(f) *Defects unavoidable under compulsion.*—So long as compulsion is retained, inequity, waste, and interference with freedom are inevitable. A lottery would only make the arbitrary element in the present system overt. Universal national service would only compound the evil—regimenting all young men, and perhaps women, to camouflage the regimentation of some.

2. The Situation in Time of Major War

If a very large fraction of the young men of the relevant age groups are required—or will be used whether required or not—in the military services, the advantages of a voluntary army become very small. It would still be technically possible to have a voluntary army, and there would still be some advantages, since it is doubtful that literally 100 percent of the potential candidates will in fact be drawn into the army. But if nearly everyone who is physically capable will serve anyway, there is little room for free choice, the avoidance of uncertainty, and so on. And to rely on volunteers under such conditions would then require very high pay in the armed services, and very high burdens on those who do not serve, in order to attract a sufficient number into the armed forces. This would involve serious political and administrative problems. To put it differently, and in terms that will become fully clear to non-economists only later, it might turn out that the implicit tax of forced service is less bad than the alternative taxes that would have to be used to finance a voluntary army.

Hence for a major war, a strong case can be made for compulsory service. And indeed, compulsory service has been introduced in the United States only under such conditions—in the Civil War, World War I, and World War II. It is hardly conceivable that it would have been introduced afresh in, say, 1950, if a system of compulsory service had not so recently been in full swing. As it was, the easiest thing to do when military needs for manpower rose was to reactivate the recent wartime technique.

3. POSSIBLE DISADVANTAGES OF A VOLUNTARY ARMY

(a) *Is a voluntary army feasible?*—Under present conditions, the number of persons who volunteer for armed service is inadequate to man the armed forces, and even so, many who volunteer do so only because they anticipate being drafted. The number of "true" volunteers is clearly much too small to man armed forces of our present size. This undoubted fact is repeatedly cited as evidence that a voluntary army is unfeasible.

It is evidence of no such thing. It is evidence rather that we are now grossly underpaying our armed forces. The starting pay for young men who enter the armed forces is now about $45 a week—including not only cash pay and allotments but also the value of clothing, food, housing and other items furnished in kind. When the bulk of young men can command at least twice this sum in civilian life, it is little wonder that volunteers are so few. Indeed, it is somewhat surprising that there are as many as there are—testimony to the drives other than pecuniary reward that lead some young men to choose military service either as a career or for a few years.

To man our armed forces with volunteers would require making conditions of service more attractive—not only higher pay but also better housing facilities and improved amenities in other respects. It will be replied that money is not the only factor young men consider in choosing their careers. That is certainly true—and equally certainly irrelevant. Adequate pay alone may not attract, but inadequate pay can certainly deter. Military service has many non-monetary attractions to young men—the chance to serve one's country, adventure, travel, opportunities for training, and so on. Not the least of the advantages of a voluntary army is that the military would have to improve their personnel policies and pay more attention to meeting the needs of the enlisted men. They now need pay little attention to them, since they can fill their ranks with conscripts serving under compulsion. Indeed, it is a tribute to their humanitarianism—and the effectiveness of indirect pressures via the political process—that service in the armed forces is not made even less attractive than it now is.

The personnel policies of the armed forces have been repeatedly criticized—and, with no spur, repeatedly left unreformed. Imaginative policies designed to make the armed forces attractive to the kind of men the armed services would like to have—plus the elimination of compulsion which now makes military service synonomous with enforced incarceration—could change drastically the whole image that the armed services present to young men. The air force, because it has relied so heavily on "real" volunteers, perhaps comes closest to demonstrating what could be done.

The question how much more we would have to pay to attract sufficient volunteers has been studied intensively in the Department of Defense study of military recruitment. Based on a variety of evidence collected in that study, Walter Oi estimates in his paper that a starting pay (again including pay in kind as well as in cash) of something like $4,000 to $5,500 a year—about $80 to $100 a week—would suffice. This is surely not an unreasonable sum. Oi estimates that the total extra payroll costs (after allowing for the savings in turnover and men employed in training) would be around $3 billion to $4 billion a year for armed forces equivalent to 2.7 million men under present methods of recruitment and not more than $8 billion a year for armed forces equivalent to the present higher number of men (around 3.1 or 3.2 million men). Based on the same evidence, the Defense Department has come up with estimates as high as $17.5 billion. Even the highest of these estimates is not in any way unfeasible in the context of total federal government expenditures of more than $175 billion a year.

Whatever may be the exact figure, it is a highly misleading indication of the cost incurred in shifting from compulsion to a voluntary army. There are net advantages, not disadvantages, in offering volunteers conditions sufficiently attractive to recruit the number of young men required.

This is clearly true on the level of individual equity: the soldier no less than the rest of us is worth his hire. How can we justify paying him less than the amount for which he is willing to serve? How can we justify, that is, involuntary servitude except in times of the greatest national emergency? One of the great gains in the progress of civilization was the elimination of the power of the noble or the sovereign to exact compulsory servitude.

On a more mundane budgetary level, the argument that a voluntary army would cost more simply involves a confusion of apparent with real cost. By this argument, the construction of the Great Pyramid with slave labor was a cheap project. The real cost of conscripting a soldier who would not voluntarily serve on present terms is not his pay and the cost of his keep. It is the amount for which he would be willing to serve. He is paying the difference. This is the extra cost to him that must be added to the cost borne by the rest of us. Compare, for example, the cost to a star professional football player and to an unemployed worker. Both might have the same attitudes toward the army and like—or dislike—a military career equally. But because the one has so much better alternatives than the other, it would take a much higher sum to attract him. When he is forced to serve, we are in effect imposing on him a tax in kind equal in value to the difference between what it would take to attract him and the military pay he actually receives. This implicit tax in kind should be added to the explicit taxes imposed on the rest of us to get the real cost of our armed forces.

If this is done, it will be seen at once that abandoning the draft would almost surely reduce the real cost—because the armed forces would then be manned by men for whom soldiering was the best available career, and hence who would require the lowest sums of money to induce them to serve. Abandoning the draft might raise the apparent money cost to the government but only because it would substitute taxes in money for taxes in kind.

Moreover, there are some important offsets even to the increase in apparent money cost. In addition to the lower turnover, already taken into account in the estimates cited, the higher average level of skill would permit further reductions in the size of the army, saving monetary cost to the government. Because manpower is cheap to the military, they now tend to waste it, using enlisted men for tasks that could be performed by civilians or machines, or eliminated entirely. Moreover, better pay at the time to volunteers might lessen the political appeal of veteran's benefits that we now grant after the event. These now cost us over $6 billion a year or one-third as much as current annual payroll costs for the active armed forces—and they will doubtless continue to rise under present conditions.

There are still other offsets. Colleges and universities would be saved the cost of housing, seating, and entertaining hundreds of thousands of young men. Total output of the community would be higher both because these men would be at work and because the young men who now go to work could be used more effectively. They could be offered and could accept jobs requiring considerable training instead of having to take stop-gap jobs while awaiting a possible call to service. Perhaps there are some effects in the opposite direction, but I have not been able to find any.

Whatever happens to the apparent monetary cost, the real cost of a voluntary army would almost surely be less than of the present system and it is not even clear that the apparent monetary cost would be higher—if it is correctly measured for the community as a whole. In any event, there can be little doubt that wholly voluntary armed forces of roughly the present size are entirely feasible on economic and fiscal grounds.

(b) *Would a voluntary army be racially unbalanced?*—It has been argued that a military career would be so much more attractive to the poor than the well-to-do that volunteer armed services would be staffed disproportionately by the poor. Since Negroes constitute a high proportion of the poor, it is further argued that volunteer armed forces would be largely Negro.

There is first a question of fact. This tendency is present today in exaggerated form—the present levels of pay are *comparatively* more attractive to Negroes than the higher levels of pay in voluntary armed forces would be. Yet the fraction of persons in the armed forces who are Negro is roughly the same as in the population at large. It has been estimated that even if every qualified Negro who does not now serve were to serve, whites would still constitute a substantial majority of the armed forces. And this is a wholly unrealistic possibility. The military services require a wide variety of skills and offer varied opportunities. They have always appealed to people of varied classes and backgrounds and they will continue to do so. Particularly if pay and amenities were made more attractive, there is every reason to expect that they would draw from all segments of the community.

In part, this argument involves invalid extrapolation from the present conscripted army to a voluntary army. Because we conscript, we pay salaries that are attractive only to the disadvantaged among us.

Beyond this question of fact, there is the more basic question of principle. Clearly, it is a good thing not a bad thing to offer better alternatives to the currently disadvantaged. The argument to the contrary rests on a political judgment: that a high ratio of Negroes in the armed services would exacerbate racial tensions at home and provide in the form of ex-soldiers a militarily trained group to foment violence. Perhaps there is something to this. My own inclination is to regard it as the reddest of red herrings. Our government should discriminate neither in the civil nor in the military services. We must handle our domestic problems as best we can and not use them as an excuse for denying Negroes opportunities in the military service.

(c) *Would a voluntary army have sufficient flexibility?*—One of the advantages cited for conscription is that it permits great flexibility in the size of the armed services. Let military needs suddenly increase, and draft calls can be rapidly stepped up, and conversely.

This is a real advantage—but can easily be overvalued. Emergencies must be met with forces in being, however they are recruited. Many months now elapse between an increase in draft calls, and the availability of additional trained men.

The key question is how much flexibility is required. Recruitment by voluntary means could provide considerable flexibility—at a cost. The way to do so would be to make pay and conditions of service more attractive than is required to recruit the number of men that it is anticipated will be needed. There would then be an excess of volunteers—queues. If the number of men required increased, the queues could be shortened and conversely.

The change in scale involved in a shift from conditions like the present to a total war is a very different matter. If the military judgment is that, in such a contingency, there would be time and reason to expand the armed forces manyfold, either universal training, to provide a trained reserve force, or stand-by provisions for conscription could be justified. Both are very different from the use of conscription to man the standing army in time of peace or brush-fire wars or wars like that in Viet Nam which require recruiting only a minority of young men.

The flexibility provided by conscription has another side. It means that, at least for a time, the administration and the military services can proceed fairly arbitrarily in committing U.S. forces. The voluntary method provides a continuing referendum of the public at large. The popularity or unpopularity of the activities for which the armed forces are used will clearly affect the ease of recruiting men. This is a consideration that will be regarded by some as an advantage of conscription, by others, including myself, as a disadvantage.

(d) *Is a "professional army" a political danger?*—There is little question that large armed forces plus the industrial complex required to support them constitute an ever-present threat to political freedom. Our free institutions would certainly be safer if the conditions of the world permitted us to maintain far smaller armed forces.

This valid fear has been converted into an invalid argument against voluntary armed forces. They would constitute a professional army, it is said, that would lack contact with the populace and become an independent political force, whereas a conscripted army regains basically a citizen army. The fallacy in this argument is that the danger comes primarily from the officers, who are now and always have been a professional corps of volunteers. A few examples from history will show that the danger to political stability is largely unrelated to the method of recruiting enlisted men.

Napoleon and Franco both rose to power at the head of conscripts. The recent military takeover in Argentina was by armed forces recruiting enlisted men by conscription. Britain and the U.S. have maintained freedom while relying primarily on volunteers: Switzerland and Sweden, while using conscription. It is hard to find any relation historically between the method of recruiting enlisted men and the political threat from the armed forces.

However we recruit enlisted men, it is essential that we adopt practices that will guard against the political danger of creating a military corps with loyalties of its own and out of contact with the broader body politic. Fortunately, we have so far largely avoided this danger. The broad basis of recruitment to the military academies, by geography as well as social and economic factors, the ROTC programs in the colleges, the recruitment of officers from enlisted men, and similar measures, have all contributed to this result.

For the future, we need to follow policies that will foster lateral recruitment into the officer corps from civilian activities—rather than primarily promotion from within. The military services no less than the civil service need and will benefit from in-and-outers. For the political gain, we should be willing to bear the higher financial costs involved in fairly high turnover and rather short average terms of service for officers. We should follow personnel policies that will continue to make at least a period of military service as an officer attractive to young men from many walks of life.

There is no way of avoiding the political danger altogether. But it can be minimized as readily with a volunteer as with a conscripted army.

4. The Transition to a Volunteer Army

Given the will, there is no reason why the transition to volunteer armed forces cannot begin at once and proceed gradually by a process of trial and error. We do not need precise and accurate knowledge of the levels of pay and amenities that will be required. We need take no irreversible step.

Out of simple justice, we should in any event raise the pay and improve the living conditions of enlisted men. If it were proposed explicitly that a special income tax of 50 per cent be imposed on enlisted men in the armed services, there would be cries of outrage. Yet that is what our present pay scales plus conscription amount to. If we started rectifying this injustice, the number of "real" volunteers would increase, even while conscription continued. Experience would show how responsive the number of volunteers is to the terms offered and how much these terms would have to be improved to attract enough men. As the number of volunteers increased, the lash of compulsion could fade away.

This picture is overdrawn in one important respect. Unless it is clear that conscription is definitely to be abolished in a reasonably short time, the armed services will not have sufficient incentive to improve their recruitment and personnel policies. They will be tempted to procrastinate, relying on the crutch of conscription. The real survival strength of conscription is that it eases the life of the top mlitary command. Hence, it would be highly desirable to have a definite termination date set for conscription.

5. CONCLUSION

The case for abolishing conscription and recruiting our armed forces by voluntary methods seems to me overwhelming. One of the greatest advances in human freedom was the commutation of taxes in kind to taxes in money. We have reverted to a barbarous custom. It is past time that we regain our heritage.

52

Draft resistance, which broadened and intensified as the war in Vietnam escalated, assumed a more organized structure in October, 1967, when forty relatively small groups which had been engaged in sporadic opposition to the draft formed "the Resistance," an organization committed to confronting and challenging the Selective Service System. That same month, "A Call to Resist Illegitimate Authority" was issued, having among its original sponsors Herbert Marcuse, Bishop James Pike, Doctor Benjamin Spock, Reverend William Sloane Coffin, and scores of other leading educators, artists, and religious leaders. This statement, and its impressive roster of supporters, helped to "legitimize" the resistance movement for many who had previously been rather hesitant in their support of it and aided its expansion from a series of isolated, individual actions to the "Hell no, we won't go!" chanted on scores of American campuses.

A Call to Resist Illegitimate Authority

1. An ever growing number of young American men are finding that the American war in Vietnam so outrages their deepest moral and religious sense that they cannot contribute to it in any way. We share their moral outrage.

2. We further believe that the war is unconstitutional and illegal. Congress has not declared a war as required by the Constitution. Moreover, under the Constitution, treaties signed by the President and ratified by the Senate have the same force as the Constitution itself. The Charter of the United Nations is such a treaty. The Charter specifically obligates the United States to refrain from force or the threat of force in international relations. It requires member states to exhaust every peaceful means of settling disputes and to submit disputes which cannot be settled peacefully to the Security Council. The United States has systematically violated all of these Charter provisions for thirteen years.

3. Moreover, this war violates international agreements, treaties and principles of law which the United States Government has solemnly endorsed. The combat role of the United States troops in Vietnam violates the Geneva Accords of 1954 which our government pledges to support but has since subverted. The destruction of rice, crops and livestock; the burning and bulldozing of entire villages consisting exclusively of civilian structures; the interning of civilian non-combatants in concentration camps; the summary executions of civilians in captured villages who could not produce satisfactory evidence of their loyalties or did not wish to be removed to concentration camps; the slaughter of peasants who dared to stand up in their fields and shake their fists at American helicopters;—these are all actions of the kind which the United States and the other victorious powers of World War II declared to be crimes against humanity for which individuals were to be held personally responsible even when acting under the orders of their governments and for which Germans were sentenced at Nuremberg to long prison terms and death. The prohibition of such acts as war crimes was incorporated in treaty law by the Geneva Conventions of 1949, ratified by the United States. These are commitments to the other countries and to Mankind, and they would claim our allegiance even if Congress should declare war.

4. We also believe it is an unconstitutional denial of religious liberty and equal protection of the laws to withhold draft exemption from men

Reprinted from the *New York Review of Books*, Vol. 9 (October 12, 1967).

whose religious or profound philosophical beliefs are opposed to what in the Western religious tradition have long been known as unjust wars.

5. Therefore, we believe on all these grounds that every free man has a legal right and a moral duty to exert every effort to end this war, to avoid collusion with it, and to encourage others to do the same. Young men in the armed forces or threatened with the draft face the most excruciating choices. For them various forms of resistance risk separation from their families and their country, destruction of their careers, loss of their freedom and loss of their lives. Each must choose the course of resistance dictated by his conscience and circumstances. Among those already in the armed forces some are refusing to obey specific illegal and immoral orders, some are attempting to educate their fellow servicemen on the murderous and barbarous nature of the war. Among those not in the armed forces some are applying for status as conscientious objectors to American aggression in Vietnam, some are refusing to be inducted. Among both groups, some are resisting openly and paying a heavy penalty, some are organizing more resistance within the United States and some have sought sanctuary in other countries.

6. We believe that each of these forms of resistance against illegitimate authority is courageous and justified. Many of us believe that open resistance to the war and the draft is the course of action most likely to strengthen the moral resolve with which all of us can oppose the war and most likely to bring an end to the war.

7. We will continue to lend our support to those who undertake resistance to this war. We will raise funds to organize draft resistance unions, to supply legal defense and bail, to support families and otherwise aid resistance to the war in whatever ways may seem appropriate.

8. We firmly believe that our statement is the sort of speech that under the First Amendment must be free, and that the actions we will undertake are as legal as is the war resistance of the young men themselves. In any case, we feel that we cannot shrink from fulfilling our responsibilities to the youth whom many of us teach, to the country whose freedom we cherish, and to the ancient traditions of religion and philosophy which we strive to preserve in this generation.

9. We call upon all men of good will to join us in this confrontation with immoral authority. Especially we call upon the universities to fulfill their mission of enlightenment and religious organizations to honor their heritage of brotherhood. Now is the time to resist!

53

In response to a rash of public burnings of draft cards, Congress enacted a law in August, 1965, making such actions punishable by up to five years' imprisonment and a $10,000 fine. This new law did not seem to significantly limit the numbers of persons who burned or mutilated their cards. As opposition to the war in Vietnam mounted, the burnings also increased. Those who favored such action saw it as a dramatic means of making a symbolic statement and, hence, protected by the First Amendment.

The test of the law's constitutionality came on May 27, 1968, when the Supreme Court decided the case of *United States* v. *O'Brien*. David O'Brien had burned his draft card on March 31, 1966, on the steps of the South Boston Court House and had been found guilty in the District Court. The Court of Appeals had overturned his conviction on constitutional grounds, and the government then carried an appeal to the Supreme Court. The Court decided, 7–1, that the law was constitutional. The following excerpts are from Chief Justice Earl Warren's majority opinion and Justice William Douglas's dissent.

United States v. O'Brien, 1968

Opinion of the Court

On the morning of March 31, 1966, David Paul O'Brien and three companions burned their Selective Service registration certificates on the steps of the South Boston Courthouse. . . .

For this act, O'Brien was indicted, tried, convicted, and sentenced. . . . He did not contest the fact that he had burned the certificate. He stated in argument to the jury that he burned the certificate publicly to influence others to adopt his antiwar beliefs, as he put it, "so that other people would reevaluate their positions with Selective Service, with the armed forces, and reevaluate their place in the culture of today, to hopefully consider my position. . . .

In the District Court, O'Brien argued that the 1965 amendment prohibiting the knowing destruction or mutilation of certificates was unconstitutional because it was enacted to abridge free speech, and because it served no legitimate legislative purpose. The District Court rejected

Reprinted from *United States* v. *O'Brien*, 391 U.S. 367 [citations deleted].

these arguments, holding that the statute on its face did not abridge
First Amendment rights, that the court was not competent to inquire
into the motives of Congress in enacting the 1965 amendment, and
that the amendment was a reasonable exercise of the power of Congress to raise armies. . . .

I

. . . Congress demonstrated its concern that certificates issued by the
Selective Service System might be abused well before the 1965 amendment here challenged. . . . In addition, as previously mentioned, regulations of the Selective Service System required registrants to keep both
their registration and classification certificates in their personal possession at all times. And section 12 (b) (6) of the Act, made knowing violation of any provision of the Act or rules and regulations promulgated
pursuant thereto a felony. . . .

II

O'Brien first argues that the 1965 Amendment is unconstitutional as
applied to him because his act of burning his registration certificate
was protected "symbolic speech" within the First Amendment. His argument is that the freedom of expression which the First Amendment
guarantees includes all modes of "communications of ideas by conduct,"
and that his conduct is within this definition because he did it in "demonstration against the war and against the draft."

We cannot accept the view that an apparently limitless variety of
conduct can be labeled "speech" whenever the person engaging in the
conduct intends thereby to express an idea. However, even on the assumption that the alleged communicative element in O'Brien's conduct
is sufficient to bring into play the First Amendment, it does not necessarily follow that the destruction of a registration certificate is constitutionally protected activity. This Court has held that when "speech"
and "nonspeech" elements are combined in the same course of conduct,
a sufficiently important governmental interest in regulating the nonspeech element can justify incidental limitations on First Amendment
freedoms. To characterize the quality of the governmental interest which
must appear, the Court has employed a variety of descriptive terms:
compelling; substantial; subordinating; paramount; cogent; strong.
Whatever imprecision inheres in these terms, we think it clear that a
government regulation is sufficiently justified if it is within the constitutional power of the Government; if it furthers an important or substantial governmental interest; if the governmental interest is unrelated

to the suppression of free expression; and if the incidental restriction on alleged First Amendment freedoms is no greater than is essential to the furtherance of that interest. We find that the 1965 Amendment to Section 2 (b) (3) of the Universal Military Training and Service Act meets all of these requirements, and consequently that O'Brien can be constitutionally convicted for violating it.

The constitutional power of Congress to raise and support armies and to make all laws necessary and proper to that end is broad and sweeping. The power of Congress to classify and conscript manpower for military service is "beyond question." Pursuant to this power, Congress may establish a system of registration for individuals liable for training and service, and may require such individuals within reason to cooperate in the registration system. The issuance of certificates indicating the registration and eligibility classification of individuals is a legitimate and substantial administrative aid in the functioning of this system. And legislation to insure the continuing availability of issued certificates serves a legitimate and substantial purpose in the system's administration.

O'Brien's argument to the contrary is necessarily premised upon his unrealistic characterization of Selective Service certificates. He essentially adopts the position that such certificates are so many pieces of paper designed to notify registrants of their registration or classification, to be retained or tossed in the wastebasket according to the convenience or taste of the registrant. Once the registrant has received notification, according to this view, there is no reason for him to retain the certificates. O'Brien notes that most of the information on a registration certificate serves no notification purpose at all; the registrant hardly needs to be told his address and physical characteristics. We agree that the registration certificate contains much information of which the registrant needs no notification. This circumstance, however, does not lead to the conclusion that the certificate serves no purpose but that like the classification certificate, it serves purposes in addition to initial notification. . . .

The many functions performed by Selective Service certificates establish beyond doubt that Congress has a legitimate and substantial interest in preventing their wanton and unrestrained destruction and assuring their continuing availability by punishing people who knowingly and willfully destroy or mutilate them. And we are unpersuaded that the pre-existence of the nonpossession regulations in any way negates this interest. . . .

We think it apparent that the continuing availability to each registrant of his Selective Service certificates substantially furthers the smooth and proper functioning of the system that Congress has established to raise armies. We think it is also apparent that the Nation has a vital interest in having a system for raising armies that functions with maximum efficiency and is capable of easily and quickly responding to continually changing circumstances. For these reasons, the Government has a substantial interest in assuring the continuing availability of issued Selective Service certificates.

It is equally clear that the 1965 amendment specifically protests this substantial governmental interest. We perceive no alternative means that would more precisely and narrowly assure the continuing availability of issued Selective Service certificates than a law which prohibits their wilful mutilation or destruction. The 1965 amendment prohibits such conduct and does nothing more. In other words, both the governmental interest and the operation of the 1965 amendment are limited to the noncommunicative aspect of O'Brien's conduct. The governmental interest and the scope of the 1965 amendment are limited to preventing harm to the smooth and efficient functioning of the Selective Service System. When O'Brien deliberately rendered unavailable his registration certificate, he wilfully frustrated this governmental interest. For this noncommunicative impact of his conduct, and for nothing else, he was convicted. . . .

III

O'Brien finally argues that the 1965 amendment is unconstitutional as enacted because what he calls the "purpose" of Congress was "to suppress freedom of speech." We reject this argument because under settled principles the purpose of Congress, as O'Brien uses that term, is not a basis for declaring this legislation unconstitutional. . . .

JUSTICE DOUGLAS'S DISSENT

The Court states that the constitutional power of Congress to raise and support armies is "broad and sweeping" and that Congress' power "to classify and conscript manpower for military service is 'beyond question.'" This is undoubtedly true in times when, by declaration of Congress, the Nation is in a state of war. The underlying and basic problem in this case, however, is whether conscription is permissible in absence of a declaration of war. That question has not been briefed nor was it presented in oral argument; but it is, I submit, a question upon which the litigants and the country are entitled to a ruling. . . . It is time that we made a ruling. . . .

54

Early in 1969, President Nixon appointed a commission headed by former Secretary of Defense Gates to examine the feasibility of an all-volunteer army. The committee issued a report on February 20, 1970, in which it unanimously endorsed moving toward a volunteer army, arguing that the conversion could be achieved with a $2.7 billion initial increase in the defense budget and that such a conversion plan would actually be cheaper in the long run.

In addition, a volunteer army would allow a much more intelligent and efficient use of manpower, since only a small number of draftees and draft-motivated volunteers reenlisted, and much of the army's time and energy was expended on training men who were then discharged precisely when their skills became valuable. The commission concluded that a 2,500,000-man force could be maintained with an annual addition of 325,000 volunteers. This figure, it was felt, could easily be met through increased pay, improved conditions of service, and more vigorous recruiting.

The report offered evidence that such a force would not be composed mainly of minority groups and insisted that the plan, rather than encouraging a trend toward militarism, would in fact serve as a real check upon military adventuring.

Gates Commission Report, 1970

Since the founding of the republic, a primary task of the government of the United States has been to provide for the common defense of a society established to secure the blessings of liberty and justice. Without endangering the nation's security, the means of defense should support the aims of the society.

The armed forces today play an honorable and important part in promoting the nation's security, as they have since our freedoms were won

Reprinted from U.S. President's Commission on an All-Volunteer Armed Force, *Report* (Washington, D.C.: Government Printing Office, 1970), pp. 5–10.

on the battlefield at Yorktown. A fundamental consideration that has guided this Commission is the need to maintain and improve the effectiveness, dignity, and status of the armed forces so they may continue to play their proper role.

The Commission has not attempted to judge the size of the armed forces the nation requires. Instead, it has accepted a range of estimates made for planning purposes which anticipate maintaining a total force in the future somewhere between 2,000,000 and 3,000,000 men.

We unanimously believe that the nation's interests will be better served by an all-volunteer force, supported by an effective standby draft, than by a mixed force of volunteers and conscripts; that steps should be taken promptly to move in this direction; and that the first indispensable step is to remove the present inequity in the pay of men serving their first term in the armed forces.

The United States has relied throughout its history on a voluntary armed force except during major wars and since 1948. A return to an all-volunteer force will strengthen our freedoms, remove an inequity now imposed on the expression of the patriotism that has never been lacking among our youth, promote the efficiency of the armed forces, and enhance their dignity. It is the system for maintaining standing forces that minimizes government interference with the freedom of the individual to determine his own life in accord with his values.

The Commission bases its judgments on long-range considerations of what method of recruiting manpower will strengthen our society's foundations. The Commission's members have reached agreement on their recommendations only as the result of prolonged study and searching debate, and in spite of initial division. We are, of course, fully aware of the current and frequently emotional public debate on national priorities, foreign policy, and the military, but are agreed that such issues stand apart from the question of when and how to end conscription. . . .

The draft has been an accepted feature of American life for a generation, and its elimination will represent still another major change in a society much buffeted by change and alarmed by violent attacks on the established order. Yet the status quo can be changed constructively and the society improved peacefully, by responsible and responsive government. It is in this spirit that the Commission has deliberated and arrived at its recommendations. However necessary conscription may have been in World War II, it has revealed many disadvantages in the past generation. It has been a costly, inequitable, and divisive procedure for recruiting men for the armed forces. It has imposed heavy burdens on a small minority of young men while easing slightly the tax burden on the rest of us. It has introduced needless uncertainty into the lives of all our young men. It has burdened draft boards with painful decisions about who shall be compelled to serve and who shall be deferred. It has weakened the political fabric of our society and impaired the delicate web of shared values that alone enables a free society to exist.

These costs of conscription would have to be borne if they were a necessary price for defending our peace and security. They are intolerable when there is an alternative consistent with our basic national values.

The alternative is an all-volunteer force, and the Commission recommends these steps toward it:

1. Raise the average level of basic pay for military personnel in the first two years of service from $180 a month to $315 a month, the increase to become effective on July 1, 1970. This involves an increase in total compensation (including the value of food, lodging, clothing, and fringe benefits) from $301 a month to $437 a month. The basic pay of officers in the first two years should be raised from an average level of $428 a month to $578 a month, and their total compensation from $717 a month to $869 a month.

2. Make comprehensive improvements in conditions of military service and in recruiting as set forth elsewhere in the report.

3. Establish a standby draft system by June 30, 1971, to be activated by joint resolution of Congress upon request of the President.

55

On April 23, 1970, President Nixon sent a special message to Congress outlining a phased implementation of the Gates Commission report. Such a program would gradually terminate the draft and demonstrate a "continuing commitment to the maximum freedom for the individual, enshrined in our earliest traditions and documents."

Senators Mark Hatfield and Barry Goldwater sponsored a bill which would have immediately provided the pay increases recommended in the commission's report, but it failed to pass on August 25, 1970. The administration, which had opposed the measure on the grounds that it was too expensive and that a volunteer army could not be introduced while the war in Vietnam was in progress, eventually set July 1, 1973, as a realistic target date for the implementation of "zero draft."

Nixon's Message on the Draft, 1970

To the Congress of the United States:

The draft has been with us now for many years. It was started as a temporary, emergency measure just before World War II. We have lived with the draft so long, and relied on it through such serious crises, that too many of us now accept it as a normal part of American life.

It is now time to embrace a new approach to meeting our military manpower requirements. I have two basic proposals.

—The first deals with the fundamental way this nation should raise the armed force necessary to defend the lives and the rights of its people, and to fulfill its existing commitments abroad.

—The second deals with reforming the present recruitment system— part volunteer, part drafted—which, in the immediate future, will be needed to maintain our armed strength.

To End the Draft

On February 21, I received the report of the Commission on an All-Volunteer Armed Force, headed by former Defense Secretary Thomas S. Gates. The Commission members concluded unanimously that the interests of the nation will be better served by an all-volunteer force than by a mixed force of volunteers and draftees, and that steps should be taken in this direction.

I have carefully reviewed the report of the Commission and have discussed the subject with many others knowledgeable in this field. The preeminent consideration in any decision I make involving the American Armed Forces must be the security of the United States. I have had to weigh carefully how our responsibilities in Vietnam and our overall foreign policy would be affected by ending the draft. I also had to consider the budgetary impact, and the possible effect on our economy.

On the other hand, we have all seen the effect of the draft on our young

Reprinted from *Public Papers of the Presidents of the United States: Richard M. Nixon, 1970* (Washington, D.C.: Government Printing Office, 1971), pp. 394–98.

people, whose lives have been disrupted first by years of uncertainty, and then by the draft itself. We all know the unfairness of the present system, no matter how just we try to make it.

After careful consideration of the factors involved, I support the basic conclusion of the Commission. I agree that we should move now toward ending the draft.

From now on, the objective of this Administration is to reduce draft calls to zero, subject to the overriding considerations of national security.

In proposing that we move toward ending the draft, I must enter three cautions: First, the draft cannot be ended all at once. It must be phased out, so that we can be certain of maintaining our defense strength at every step. Second, existing induction authority expires on July 1, 1971, and I expect that it will be necessary for the next Congress to extend this authority. And third, as we move away from reliance on the draft, we must make provisions to establish a standby draft system that can be used in case of emergency.

To move toward reducing draft calls to zero, we are proceeding with a wide array of actions and proposals:

—This Administration proposed, and the Congress has approved, a six percent across-the-board pay increase for Federal employees, retroactive to the first of this year. This raises the pay of members of the Armed Forces by $1.2 billion a year.

—I shall propose an additional 20 percent pay increase for enlisted men with less than two years of service, to be effective January 1, 1971. This action, if approved by the Congress, will raise the annual pay of enlisted men with less than two years of service by $500 million a year, and is a first step in removing the present inequity in pay of men serving their first two years in the Armed Forces. The cost for Fiscal Year 1971 will be $250 million.

—In January 1971 I shall recommend to the Congress, in the Fiscal Year 1972 budget, an additional $2.0 billion for added pay and other benefits—especially for those serving their first two years— to help attract and retain the personnel we need for our Armed Forces.

—I have today directed the Secretary of Defense to give high priority to the expansion of programs designed to increase enlistments and retentions in the services. Further, I have directed that he give me a report every quarter on the progress of this program. Other agencies have been directed to assist in the effort.

—I am also directing the Secretary of Defense to review the policies and practices of the military services to give new emphasis to recognition of the individual needs, aspirations and capabilities of all military personnel.

No one can predict with precision whether or not, or precisely when, we can end conscription. It depends, in part, on the necessity of maintaining required military force levels to meet our commitments in Vietnam and elsewhere. It also depends on the degree to which the combination of military pay increases and enhanced benefits will attract and hold enough volunteers to maintain the forces we need, the attitude of young people toward military service, and the availability of jobs in the labor market.

However, I am confident that, barring any unforeseen developments, this proposed program will achieve our objective.

The starting pay of an enlisted man in our Armed Forces is—taking the latest raise into account—less than $1,500 a year. This is less than half of the minimum wage in the private sector. Of course, we should add to this the value of the food, uniforms and housing that is provided free. But it is hardly comparable to what most young men can earn as civilians. Even with special allowances, some married enlisted men have been forced to go on welfare to support their families.

The low pay illustrates another inequity of the draft. These men, in effect, pay a large hidden tax—the difference between their military pay and what they could earn as civilians. Therefore, on the grounds of equity alone, there is good reason to substantially increase pay.

While we focus on removing inequities in the pay of men serving their first few years in the military, we must not neglect the career servicemen. They are the indispensable core of our Armed Forces. The increasing technological complexity of modern defense, and the constantly changing international situation, make their assignments ever more difficult—and critical. We shall continue to make every effort to ensure that they are fairly treated and justly compensated.

There is another essential element—beyond pay and benefits, beyond the best in training and equipment—that is vital to the high morale of any armed force in a free society. It is the backing, support and confidence of the people and the society the military serves. While government can provide the economic justice our men in arms deserve—moral support and backing can come only from the American people. At few times in our history has it been more needed than today.

The consideration of national security contains no argument against these historic actions; the considerations of freedom and justice argue eloquently in their behalf.

To Reform the Draft

As we move toward our goal of ending the draft in the United States, we must deal with the draft as it now exists. This nation has a right to expect that the responsibility for national defense will be shared equitably and consistently by all segments of our society. Given this basic principle, I believe that there are important reforms that we must make in our present draft system.

It is my judgment, and that of the National Security Council, that future occupational, agricultural and student deferments are no longer dictated by the national interest. I am issuing today an Executive Order [11527] to direct that no future deferments shall be granted on the basis of employment. Very few young men at age 19 are in such critical positions that they cannot be replaced. All those who held occupational deferments before today, as well as any who may be granted such deferments from pending applications filed before today, will be deferred as they were previously.

This same Executive Order will also eliminate all future paternity deferments—except in those cases where a local draft board determines that extreme hardship would result. All those who held paternity deferments before today, as well as any who may be granted deferments from pending applications filed before today, will be deferred as long as they are living with and supporting child dependents.

I am also asking the Congress today to make some changes in the Military Selective Service Act of 1967.

The first would restore to the President discretionary authority on the deferment of students seeking baccalaureate degrees. If the Congress restores this authority, I shall promptly issue a second Executive Order that would bar all undergraduate deferments, except for young men who are undergraduate students prior to today. These young men would continue to be eligible for deferment under present regulations during their undergraduate years. This Executive Order would also end deferments for young men in junior college, and in apprentice and technical training programs, except for those who entered before today. Men participating in such programs before today would continue to be deferred until they complete them.

Should Congress pass the legislation I have requested, those young men who start college or enter apprentice or other technical training today or hereafter, and subsequently receive a notice of induction, will have their entry into service postponed until the end of the academic semester, or for apprentices and trainees, until some appropriate breaking point in their program.

Even if college deferments are phased out, college men who through ROTC or other military programs have chosen to obligate themselves to enter military service at a later date would be permitted to postpone their active duty until completion of their study program.

In each instance, I have spoken of the phasing out—not the elimination—of existing deferments. The sudden elimination of existing deferments would disrupt plans made in good faith by individuals, companies, colleges and local school systems on the basis of those deferments.

My second legislative proposal would establish a direct national call, by lottery sequence numbers each month, to improve the operation of the random selection system. We need to ensure that men throughout the country with the same lottery number have equal liability to induction.

Under the present law, for example, a man with sequence number 185 may be called up by one draft board while a man with a lower number in a different board is not called. This can happen because present law does not permit a national call of young men by lottery sequence numbers.

Some local draft boards may not have enough low numbers to fill their assigned quota for the month. As a result, these local boards are forced to call young men with higher numbers. At the same time, other draft boards throughout the country will have more low numbers than necessary to fill their quotas.

I am recommending to the Congress an amendment to suspend this quota requirement while the random selection system is in effect. If the Congress adopts this amendment, I will authorize the Selective Service System to establish a plan under which the draft call each month will be on a national basis, with the same lottery sequence numbers called throughout the country. This will result in a still more equitable draft system.

As long as we need the draft, it is incumbent upon us to make it as fair and equitable as we can. I urge favorable Congressional action on these legislative proposals for draft reform.

CONCLUSION

While I believe that these reforms in our existing draft system are essential, it should be remembered that they are improvements in a system to be used only as long as conscription continues to be necessary.

Ultimately, the preservation of a free society depends upon both the willingness of its beneficiaries to bear the burden of its defense—and the willingness of government to guarantee the freedom of the individual.

With an end to the draft, we will demonstrate to the world the responsiveness of republican government—and our continuing commitment to the maximum freedom for the individual, enshrined in our earliest traditions and founding documents. By upholding the cause of freedom without conscription we will have demonstrated in one more area the superiority of a society based upon belief in the dignity of man over a society based on the supremacy of the State.

56

On January 27, 1973, Secretary of Defense Melvin Laird announced that "zero draft" would be implemented immediately. This statement, issued the same day the peace agreement was signed in Paris and five months ahead of the administration's timetable, was read by many as an end to the draft. In fact, as eventually became clear, the Selective Service System would continue with almost all of its responsibilities, but no calls would be made upon its registrants.

Melvin Laird Announces "Zero Draft," 1973

With the signing of the peace agreement in Paris today, and after receiving a report from the Secretary of the Army that he foresees no need for further inductions, I wish to inform you that the Armed Forces henceforth will depend exclusively on volunteer soldiers, sailors, airmen and Marines. Use of the draft has ended.

This means that we have beaten President Nixon's objective of zero draft calls by five months.

I know that each of you will continue to do whatever is appropriate to support legislation to insure approval of additional incentives for our men and women as proposed in the Special Pay Incentives legislation. I am particularly concerned that without such legislation, it will be extremely difficult, if not impossible, to maintain the National Guard and

Reprinted from a news release of the Office of the Assistant Secretary of Defense (Pubic Affairs), January 27, 1973.

Reserve at levels mandated by the Congress and as required by our Total Force Concept.

I am confident that the Congress will continue to support those programs necessary to allow us to continue the zero-draft status we assume today.

I am particularly hopeful that the Senate will promptly follow the lead of the House and enact the legislation giving added incentives for service from members of the health professions, so that the requirements for health services personnel can also be put on a volunteer basis.

I want to congratulate you and your organizations for the magnificent work which has been done during the past four years in moving us from an armed force which was drafting 300,000 men a year to my decision today that use of the draft for our soldiers, sailors, airmen and Marines is finished, and that the all-volunteer era—which our Commander-in-Chief, President Nixon, has promised the American people—is upon us.

Bibliography

☆

Bernardo, Joseph C., and Eugene H. Bacon. *American Military Policy: Its Development since 1775.* Harrisburg, Pa.: Military Service Publishing Co., 1955.

Blum, Albert A. *Drafted or Deferred: Practices Past and Present.* Ann Arbor: Bureau of Industrial Relations, University of Michigan, 1967.

Boulding, Kenneth E., et al. *The Draft.* New York: Hill and Wang Co., 1968.

Brock, Peter. *Pacifism in the United States: From the Colonial Era to the First World War.* Princeton: Princeton University Press, 1968.

Carper, Jean. *Bitter Greetings: The Scandal of the Military Draft.* New York: Grossman Publishers, 1967.

Chapman, Bruce. *Wrong Man in Uniform.* New York: Trident Press, 1967.

Chatfield, Charles. *For Peace and Justice: Pacifism in America, 1914–1941.* Knoxville: The University of Tennessee Press, 1971.

Chomsky, Noam, et al. *Trials of the Resistance.* New York: Random House, Inc., 1970.

Clifford, John Garry. *The Citizen Soldiers: The Plattsburg Training Camp Movement, 1913–1920.* Lexington: University Press of Kentucky, 1972.

Crowder, Enoch H. *The Spirit of Selective Service.* New York: The Century Company, 1920.

Cunliffe, Marcus. *Soldiers and Civilians: The Martial Spirit in America, 1775–1865.* Boston: Little, Brown and Company, 1968.

Davis, James W., and Kenneth M. Dolbeare. *Little Groups of Neighbors: The Selective Service System.* Chicago: Markham Publishing Co., 1968.

Duggan, J. C. *Legislative and Statutory Development of the Federal Concept of Conscription for Military Service.* Washington, D.C.: Catholic University Press, 1946.

Eberly, Donald J., ed. *A Profile on National Service.* New York: Overseas Educational Service, 1966.

Ekirch, Arthur A., Jr. *The Civilian and the Military: A History of the American Anti-Militarist Tradition.* New York: Oxford University Press, 1956.

Evers, Alf. *Selective Service: A Guide to the Draft.* Philadelphia: J. B. Lippincott Co., 1957.

Ferber, Michael, and Staughton Lynd. *The Resistance.* Boston: Beacon Press, 1971.

Finn, James, ed. *A Conflict of Loyalties: The Case for Selective Conscientious Objection.* New York: Pegasus, 1968.

Fitzpatrick, Edward A. *Conscription and America.* Milwaukee: Richards Publishing Co., 1940.

French, Paul C. *We Won't Murder: Being the Story of Men Who Followed Their Conscientious Scruples and Helped Give Life to Democracy.* New York: Hastings House, 1940.

Friedman, Leon. *The Wise Minority.* New York: The Dial Press, 1971.

Gaylin, Willard. *In the Service of Their Country: War Resisters in Prison.* New York: The Viking Press, 1970.

Gerhardt, J. M. *The Draft and Public Policy: Issues in Military Manpower Procurement, 1945–1970.* Columbus: Ohio State University Press, 1971.

Gray, Harold S. *Character "Bad": The Story of a Conscientious Objector.* New York: Harpers, 1934.

Hassler, R. Alfred. *Conscripts of Conscience: The Story of Sixteen Objectors to Conscription.* New York: Fellowship of Reconciliation, 1942.

Huntington, Samuel. *The Soldier and the State: The Theory and Politics of Civil-Military Relations.* Cambridge: Harvard University Press, 1961.

Jacobs, Clyde E., and John F. Gallagher. *The Selective Service Act: A Case Study of the Governmental Process.* New York: Dodd, Mead and Company, 1967.

Kellogg, Walter Guest. *The Conscientious Objector.* New York: Boni and Liveright, 1919.

Lauter, Paul, and Florence Howe. *The Conspiracy of the Young.* New York: The World Publishing Company, 1970.

Leach, Jack F. *Conscription in the United States.* Rutland, Vt.: Charles E. Tuttle Publishing Company, 1952.

Little, Roger, ed. *Selective Service and American Society.* New York: Russell Sage Foundation, 1969.

Lockmiller, David A. *Enoch H. Crowder: Soldier, Lawyer and Statesman.* Columbia: University of Missouri Press, 1955.

Long, Edward L., Jr. *War and Conscience in America.* Philadelphia: Westminster Press, 1968.

Lynd, Alice, ed. *We Won't Go: Personal Accounts of War Objectors.* Boston: Beacon Press, 1968.

Marmion, Harry. *The Case against a Volunteer Army.* Chicago: Quadrangle Books, 1971.

———. *Selective Service in America: Conflict and Compromise.* New York: John Wiley & Sons, 1968.

Miller, James C., III, et. al., eds. *Why the Draft? The Case for a Volunteer Army.* Baltimore: Penguin Books, Inc., 1968.

Millis, Walter. *Arms and Men: A Study in American Military History.* New York: New American Library of World Literature, Inc., 1958.

————. *Individual Freedom and the Common Defense.* New York: The Fund for the Republic, Consultants on the Basic Issues, 1957.

————, ed. *American Military Thought.* Indianapolis: The Bobbs-Merrill Company, 1966.

Mitford, Jessica. *The Trial of Dr. Spock.* New York: Alfred A. Knopf, 1969.

Moore, Albert Burton. *Conscription and Conflict in the Confederacy.* New York: Macmillan Company, 1924.

Murdock, Eugene C. *One Million Men: The Civil War Draft in the North.* Madison: State Historical Society of Wisconsin, 1971.

Palmer, John McAuley. *America in Arms.* New Haven: Yale University Press, 1941.

Peterson, Horace C., and Gilbert C. Fite. *Opponents of War, 1917–1918.* Madison: University of Wisconsin Press, 1957.

Reedy, George E. *Who Will Do Our Fighting for Us?* New York: The World Publishing Company, 1969.

Reeves, Thomas, and Karl Hess. *The End of the Draft: The Feasibility of Freedom.* New York: Random House, Inc., 1970.

Sanders, Jacquin. *The Draft and the Vietnam War.* New York: Walker and Co., 1966.

Schlissel, Lillian, ed. *Conscience in America: A Documentary History of Conscientious Objection in America, 1757–1967.* New York: E. P. Dutton & Co., 1968.

Shapiro, Andrew O., and John M. Striker. *Mastering the Draft: A Comprehensive, Easy-Reference Guide for Solving Draft Problems.* Boston: Little, Brown and Company, 1970.

Sibley, Mulford Q., and Philip E. Jacob. *Conscription of Conscience: The American State and the Conscientious Objector, 1940–1947.* Ithaca: Cornell University Press, 1952.

Stafford, Robert T., et al. *How to End the Draft.* Washington, D.C.: The National Press Inc., 1967.

Stern, Frederick Martin. *The Citizen Army: Key to Defense in the Atomic Age.* New York: St. Martin's Press, 1957.

Swomley, John M. *The Military Establishment.* Boston: Beacon Press, Inc., 1964.

Tax, Sol, ed. *The Draft: A Handbook of Facts and Alternatives.* Chicago: University of Chicago Press, 1967.

Thomas, Norman. *The Conscientious Objector in America.* New York: B. W. Huebsch, Inc., 1923.

————. *Is Conscience A Crime?* New York: Vanguard, 1927.

Trytten, M. H. *Student Deferment in Selective Service: A Vital Factor in National Security.* Minneapolis: University of Minnesota Press, 1952.

U.S. National Advisory Commission on Selective Service. *In Pursuit of Equity: Who Serves when Not All Serve?* Washington, D.C.: Government Printing Office, 1967.

U.S. President's Advisory Commission on Universal Training. *A Program for National Security.* Washington, D.C.: Government Printing Office, 1947.

U.S. President's Commission on an All-Volunteer Armed Force. *Report.* Washington, D.C.: Government Printing Office, 1970.

———. *Studies Prepared for the President's Commission on an All-Volunteer Armed Force.* 2 vols. Washington, D.C.: Government Printing Office, 1970.

U.S. Selective Service System. Reports of the Director. Washington, D.C.: Government Printing Office.

Selective Service in Peacetime. 1942.

Selective Service in Wartime. 1943.

Selective Service as the Tide of War Turns. 1945.

Selective Service and Victory. 1948.

———. Special Monographs. Washington, D.C.: Government Printing Office.

No. 1. *Backgrounds of Selective Service: A Historical Review of the Principle of Citizen Compulsion in the Raising of Armies.* 2 vols. 1947 and 1949.

No. 2. *The Selective Service Act.* 5 vols. 1954.

No. 3. *Organization and Administration of the System.* 2 vols. 1951.

No. 4. *Registration and Selective Service.* 1946.

No. 5. *The Classification Process.* 3 vols. 1950.

No. 6. *Industrial Deferment.* 3 vols. 1948.

No. 7. *Agricultural Deferment.* 1947.

No. 8. *Dependency Deferment.* 1947.

No. 9. *Age in the Selective Service Process.* 1946.

No. 10. *Special Groups.* 2 vols. 1953.

No. 11. *Conscientious Objection.* 2 vols. 1950.

No. 12. *Quotas, Calls, and Inductions.* 2 vols. 1948.

No. 13. *Reemployment and Selective Service.* 2 vols. 1949.

No. 14. *Enforcement of the Selective Service Law.* 1950.

No. 15. *Physical Examination of the Selective Service Registrants.* 3 vols. 1948.

No. 16. *Problems of Selective Service.* 3 vols. 1952.

No. 17. *Operation of Selective Service.* 2 vols. 1955.

No. 18. *Evaluation of the Selective Service Program.* 3 vols. 1967.

U.S. Task Force on the Structure of the Selective Service System. *Report.* Washington, D.C.: Government Printing Office, 1967.

Upton, Emory. *The Military Policy of the United States.* Washington, D.C.: Government Printing Office, 1912.

Walton, George. *Let's End the Draft Mess.* New York: David McKay Co., Inc., 1967.

Wamsley, Gary L. *Selective Service and a Changing America*. Columbus, Ohio: Charles E. Merrill Publishing Company, 1969.

Weigley, Russell F. *History of the United States Army*. New York: The Macmillan Company, 1967.

————. *Towards an American Army: Military Thought from Washington to Marshall*. New York: Columbia University Press, 1962.

Willenz, June A., ed. *Dialogue on the Draft*. Washington, D.C.: American Veterans Committee, 1967.

Wittner, Lawrence S. *Rebels against War: The American Peace Movement since 1941*. New York: Columbia University Press, 1969.

Wood, Leonard. *The Military Obligation of Citizenship*. Princeton: Princeton University Press, 1915.

————. *Our Military History*. Chicago: The Reilly and Britton Company, 1916.

Wright, Edward N. *Conscientious Objectors in the Civil War*. Philadelphia: University of Pennsylvania Press, 1931.

Index

☆

American Union against Militarism, 130
Army, regular: 102–3, 104
Army, standing: *See* Standing army; Universal military training
Army Reorganization Bill of 1919, 106

Baldwin, Roger, 131
Berrigan brothers, 226–27
Blacks: excluded from early militia, 23; drafted by Confederates, 58; Union regiments in Civil War, 59
Bounties: Revolutionary War, 7; Civil War, 58
Brooks, Arle, 186

Calhoun, John C., 50
"Channeling" (Selective Service work assignments), 239–45
Civilian Public Service Camps, 186
Clark, Grenville, 156
Coffin, William S.: acts of draft resistance, 225; part of "the Resistance" in 1967, 263
Commutation fee, 57
Conscientious objection: reconsidered in 1967, 221; selective, 223
Conscientious objectors: Civil War, 77; World War I, 106, 137; Leavenworth strike of, 137; treatment in 1940 draft law, 158, 186; case of

Daniel Seeger, 221; case of Elliott Welsh II, 222
Conscription: supported by Calhoun in 1816, 50; opposed by Webster, 44–50; Confederate law for, 61–62; first federal, 62; by the North in Civil War, 62–66; of wealth and manpower, 152; universal abolition of, 153, 203; nonviolent noncooperation, 226. *See also* Draft
Constitutional Convention, 21–22
Continental Army: manpower problems, 6, 15–16; desertion from, 9

Desertions: after 1755 draft law, 5; from Continental Army, 9; increased in Vietnam War, 227
Dick Act of 1903 (Militia Act), 103
Draft: arguments for today, xviii–xix; in each colonial state, 7–8; by Virginia in 1770's, 8; 1827 constitutionality decision, 24n; Seymour against, 70; failure of, 93; first peacetime, 157; supported by 1940 candidates, 157; Forrestal on, 159; Norman Thomas on, 159; maintenance after World War II, 160; as 1956 campaign issue, 208–9; effect of Vietnam on attitudes toward, 220; 1960 attitude toward, 220; Army officers opposed to, 227; proposed changes to